UNION PACIFIC 1977-1980

Extra 3379 West departs Green River, WY on 30 September 1977.

Photographs and text
by
GEORGE R. COCKLE

Overland Models, Inc.

RR 12, Box 445, Muncie, Indiana 47302

Copyright 1980
International Standard Book Number 0-916160-03-3
Library of Congress Card Number 77-81546

Typesetting by Tyler Type Service,
   Lincoln, Nebraska
Graphics by American Litho Graphic Corporation, Inc.
   Omaha, Nebraska
Printing by Precision Service, Inc.
   Council Bluffs, Iowa

ACKNOWLEDGMENTS

   A project of this magnitude requires considerable help to be successful. The ideas, support and efforts of persons too numerous to mention went into the making of this book.

   We have been fortunate to have enthusiastic support from the Union Pacific Railroad. Special acknowledgment must be made for their permission to use the corporate herald and other identifiable designs, the "Great Big Rollin' Railroad" verses, and all the mechanical drawings used in the locomotive presentations plus the Energy Slogan featurette. Especially supportive were Messrs. Frederic Christensen, Barry Combs, Earl Cure, Richard Lohr, Don Mears, Richard Prince, John Rieschl, Edwin Schafer, and . . . in particular, John Witherbee.

   Our sincere thanks and appreciation is extended to the following contributors: Norman E. Anderson, Kenneth M. Ardinger, Gerald J. Bosanek, Martin Bosynak, Greg B. Davies, James R. Dougherty, Ben Fredericks, Brian Greibenow, Paul Guernsey, Brian T. Marsh, Jim Nelson, Robert Personett, Vic F. Reyna, Richard Stephenson, Charles W. Stortz, Jr., James W. Watson, and A. J. Wolff.

   The professional assistance from American Litho Graphic Corporation and the personal interest by its President, Mr. Bob Gittins, made the organization of this volume an easier task. Mr. Gerrit "Van" Tyler of Tyler Type Service provided his valuable typesetting experience in converting the reams of tabular data and copy into readable text. Mr. Tom Kruger and the production staff at Precision Services are acknowledged for their technical assistance and excellence in the print trade.

   Finally, it is with great appreciation that we acknowledge the understanding, encouragement and support our wives . . . Janice and Roberta . . . have given this project.

THOMAS E. MARSH Muncie, Indiana	— November 1980 —	**GEORGE R. COCKLE** Omaha, Nebraska

COVER: Noted western artist Harry W. Brunk captures big railroading flavor at North Platte, Nebraska in 1978. The ever-changing scene at this large servicing area shows an EMD "fast forty" on the front; on the back is an originally-numbered General Electric C30-7.

AN OVERLAND RAILBOOK

UNION PACIFIC CA-11 CABOOSES
CENTENNIALS IN ACTION
UNION PACIFIC . . . 1977-1980

OVERLAND RAILBOOKS is soliciting photographic materials for future publications covering the western railroading scene. We are interested in black and white photographs that are technically well printed and which are aesthetically pleasing. We will gladly print from your negative materials. Current needs can be determined by contacting us.

All photographs taken by George R. Cockle unless otherwise so credited.

UNION PACIFIC... 1977-1980

The posture of the Union Pacific Railroad today was established by some broad sweeping instructions first issued in the early 1970's. It has taken almost ten years to implement those executive concepts into reality... but they have taken shape through streamlining of the locomotive fleet, improvement of the rolling equipment, restructuring two classification yards to expedite the orderly flow of traffic, capital track and roadbed initiatives including the relaying of miles of continuous welded rail, extending existing centralized traffic control and considering mergers with two adjacent rail systems to provide faster and more efficient service west of the Mississippi River.

While the Union Pacific Railroad is a "people-oriented" operation, one must look to the source for this dynamic strength... This book is dedicated to two such operating officials who had the vision and exercised the opportunity to make the Union Pacific Railroad a leader in the transportation field... its President, Mr. John C. Kenefick and recently retired Chief Mechanical Officer, Mr. Frank D. Acord.

Sketches by Randi Brinkman

FRANK D. ACORD   JOHN C. KENEFICK

This presentation has been reduced to outlining one facet of Union Pacific's vitalization schedule in the 1970's... its motive power. The general direction and manner of achievement was established in the early 1970's, when Mr. Acord was appointed the Chief Mechanical Officer by Mr. Kenefick. The previous CMO, Mr. D. S. Neuhart, had been an advocate of *super power* to conquer the west.

Some of his behemoths worked, and some didn't fare so well. His idea to mount double engines on a single chassis resulted in the successful DDA40X "Centennial," and the not-so-successful General Electric U50 versions plus the ALCo C855 set... all in the high horsepower range. He had a continuing interest in the gas electric turbine locomotives and experimented with the coal burning electric turbine. He tinkered with the lower horsepower units by turbocharging them to higher performance. He was willing to try any proposition to increase motive power performance. Because of this position, the locomotive roster was swollen with 10 of this and 10 of that model purchased to test their capabilities. The experimentation program of Mr. Neuhart is legion, but we only want to introduce the notion that the locomotive roster of the early 1970's was replete with many models and variants.

It was this variety of power that challenged Mr. Acord's management abilities upon his appointment as Chief Mechanical Officer in October 1971. While "pool power" had been in effect during the late 1960's, greater emphasis was placed on "run-throughs" and the implementation of a highly-monitored maintenance schedule to reduce failures or missed schedules. These were initial steps in making maximum use of the wide variety of power. That many of the units were not compatible with other railroads which Union Pacific had "run-through" agreements with became increasingly clear.

A trio of C30-7's pulls down the mainline at Council Bluffs, IA with a westbound empty unit coal train on 12 June 1980.

It took about two years for Mr. Acord to shake-down the motive power dilemma into manageable parameters established in his ten-year program (1971-1980). Beginning in 1975, his assistant, Mr. Jack McDonough, chaired a number of planning sessions designed to profile the system's requirements in the 1980's. Those meetings were loosely called the "McDonough Board."

From these "think-tank" sessions, the Locomotive Fleet Management Program was established. The first step of this program was to address the current locomotive situation. Even though new units were being added to the fleet, the average locomotive age steadily increased. The budgeted maintenance dollars were inadequate to sustain the new locomotives because the unscheduled heavy repairs became more frequent on the older locomotives. The 1976 fleet rostered too many different kinds of locomotives with the attendant problems of poor compatibility, the excessive inventory of different repair parts and the diverse shop skills necessary to maintain an operational fleet.

The resulting answer began to appear in 1976 with the replacement of older locomotives of low horsepower and poor technology as they required heavy repairs. The theory of using less high horsepower units to do the same amount of work was beginning to take shape.

It was about this time that the proposed locomotive fleet for the 1980's was announced. The decision was made to use Electro-Motive's SD40/SD40-2's and General Electric's U30C/C30-7's as mainline road units. The EMD GP38-2 was selected to perform branchline services. The GP40X was "nominated-in-kind" to profile the high-speed requirements. In the switcher area, the performance of the MP15 was used to set the standard; however, Union Pacific voiced dissatisfaction with any currently available switcher. Thus, the die was set.

With these parameters firmly stated, an immediate reduction of the base fleet from 1,327 units on 1 January 1976, was commenced. Using projected figures to maintain 1976 traffic levels on 1 January 1981, the fleet would be decreased to a base of 1,188 units. Taking into consideration projected growth through 1981, the fleet base would range in at about 1,375 units . . . well within the manageability of the railroad's facilities.

A quick survey of the roster on pages 6 and 7 will show the reduction, by years, of the lower horsepower units and the steady increase in the high horsepower road units . . . all in accordance with this locomotive Fleet Management Program.

The next major step involved the establishment of a preventive maintenance program. The principle of affording preferential preventive maintenance to newer locomotives has been the key in improved operating results in critical services. The idea of maximizing the availability and reliability of the units doing the most work called for creating a three-tier priority system.

Priority I loosely incorporates units less than 10 years old. These are the high horsepower locomotives having a high order of reliability and maintainability built-in through modern technology. The preferential preventive maintenance calls for servicing with new parts. 56% of the base fleet falls within this grouping and makes 76% of the mileage, with most units assigned to time-sensitive mainline traffic.

Priority II encompasses the 11- to 17.5-year-old locomotives. These are in the medium horsepower range having good technology. Required preventive maintenance is completed with second-hand or reconditioned parts. 19% of the base fleet falls within this grouping and makes 13% of the mileage, with most assigned to secondary mainline trains and locals.

Priority III lumps together all the units over 17.5 years old. These are low horsepower units with poor technology. While regular maintenance is performed, they are set aside when heavy repairs are required. 25% of the base fleet falls within this grouping and makes 11% of the mileage, with most assigned to local and switch services.

Age is the key. Older locomotives are downgraded to lower priorities because new technology produces locomotives better adapted to more demanding service. Naturally, undependable locomotives exhibiting inferior capabilities will be reduced to Priority III much quicker than the stated standards.

This priority system has permitted the railroad to set aside a considerable number of old and obsolete Priority III units as they became due for heavy overhaul. This has resulted in more maintenance dollars being diverted to Priority I and II units. The sale of unserviceable units also produced a gain in dollars.

The results of this fleet management program can be measured easily by the relative availability of the base fleet. The Mechanical Department's goal is set at 92% . . . and it was first exceeded in March 1977. Consider . . . 1% represents about 13 units!

Quickly put, the objectives of the 1980's master plan call for the average age of a road unit to be reduced from 11.4 years to 7.4 years old. By attrition, the 27 different models will be reduced to 5 distinct units. The base fleet of 1,327 units will be reduced to 1,150 road locomotives. The availability of 86.4% will be increased to 92% or better, with a reduction from an average of 157 locomotives held for repair daily to 100 units. The average number of 26.8 failures per day will be targeted at 20. While emphasis is placed on condition, mileage is still the key . . . with an anticipated average increase from 7,395 to 10,000 miles per locomotive per month.

This was the action plan Mr. Acord put in position to streamline the diesel fleet. We mention the program because it helps establish the primary editorial concept in putting Union Pacific . . . *1977-1980* together.

The huge Union Pacific servicing facilities at North Platte, NE plays host to an ever-changing horde of locomotives . . . in for a quick refueling and a new crew. Not only are Union Pacific units enmass, but a wide variety of colors from other rails which have run-through agreements with the Union Pacific are seen. 1 September 1979.

Recognizing the massive turn-over in the base fleet from many models to a chosen few, the years 1977 through 1980 represent one of the most dramatic periods in Union Pacific's motive power history. Here, for the last time, many models are making their last appearance on the roster . . . in fact, some models have been completely disposed of during this period. While there are more than five models still on the roster, it should be apparent that the numbers are quickly dropping.

The concept of offering an expanded photographic locomotive roster showing the details on each current model has met with an unequivocable approval, based on conversations with both railroaders and railfans.

While each model is covered, it still only represents a brief summary. Recommended reading includes Hol Wagner's *Union Pacific Motive Power Review, 1968-77* for the basic background leading up to this presentation; Don Dover's *Extra 2200 South, The Locomotive Newsmagazine* for current railroad happenings; national rail-oriented monthly publications to include *CTC Board, Modern Railroads, NMRA Bulletin, Pacific News, Railfan & Railroad, Railway Age* and *Trains*. A helpful reference set would be Jerry Pinkepank's *Diesel Spotter's Guide, The Second Diesel Spotter's Guide* and *Diesel Spotter's Guide-Update*. There are several specific locomotive books available on the Union Pacific: Reverend Harold Keekley's *Big Blow . . . Union Pacific's Super Turbine*, and *Roaring U50's . . . Union Pacific's Twin Diesels;* George R. Cockle's *Centennials in Action*. There is the Union Pacific Railroad Historical Society which published a monthly publication, *On The System*.

THE ROSTER

This Union Pacific expanded locomotive photographic roster covers the period from 1 January 1977 through 31 August 1980. The opening summary of locomotive ownership by year permits a quick survey of all additions and deletions within each model designation.

Following is a more detailed overview of each model which contains a detailed roster, a general arrangement drawing along with a brief description. An assortment of views for each model provides a graphic study to better understand the construction features, painting and lettering variants... without attempting to appear as a technical manual.

As with any energetic presentation covering a wide range of statistical data, the possibility of error exists. Every effort has been made to minimize any potential fault by cross-checking presented material against builder records and published data in recognized railroad periodicals.

The final authority for all roster entries is Union Pacific's "Diesel, Turbine and Electric Locomotive Historical Record," Office of the Chief Mechanical Officer, 31 December 1979, as updated through 31 August 1980.

Locomotive Series	Builder Model	Horse-power	Weight +000	January 31, 1977	January 31, 1978	January 31, 1979	January 31, 1980	August 31, 1980
1-50	EMD SD45	3600	393	—	—	39	50	49
45-53	GE U50D	5000	558	3	—	—	—	—
60	EMD SD45M	3600	406	—	—	—	—	1
70-84	EMD DD35A	5000	522	15	15	15	12	8
72B-98B	EMD DD35B	5000	520	27	27	27	6	1
99	EMD SD24M	3000	399	—	—	1	1	1
100-129	EMD GP7	1500	249	29	21	11	7	5
131-203	EMD GP9	1750	247	61	57	52	42	34
134B-204B	EMD GP9B	1750	244	19	8	—	—	—
205-244	EMD GP9	1750	246	33	31	27	17	14
245-299	EMD GP9	1750	248	45	44	38	29	21
300-348	EMD GP9M	2000	259	24	24	20	12	9
303B-348B	EMD GP9BM	2000	255	16	9	3	—	—
302-349	EMD GP9	1750	247	17	17	15	11	8
312B-347B	EMD GP9B	1750	244	4	3	—	—	—
400-429	EMD SD24	2400	386	29	21	21	20	19
400B-444B	EMD SD24B	2400	383	45	12	3	1	1
420-424	ALCo C415	1500	259	(5)	(5)	(5)	(5)	5
445-448	EMD SD24	2400	386	4	4	4	3	3
450-459	EMD SD7	1500	363	10	10	8	4	3
470-499	EMD GP20	2000	258	30	23	16	11	8
500-519	GE U28B	2800	270	—	—	—	—	20
600-630	EMD GP40	3000	266	—	—	—	—	31
631-650	EMD GP40	3000	264	—	—	—	—	20
700-735	EMD GP30	2250	263	36	36	36	36	36
700B-739B	EMD GP30B	2250	259	39	38	38	38	38
740-763	EMD GP35	2500	261	24	24	24	24	24
800-875	EMD GP30	2250	260	74	74	74	74	74
928	EMD E8A	2250	340	1	1	1	1	—
951-954	EMD E9A	2400	344	2	2	2	2	—
960	EMD E9A	2400	344	1	1	1	1	—
968B-969B	EMD E9B	2400	340	2	2	2	2	—
973B-974B	EMD E9B	2400	340	2	2	2	2	—
1003-1034	EMD NW2	1000	251	22	19	12	7	5
1036-1095	EMD NW2	1000	250	46	43	34	26	24
1200-1207	(UP) SW10	1200	251	—	—	—	—	8
1400-1409	EMD SDP35	2500	380	10	10	10	10	10

Locomotive Series	Builder Model	Horse-power	Weight +000	January 31, 1977	January 31, 1978	January 31, 1979	January 31, 1980	August 31, 1980
1800-1824	EMD SW7	1200	246	25	24	22	22	22
1825-1866	EMD SW9	1200	247	41	38	36	35	29
1839-1848	(UP) SW10	1200	251	—	—	—	2	—
1871-1877	EMD TR5	1200	260	7	7	7	7	7
1870B-1877B	EMD TR5	1200	260	7	7	7	7	7
2000-2039	EMD GP38-2	2000	269	40	40	40	40	40
2040-2059	EMD GP38-2	2000	269	20	20	20	20	20
2400-2414	GE C30-7	3000	393	—	—	15	15	15
2415-2429	GE C30-7	3000	393	—	—	15	15	15
2430-2439	GE C30-7	3000	393	—	—	10	10	10
2440-2459	GE C30-7	3000	393	—	—	20	20	20
2460-2499	GE C30-7	3000	393	—	—	—	6	40
2500-2539	GE C30-7	3000	393	—	—	—	—	17
2800-2809	GE U28C	2800	374	10	10	10	6	3
2810-2829	GE U30C	3000	391	20	20	20	20	20
2830-2869	GE U30C	3000	393	40	40	40	40	40
2870-2904	GE U30C	3000	393	35	35	35	34	34
2905-2919	GE U30C	3000	393	15	15	15	15	15
2920-2959	GE U30C	3000	393	40	40	40	40	40
2960-2974	GE C30-7	3000	393	—	15	—	—	—
3000-3082	EMD SD40	3000	393	75	74	74	74	74
3040-3047	EMD SD40	3000	393	8	8	8	8	8
3083-3122	EMD SD40-2	3000	391	40	40	40	40	40
3123-3202	EMD SD40-2	3000	391	80	79	79	79	79
3203-3242	EMD SD40-2	3000	392	37	37	37	37	38
3243-3274	EMD SD40-2	3000	390	—	—	—	—	2
3275-3287	EMD SD40-2	3000	390	13	13	13	13	13
3288-3304	EMD SD40-2	3000	390	17	17	17	17	17
3305-3334	EMD SD40-2	3000	392	—	—	—	—	8
3335-3399	EMD SD40-2	3000	390	—	64	64	64	64
3400-3409	EMD SD40-2	3000	390	—	—	—	—	—
3410-3488	EMD SD40-2	3000	390	—	—	79	79	79
3489-3498	EMD SD40-2	3000	390	—	—	10	10	10
3499-3583	EMD SD40-2	3000	390	—	—	22	85	85
3600-3649	EMD SD45	3600	393	50	50	11	—	—
3609-3768	EMD SD40-2	3000	390	—	—	—	107	160
3999	EMD SD24M	3000	399	1	1	—	—	—
5000-5039	GE U50C	5000	443	40	23	—	—	—
6900-6946	EMD DDA40X	6600	545	46	46	45	45	45
8000-8034	EMD SD40-2H	3000	390	35	35	35	35	32
8035-8064	EMD SD40-2M	3000	392	30	30	30	30	22
8065-8074	EMD SD40-2M	3000	390	—	10	10	10	10
8075-8099	EMD SD40-2M	3000	390	—	—	—	25	25
9000-9005	EMD GP40X	3500	275	—	—	6	6	6
262-281	GE U28B	2800	270	(20)	(20)	(20)	(20)	—
340-359	EMD GP40	3000	266	(20)	(20)	(20)	(20)	—
362-381	EMD GP40	3000	266	(19)	(18)	(11)	(11)	—
4700-4719	EMD GP40	3000	264	(20)	(20)	(20)	(20)	—
TOTAL UNITS OWNED				1,526	1,499	1,544	1,643	1,691

SOURCE: Union Pacific's Monthly Reports, "Locomotive Units Owned," Office of the Chief Mechanical Officer.

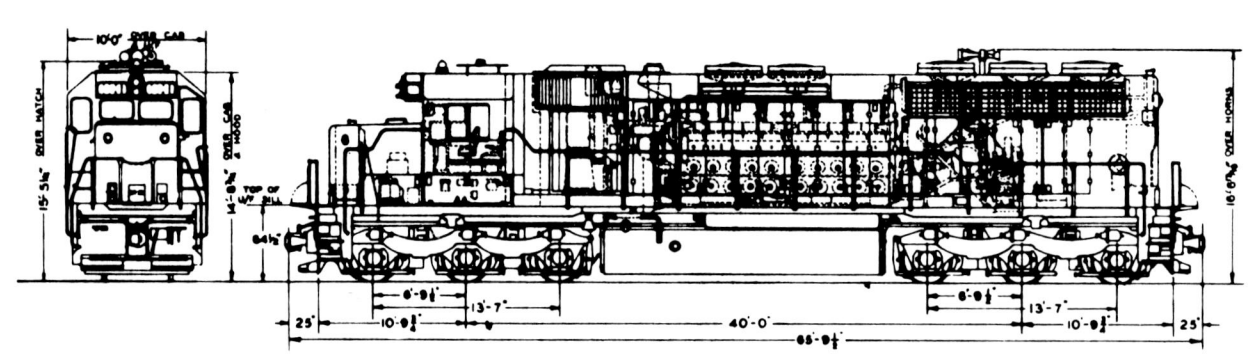

EMD SD45

GENERAL DATA
A.A.R. DESIGNATION	C-C
GEAR RATIO	62/15
WEIGHT LOADED	393,300 LBS.
LIGHT WEIGHT	353,015 LBS. APPROX.
MAXIMUM CURVATURE	17° WITH TRAIN
MAXIMUM CURVATURE	22° AS SINGLE UNIT
MAXIMUM SPEED	65 M.P.H.
MINIMUM CONT. SPEED	11 M.P.H.

SUPPLIES
FUEL	4000 GALS.
LUBE OIL	466 GALS.
COOLING WATER	288 GALS.
SAND	56 CU. FT.

DIESEL ENGINE
MODEL	20-645-E3
TURBOCHARGER	EQUIPPED
SPARK ARRESTER	NOT REQUIRED
AIR FILTER, BASIC:	
CARBODY	NOT EQUIPPED
PRIMARY	DYNAVANE
ENGINE	AAF BAG
FUEL HEATER	KELTY

BRAKES
SCHEDULE	26 L AUTOMATIC RETAINER CONTROL ON ALL UNITS
AIR COMPRESSOR	WBO
BRAKE SHOES	HI PHOS. CAST IRON
SAFETY CONTROL	FOOT PEDAL

ELECTRICAL
MULTIPLE UNIT RECEPTACLES	12-21 & 27 PT
MAIN GENERATOR	AR-10
ALTERNATOR	D-14
TRACTION MOTORS, TYPE	D-17
NUMBER OF TRACTION MOTORS	6
DYNAMIC BRAKES	POTENTIAL CONTROL
BATTERIES	64 V. 426 AMP. HRS.
HEADLIGHTS	TWIN SEALED BEAMS 200W EA.
AUXILIARY GENERATOR	10 KW
COOLING FANS	(3) 48" 9-BLADE
CAB SIGNALS	US&S TYPE 'EL'
ROTATING WARNING LIGHTS	EQUIPPED

*EXTENDED RANGE

RUNNING GEAR
DRAFT GEAR	M-381
COUPLER	TYPE 'E'
JOURNALS	6½" x 12" HYATT R.B.
WHEELS	40" DIA.
TRUCKS	6 WHL., FLEXICOIL, CLASP BRKS., HIGH CYLS.

MISCELLANEOUS
WHISTLE	LESLIE S-5 TRF
TOILET	EQUIPPED
FIRE EXTINGUISHERS	(3) 30 LB. ANSUL
WATER COOLER	EQUIPPED
FUEL FILLER	BUCKEYE
SPEED RECORDER	CP

The *One-Spot* basks in its reflection at Council Bluffs, IA on 24 November 1979. Originally delivered as UP 3601 in March 1968, it was renumbered to UP 1 in November 1978. The renumbering of the fifty SD45's cleared the 3600-series road numbers so as to sequentially continue the numbering of newly purchased SD40-2's. The odd-numbered units up through UP 35 are remote RCS units.

THE "spot number" on the Union Pacific is currently held by a remote RCS equipped SD45. Previously held one-spot units were the 1938 General Electric's oil-burning steam turbine locomotive (retired by owner-GE in 1943) and 1958 General Electric's 8500-horsepower oil-burning gas-turbine locomotive (retired in 1968). Council Bluffs, IA, 24 November 1979.

ELECTRO-MOTIVE'S SD45 ROSTER

UNIT	BUILDER DATE	BUILDER NUMBER	REMARKS
1:3	March 1968	33410	Originally UP 3601, renumbered 11/78. Remote RCS unit.
2:3	March 1968	33411	Originally UP 3602, renumbered 10/78. Control RCS unit.
3:2	March 1968	33412	Originally UP 3603, renumbered 10/78. Control RCS unit.
4:2	March 1968	33413	Originally UP 3604, renumbered 10/78. Control RCS unit.
5:2	April 1968	33414	Originally UP 3605, renumbered 10/78. Remote RCS unit.
6:2	April 1968	33415	Originally UP 3606, renumbered 11/78. Control RCS unit.
7:2	April 1968	33416	Originally UP 3607, renumbered 10/78. Remote RCS unit.
8:2	April 1968	33417	Originally UP 3608, renumbered 10/78. Control RCS unit.
9:2	April 1968	33418	Originally UP 3609, renumbered 9/78. Remote RCS unit.
10:2	April 1968	33419	Originally UP 3610, renumbered 10/78. Control RCS unit.
11:2	April 1968	33420	Originally UP 3611, renumbered 11/78. Remote RCS unit.
12:2	April 1968	33421	Originally UP 3612, renumbered 11/78. Control RCS unit.
13:2	April 1968	33422	Originally UP 3613, renumbered 10/78. Remote RCS unit.
14:2	April 1968	33423	Originally UP 3614, renumbered 12/78. Control RCS unit. Modified by and set up to receive 12-cylinder 3000hp. Sulzer engine.
15:2	April 1968	33424	Originally UP 3615, renumbered 10/78. Remote RCS unit.
16:2	April 1968	33425	Originally UP 3616, renumbered 11/78. Control RCS unit.
17:2	April 1968	33426	Originally UP 3617, renumbered 10/78. Remote RCS unit.
18:2	April 1968	33427	Originally UP 3618, renumbered 12/78. Control RCS unit.
19:2	April 1968	33428	Originally UP 3619, renumbered 11/78. Remote RCS unit.
20:2	April 1968	33429	Originally UP 3620, renumbered 11/78. Control RCS unit.
21:2	April 1968	33430	Orginally UP 3621, renumbered 9/78. Remote RCS unit.
22:2	April 1968	33431	Originally UP 3622, renumbered 12/78. Control RCS unit.
23:2	April 1968	33432	Originally UP 3623, renumbered 12/78. Remote RCS unit.
24:2	March 1968	33433	Originally UP 3624, renumbered 10/78. Control RCS unit.
25:2	March 1968	33434	Originally UP 3625, renumbered 11/78. Remote RCS unit.
26:2	April 1968	33435	Originally UP 3626, renumbered 10/78. Control RCS unit.
27:2	March 1968	33436	Originally UP 3627, renumbered 11/78. Remote RCS unit.
28:2	March 1968	33437	Originally UP 3628, renumbered 12/78. Control RCS unit.
29:2	March 1968	33438	Originally UP 3629, renumbered 10/78. Remote RCS unit.
30:2	March 1968	33439	Originally UP 3630, renumbered 12/78. Control RCS unit.
31:2	March 1968	33440	Originally UP 3631, renumbered 11/78. Remote RCS unit.
32:2	March 1968	33441	Originally UP 3632, renumbered 10/78. Control RCS unit.
33:2	March 1968	33442	Originally UP 3633, renumbered 10/78. Remote RCS unit.
34:2	March 1968	33443	Originally UP 3634, renumbered 11/78. Control RCS unit. Modified by Morrison-Knudsen, Boise, ID to receive 12-cylinder 3000hp. Sulzer engine. Renumbered UP 60 7/80.
35:2	March 1968	33444	Originally UP 3635, renumbered 11/78. Remote RCS unit.
36:2	March 1968	33445	Originally UP 3636, renumbered 11/78. Control RCS unit.
37:2	March 1968	33446	Originally UP 3637, renumbered 10/78.
38:2	March 1968	33447	Originally UP 3638, renumbered 3/79.
39:2	March 1968	33448	Originally UP 3629, renumbered 4/79.
40:2	March 1968	34016	Originally UP 3640, renumbered 4/79.
41:2	March 1968	34017	Originally UP 3641, renumbered 12/78.
42:2	March 1968	34018	Originally UP 3642, renumbered 4/79.
43:2	March 1968	34019	Originally UP 3643, renumbered 4/79.
44:2	March 1968	34020	Originally UP 3644, renumbered 3/79.
45:2	March 1968	34021	Originally UP 3645, renumbered 3/79.
46:2	March 1968	34022	Originally UP 3646, renumbered 3/79.
47:2	March 1968	34023	Originally UP 3647, renumbered 3/79.
48:2	April 1968	34024	Originally UP 3648, renumbered 3/79.
49:2	April 1968	34025	Originally UP 3649, renumbered 3/79.
50:3	March 1968	33409	Originally UP 3600, renumbered 9/78. Control RCS unit.

The right rear view shows off the just-out-of-the-shop C-type truck assembly. The original gear ratio of 59/18 permitted a maximum speed of 80-mph. They were changed out to 62/15 for a lower maximum speed of 65-mph when the "fast-forties" were introduced. Note the location of the "firecracker-styled" antenna which was moved aft when the remote control antennae were installed over the cab. On the diesel service lead at Council Bluffs, IA, 6 January 1979.

Pulling up-hill on Mainline 1, UP 9 is at Summit in Omaha, NE on 28 September 1978. This down-on view provides a detailed study of the roof features and the RCS antenna installation. The fresh paint job adds to the scene.

A non-RCS equipped SD45 awaits assignment at Las Vegas, NV on 16 May 1980. Forward mounted horns are part of Union Pacific's efforts to increase the locomotive's audible effectiveness. *Photo by Martin Bosnyak.*

Lucky Seven faces east at Council Bluffs, IA on 28 October 1978. It has just been retrucked at Omaha Shops, evidenced by its bright silver sideframes. These units never received pilot snow plows even though their assignments were usually in snow-prone territories. Fully loaded operating weight of these SD45's is 393,000 pounds with 4000 gallons of diesel fuel, 466 gallons of lubricating oil, 288 gallons of cooling water and 56 cubic feet of sand on board.

Two different views of UP 6 give some advantage in studying the antennae arrangements.

The overhead cab installation is the control RCS antenna arrangement housed on a large ground plane, oft referred to as the "ping pong table." As the even-numbered units up through UP 36, and UP 50 are control units, performance demands are transmitted from these units to the remote unit for response. Due to a number of electronic considerations, the use of remote control mid-train service has all but been abandoned.

Normal VHF train communications is handled by the "firecracker-styled" antenna which was moved aft when the RCS equipment was installed.

Both views at Council Bluffs, IA on 19 November 1978.

A rear view shows off the "fireman's side" of the SD45. This is the last control RCS unit in the even-numbered group, except for UP 50. While considered high-horsepower units . . . 3600 horsepower . . . they seldom operated in concert with other high-horsepowered units. On this day; however, a DDA40X "Centennial" is in the lead position! Council Bluffs, IA, 8 February 1980.

Awaiting assignment at Pocatello, ID on 22 May 1979, UP 33 is starting to show sign of heavy wear. These units run-up high monthly mileages with good marks in the availability column. Their high reliability has kept them from being stored serviceable during any downturns in traffic over the years. *Photo by Gerald J. Bosanek.*

Two differing views of the remote RCS antenna installation provide a better appreciation of its overhead mounting.

The frontal cab view of UP 19 shows the feet and table of the ground plane installation. The transmit and receive antennae are fed by the coaxial leads coming from the cab. Council Bluffs, IA, 4 January 1980.

Extra 11 East, rounds the turn at Omaha, NE on 28 January 1979. It is very cold! The crew will soon cross the Missouri River and "yard" their train at Council Bluffs, IA. Trainmen on the Nebraska's First Subdivision are use to the harsh prairie winters and can truly say . . . "We Can Handle It."

Originally the first SD45, delivered as UP 3600, it was renumbered and is now the last in the series as UP 50. Shown on the diesel service tracks at Council Bluffs, IA on 8 February 1980.

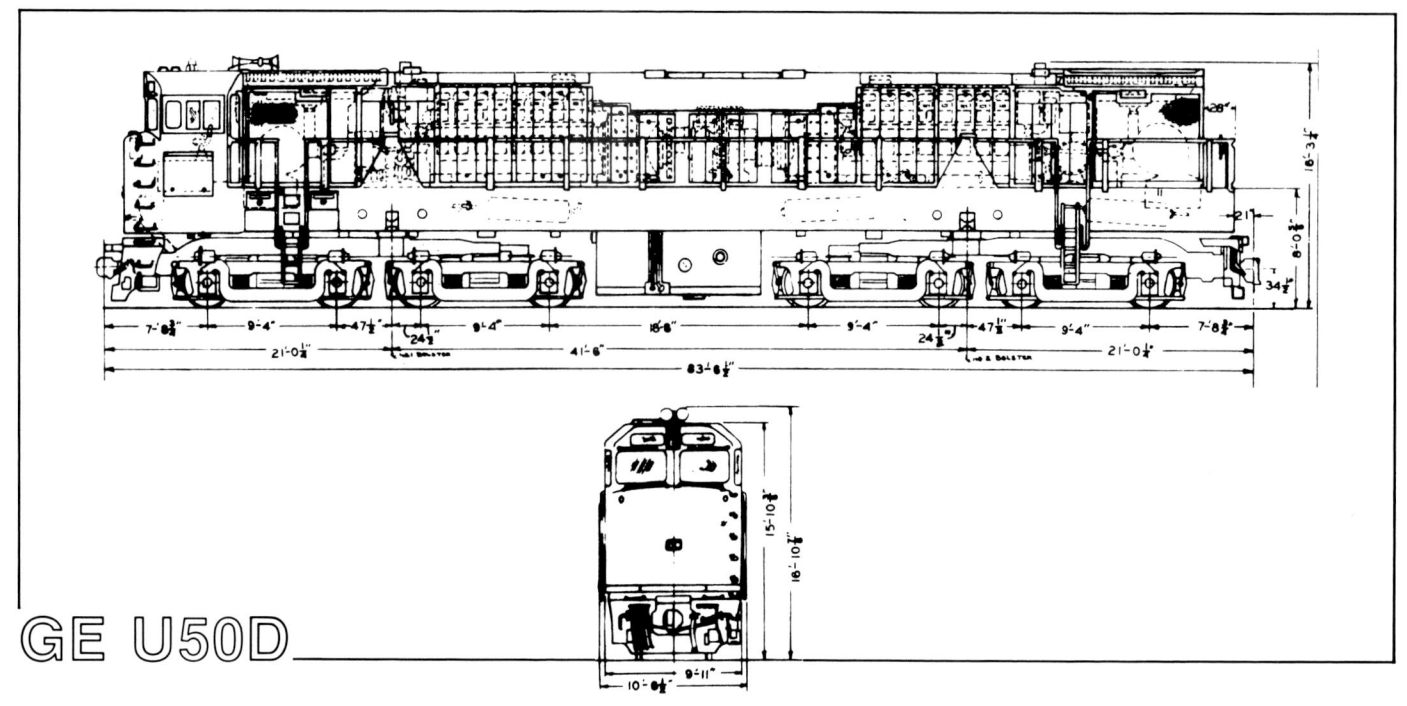

GE U50D

GENERAL DATA
A.A.R. DESIGNATION	B-B-B-B
GEAR RATIO	74/18
WEIGHT LOADED	557,960 LBS.
LIGHT WEIGHT	504,546 LBS. APPROX.
MAXIMUM CURVATURE	WITH TRAIN
MAXIMUM CURVATURE	21° AS SINGLE UNIT
MAXIMUM SPEED	71 M.P.H.
MINIMUM CONT. SPEED	14.7 M.P.H.

SUPPLIES
FUEL	5850 GALS.
LUBE OIL	385 GALS.
COOLING WATER	290 GALS.
SAND	60 CU. FT.

DIESEL ENGINE
MODEL	GE 7FDL-16
TURBOCHARGER	EQUIPPED
SPARK ARRESTER	NOT REQUIRED
AIR FILTER, BASIC:	
CARBODY	NOT EQUIPPED
PRIMARY	DYNAVANE
ENGINE	PANEL OIL BATH (AIR MAZE)
FUEL HEATER	KELTY

RUNNING GEAR
DRAFT GEAR	MF-400
COUPLER	TYPE F
JOURNALS	7" DIA. TIMKEN R.B.
WHEELS	40" DIA.
TRUCKS	(4) 4 WHL., EQUALIZER, SWINGHANGER CLASP BRK. TRKS. ON SPAN BOLSTERS

ELECTRICAL
MULTIPLE UNIT RECEPTACLES	27 PT
MAIN GENERATOR	5GT 598C4
ALTERNATOR	NOT EQUIPPED
TRACTION MOTORS, TYPE	GE 752
NUMBER OF TRACTION MOTORS	8
DYNAMIC BRAKES	POTENTIAL CONTROL*
BATTERIES	64V. 426 AMP. HRS.
HEADLIGHTS	TWIN SEALED BEAMS 200W. EA.
AUXILIARY GENERATOR	5GY27E1
COOLING FANS	MECHANICAL
CAB SIGNALS	SEE NOTE
ROTATING WARNING LIGHTS	EQUIPPED
R.C.S.	NOT EQUIPPED
EXCITER	5GY50B1

*EXTENDED RANGE
NOTES:
  UNITS 31-33, 46-48 & 50-53 .... GRS
  UNITS 34-45 & 49 .... US&S TYPE 'EL'

BRAKES
SCHEDULE	24RL
AIR COMPRESSOR	(2) 3CWDL
BRAKE SHOES	CAST IRON
SAFETY CONTROL	FOOT PEDAL

MISCELLANEOUS
WHISTLE	LESLIE 3 OR 2 CHIME
TOILET	EQUIPPED
FIRE EXTINGUISHERS	(5) 30 LB. ANSUL
WATER COOLER	EQUIPPED
FUEL FILLER	BUCKEYE
SPEED RECORDER	CP

GENERAL ELECTRIC'S U50D ROSTER

UNIT	BUILDER DATE	BUILDER NUMBER	REMARKS
45	September 1964	35105	Sold 5/77 to Erman Corporation, Turner, KS.
51:2	July 1965	35649	Sold 8/77 to Erman Corporation, Turner, KS.
53:2	August 1965	35651	Sold 5/77 to Erman Corporation, Turner, KS.

Standing proud, but disused, is one of three U50's that stayed on the roster through the mid-1977's. Like the diesel house and the water tank that have been torn down, so it was that these giants of the rail are gone too . . . victims of advanced locomotive technology. Council Bluffs, IA, 26 July 1975.

Striking a classic pose, the two styles of General Electric 5,000-horsepower double-engined, single-chassis U50's stand behind the old Council Bluffs diesel house on 26 July 1975.

The UP 45 rides on a pair of double-set trucks, connected by a span bolster to support the massive unit. These were identified initially as U50's; however, many added the wheel arrangement in parenthesis (B+B–B+B). When General Electric brought out the U50C, the first edition became identified as the U50D.

The overhead rear view of the same units shows off the differing rooflines . . . especially in the radiator design where the U50D had two opposing end groups while the U50C had a combined centralized group at its mid-section.

Showing all sign of defeat, UP 53 sits outside the Omaha Shops on 28 April 1977, readied for movement to Erman Corporation, Turner, KS. The shop forces marked out all Union Pacific identification with black spray paint as the last act of stripping the unit of any useable parts. This Kansas scrapper bought all of the U50C's and these three remaining U50D's. Most of them have not been "torched" as yet . . . sitting in long storage lines beside the Santa Fe's mainline just west of Kansas City, KS.

When viewing UP 34, modified by Morrison-Knudsen to their TE83-6S standards, it appears similar to the standard SD45. Closer examination will disclose two major differences. The car body door panels along the side of the engine are new to space openings for best access to the Sulzer engine. The door panels are set out 2 inches from the rest of the car body to provide adequate clearance for the engine. The other spotting feature is only on the left side of the locomotive and is mentioned below. Boise, ID, 28 July 1980.—*Photo by Norman E. Anderson.*

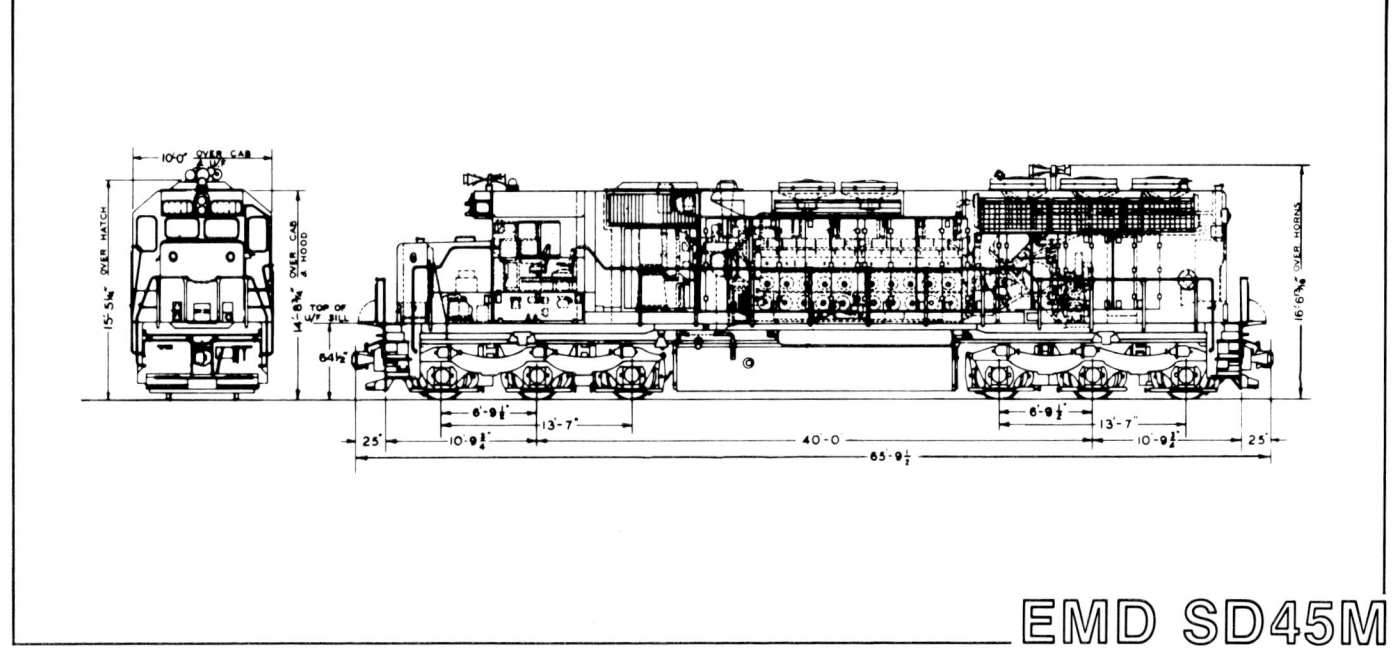

THE GENERAL ARRANGEMENT DIAGRAM APPEARS WITH RENUMBERED "SPOT-CLASS" PRESENTATION.

ELECTRO-MOTIVE'S SD45M ROSTER

UNIT	BUILDER DATE	BUILDER NUMBER	REMARKS
60	March 1968	33443	Converted from UP 34 by Morrison-Knudsen, Boise, ID. A 16-cylinder Sulzer engine has been installed on a test basis. Renumbered 8/80.

The first of six units to be fitted with the Sulzer 16-ASV 25/30 diesel engine was scheduled to be painted and renumbered as UP 60 on completion of the conversion by Morrison-Knudsen. At the 11th hour, Union Pacific decided to have the unit repainted and lettered at North Platte, so the unit was hastily completed and shipped in primer paint as UP 34 from Boise, ID on 28 July 1980.

The other major spotting feature is the air filtering modification applied to the rear door. An extra primary filter has been located in the door to provide filtered air to the clean air compartment. —*Photo by Norman E. Anderson.*

When viewing the modified SD45's left side, the easiest spotting feature is the extra primary air filter located in the last door opening in the car body. In the future, relocating the turbocharger to the rear of the Sulzer diesel engine will allow taking combustion air from the EMD clean air compartment, thus eliminating the need for the extra primary air filter. Pictured at Morrison-Knudson Company, Boise, ID, 28 July 1980.

Due to the current location of the two turbochargers at the front of the Sulzer 16-ASV 25/30 diesel engine, the combustion air could not be conveniently drawn from the EMD clean air compartment. Therefore, Morrison-Knudsen removed the last carbody door and installed a new primary air filter to pre-filter the combustion air. A new wall was installed in the carbody behind the air compressor and the engine air filter located above the compressor to draw air out of the new intake air compartment. Shown at Boise, ID, 28 July 1980.

Photographs on both pages by
NORMAN E. ANDERSON

The new door panels on UP 34 in the area of the diesel engine between the clear air compartment and radiator section are set-out 2-inches. This provides clearance for the newly installed Sulzer 16-ASV 25/30 diesel engine. The locomotive was given a primer coat shortly after this 26 July 1980 photograph at Boise, ID.

Freshly painted, UP 60 idles at Weiser, ID on 14 August 1980, while the crew of the "Huntington Local" are at "beans." This view clearly shows the additional primary air filter. A closer examination shows the new door arrangement, set-out 2-inches, to accomodate the Sulzer diesel engine.

This left rear pose provides a good view of the added primary air filter and a good angle to note the angled transition, between the "6" and "0," between the old carbody width and the new carbody door panels adjacent to the engine. The 2-inch extension is obvious. Weiser, ID, 14 August 1980.

Shown switching in Weiser, ID on 14 August 1980, it is working the "Huntington Local." This right-side rear view shows the application of Union Pacific's new simplified paint scheme to the slightly modified SD45 carbody.

Viewed from the right front, the new engine room door panel is clearly seen. The door panel is 2-inches wider than the old carbody on both sides. The panel comes straight out from the old carbody at the front, directly behind the clean air compartment. At the rear, a transition piece brings the panel back to the old carbody. The outset of the door panel is also visible at the dynamic brake hatch and directly above the walkway. Weiser, ID, 14 August 1980.

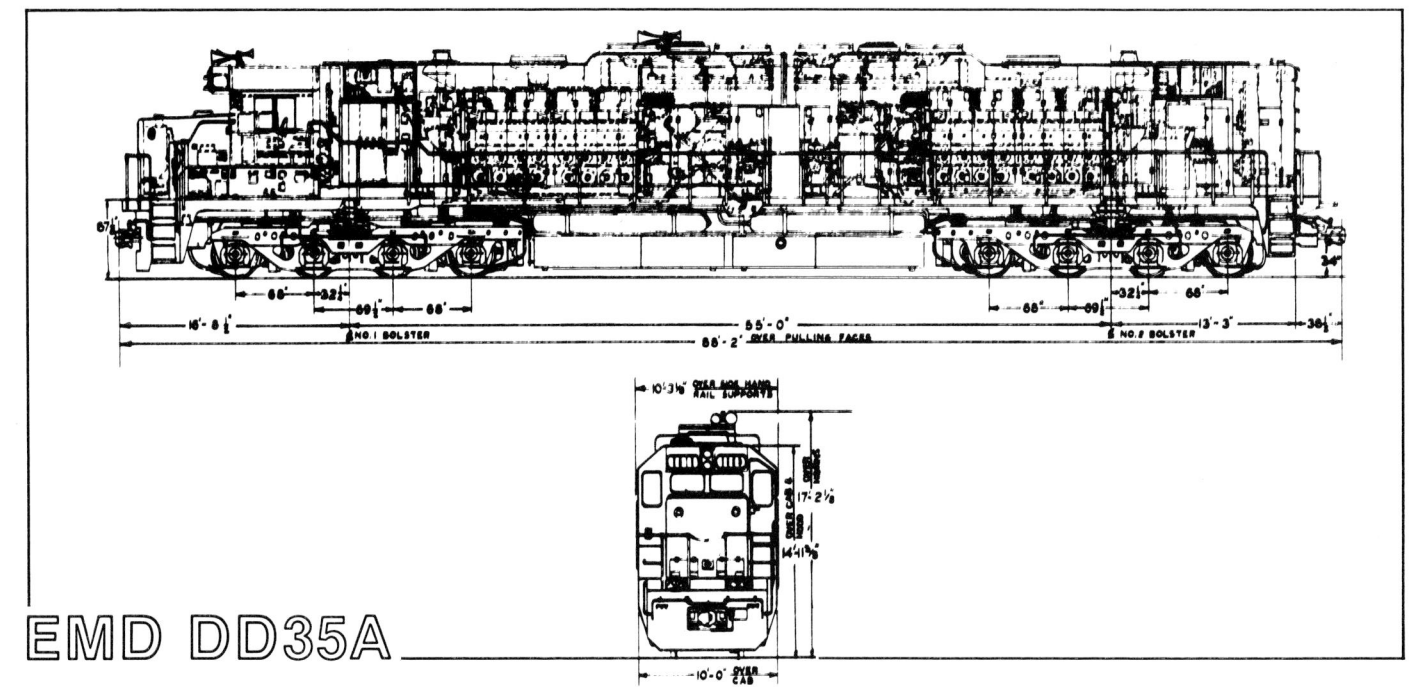

EMD DD35A

GENERAL DATA
A.A.R. DESIGNATION	D-D
GEAR RATIO	74/18
WEIGHT LOADED	521,980 LBS.
LIGHT WEIGHT	475,452 LBS. APPROX.
MAXIMUM CURVATURE	16.8° WITH TRAIN
MAXIMUM CURVATURE	19.4° AS SINGLE UNIT
MAXIMUM SPEED	65 M.P.H.
MINIMUM CONT. SPEED	12 M.P.H.

SUPPLIES
FUEL	5200 GALS.
LUBE OIL	374 GALS.
COOLING WATER	275 GALS.
SAND	40 CU. FT.

DIESEL ENGINE
MODEL	16-567-D3A
TURBOCHARGER	EQUIPPED
SPARK ARRESTER	NOT REQUIRED
AIR FILTER, BASIC:	
CARBODY	NOT EQUIPPED
PRIMARY	DYNAVANE
ENGINE	AAF BAG
FUEL HEATER	KELTY**

**SOME MODIFIED WITH FARR

RUNNING GEAR
DRAFT GEAR	M-381
COUPLER	TYPE 'E'
JOURNALS	6½" x 12" HYATT R.B.
WHEELS	40" DIA.
TRUCKS	8 WHL., FLEXCOIL, SINGLE SHOE BRKS, LOW CYLS.

ELECTRICAL
MULTIPLE UNIT RECEPTACLES	12-21 & 27 PT
MAIN GENERATOR	D-32
ALTERNATOR	D-14
TRACTION MOTORS, TYPE	GE-752E-20A
NUMBER OF TRACTION MOTORS	8
DYNAMIC BRAKES	POTENTIAL CONTROL*
BATTERIES	64V. 426 AMP. HRS.
HEADLIGHTS	SEALED BEAMS 200W. EA.
AUXILIARY GENERATOR	(2) 10 KW
COOLING FANS	(2) 48" DIA. & (1) 36" DIA.
CAB SIGNALS	NOTE
ROTATING WARNING LIGHTS	EQUIPPED
R.C.S.	NOT EQUIPPED

*EXTENDED RANGE
NOTES:
  CAB SIGNALS:
    UNITS 71 & 73 .... US&S TYPE 'EL'
    UNITS 74, 80 & 81 .... GRS

BRAKES
SCHEDULE	26L J1.4 (140%) + J1.6 (160%) RELAY VALVE
AIR COMPRESSOR	(2) WBO
BRAKE SHOES	HI FRICT. COMP.
SAFETY CONTROL	FOOT PEDAL

MISCELLANEOUS
WHISTLE	LESLIE S-3 LRF
TOILET	EQUIPPED
FIRE EXTINGUISHERS	(5) 30 LB. ANSUL
WATER COOLER	EQUIPPED
FUEL FILLER	BUCKEYE
SPEED RECORDER	CP

ELECTRO-MOTIVE'S DD35A ROSTER

UNIT	BUILDER DATE	BUILDER NUMBER	REMARKS	UNIT	BUILDER DATE	BUILDER NUMBER	REMARKS
70:2	May 1965	29984	Retired 9/79. Sold 9/79 to Naporano Iron & Metal Company, Newark, NJ.	77	June 1965	29991	
71:2	May 1965	29985		78	June 1965	29992	Retired 3/80. Held for disposition.
72:2	May 1965	29986		79	June 1965	29993	
73:2	May 1965	29987		80:2	June 1965	29994	Retired 5/80. Held for disposition.
74:2	May 1965	29988	Sold 2/80 to Naporano Iron & Metal Company, Newark, NJ.	81	June 1965	29995	
75:2	May 1965	29989	Retired 3/80. Held for disposition.	82	July 1965	29996	Retired 10/79. Sold 8/80 to Precision National Corporation, Mt. Vernon, IL.
76	May 1965	29990		83	July 1965	29997	Retired 12/79. Held for disposition.
				84	July 1965	29998	Retired 5/80. Held for disposition.

Cresting the Summit at Cajon Pass is westbound *Extra 82 West* with a long string of cars stretching out behind. The downhill run is marked by the large signs UP 82 is passing. This is Santa Fe track on which Union Pacific has operating agreements . . . between Daggett and Riverside Junction, CA.

Union Pacific has side-lined its fleet of DD35A and B-units. Based on operating expenses, units began phasing out in the late 1970's with the B-units being hit hardest. In down-turns of traffic, these units were usually the first-in and last-out of storage.

Shown here, draped in plastic sheeting over all openings, UP 74 has been prepared for long term storage and awaits movement at Omaha, NE on 26 September 1980 to the storage tracks in Council Bluffs, IA.

The "elephant-style" hook-up of UP 76 and 79 show off the rear and front construction features of the large double-engined DD35. Riding on massive D-style trucks, they otherwise appear almost like two GP35 units in line.

Electro—Motive had originally intended the DD35 to be a booster unit with a GP35 on either end. In fact, the EMD demonstration set . . . painted orange and white . . . toured in such a fashion. Union Pacific had cab versions produced in 1965 . . . basically the same as the B-units, except for the mid-section sloping radiators similiar to those found on the rear of SD45's.

Shown active at Council Bluffs, IA on 12 September 1980, shortly before being shipped to Omaha Shops for long term storage preparation.

Displaying a large-sized cab number, UP 70 awaits a westbound call on the service lead at Council Bluffs, IA, 18 July 1979. In two months it would be retired and later sold to Naporano Iron & Metal Company, Newark, NJ for scrap.

The disposition of the A-units began with **this** unit and was followed by the retirement of seven more by May 1980.

UP 71 was equipped with Performance Control allowing a lower minimum continuous speed of 11 mph.

The line-up of DD35's scheduled for long term storage are staged in front of the Omaha Shops on 26 September 1980. They will be prepared and sealed-up against the weather and then be returned to the storage lines at Council Bluffs, IA.

A total of eight DD35A's remain active: UP 71-74, 76, 77, 79 and 81. This long term storage might well spell the death knoll for these 5000-horsepower units . . . hastened by the slower economy and the arrival of newer units.

The separation of the two 16-cylinder 567-D3A diesel engines is at nearly the middle of the common underframe. The forward engine operating controls are in the cab, while the #2 engine operating controls are mounted on the forward wall . . . accessible from the gallery. The flaired radiators of both engines have a diaphragm interlock which permits flexing of the individual car bodies. This is UP 76 at Council Bluffs, IA on 12 September 1980.

The "nose-to-nose" shows the construction difference for each side as UP 81 and 76 await movement at Council Bluffs, IA on 12 September 1980 to Omaha Shops for long term storage preparations.

All DD35A's, except UP 84, have General Electric's 752E-20-A traction motors, and set with a 74:18 gear ratio for 65 mph operation. UP 84 has EMD's D67-B-1 traction motor and set with a 62:15 gear ratio for 65 mph operation.

The overhead nose shot of UP 76 shows the angular cab construction, not unlike the GP35's. The wire whip antenna mounts forward of the rotating beacon. The short hood has light green non-slip safety paint applied. Council Bluffs, IA, 7 October 1980.

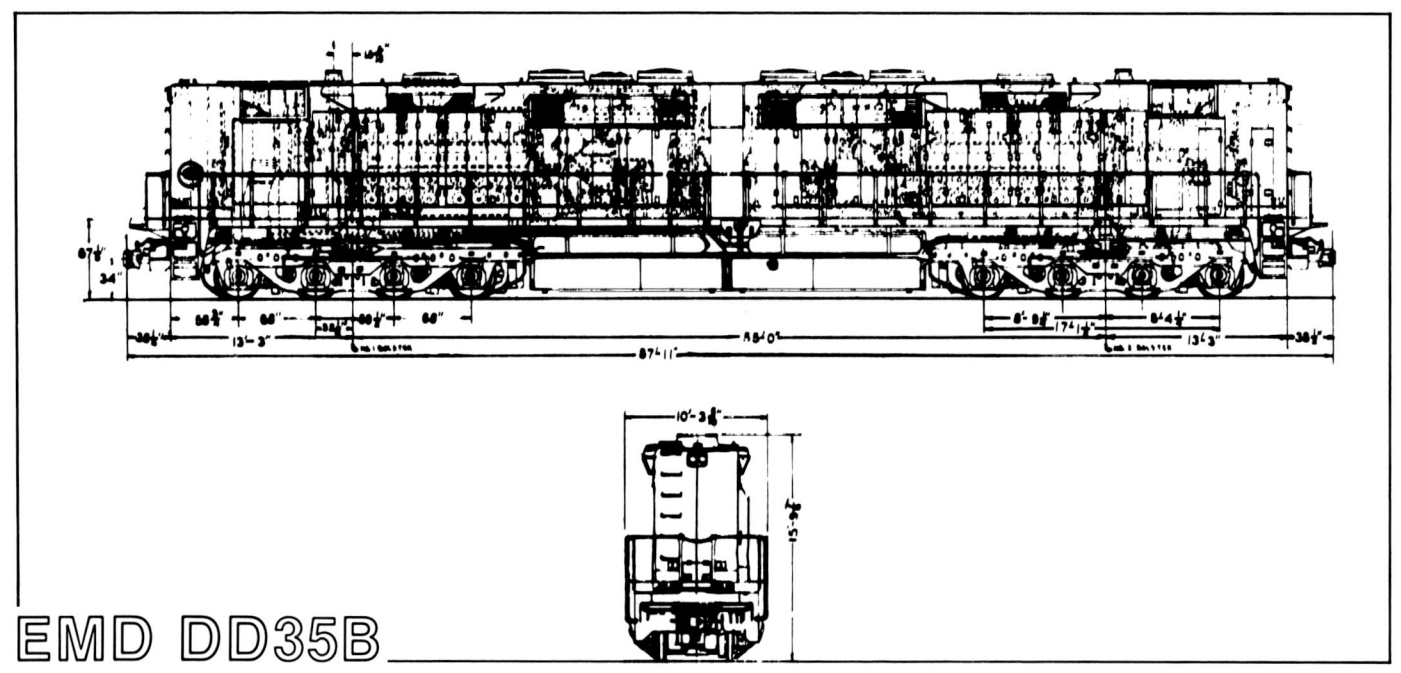

EMD DD35B

GENERAL DATA
A.A.R. DESIGNATION	D-D
GEAR RATIO	62/15
WEIGHT LOADED	519,553 LBS.
LIGHT WEIGHT	473,407 LBS. APPROX.
MAXIMUM CURVATURE	16° WITH TRAIN
MAXIMUM CURVATURE	19° AS SINGLE UNIT
MAXIMUM SPEED	65 M.P.H.
MINIMUM CONT. SPEED	12 M.P.H.

SUPPLIES
FUEL	5200 GALS.
LUBE OIL	243 GALS.
COOLING WATER	275 GALS.
SAND	46 CU. FT.

DIESEL ENGINE
MODEL	16-567-D3A
TURBOCHARGER	EQUIPPED
SPARK ARRESTER	NOT REQUIRED
AIR FILTER, BASIC:	
CARBODY	NOT EQUIPPED
PRIMARY	DYNAVANE
ENGINE	AAF BAG
FUEL HEATER	KELTY*

*SOME MODIFIED WITH FARR

BRAKES
SCHEDULE	26L J1.4 (140%) + J1.6 (160%)
AIR COMPRESSOR	(2) WBO*
BRAKE SHOES	HI FRICT. COMP.
SAFETY CONTROL	NOT EQUIPPED

*72B—(1) WBO

ELECTRICAL
MULTIPLE UNIT RECEPTACLES	12-21 & 27 PT
MAIN GENERATOR	D-32
ALTERNATOR	D-32
TRACTION MOTORS, TYPE	D-67B1
NUMBER OF TRACTION MOTORS	8
DYNAMIC BRAKES	POTENTIAL CONTROL**
BATTERIES	64V. 426 AMP. HRS.
HEADLIGHTS	TWIN SEALED BEAMS 200W. EA.
AUXILIARY GENERATOR	10 KW.
COOLING FANS	(2) 48" DIA. & (1) 36" DIA.
CAB SIGNALS	NOT EQUIPPED
ROTATING WARNING LIGHTS	NOT EQUIPPED
R.C.S.	NOT EQUIPPED

**EXTENDED RANGE

RUNNING GEAR
DRAFT GEAR	M-381
COUPLER	TYPE 'E'
JOURNALS	6½" x 12" HYATT R.B.
WHEELS	40" DIA.
TRUCKS	8 WHL., FLEXICOIL, SINGLE SHOE BRAKES, LOW CYLS.

MISCELLANEOUS
WHISTLE	NOT EQUIPPED
TOILET	NOT EQUIPPED
FIRE EXTINGUISHERS	(4) 30 LB. ANSUL
WATER COOLER	NOT EQUIPPED
FUEL FILLER	BUCKEYE
SPEED RECORDER	NOT EQUIPPED

ELECTRO-MOTIVE'S DD35B ROSTER

UNIT	BUILDER DATE	BUILDER NUMBER	REMARKS
72B	November 1963	28320	Originally EMD 5653. Purchased from EMD 6/64. Retired 6/79. Sold 11/79 to Peaker Industries, Brighton, MN.
73B	November 1963	28554	Originally EMD 5655. Purchased from EMD 6/64. Retired 4/80. Held for disposition.
74B	May 1964	29190	Retired 9/79. Sold 8/80 to Hyman-Michaels Company, Madison, IL.
75B	May 1964	29191	Retired 6/79. Sold 10/79 to Naporano Iron & Metal Company, Newark, NJ.
76B	May 1964	29192	Retired 1/80. Held for disposition.
77B	June 1964	29193	Retired 9/79. Held for disposition.
78B	June 1964	29194	Retired 12/79. Sold 5/80 to Naporano Iron & Metal Company, Newark, NJ.
79B	June 1964	29195	Retired 9/79. Sold 5/80 to Naporano Iron & Metal Company, Newark, NJ.
80B:2	June 1964	29196	Retired 3/80. Held for disposition.
81B	June 1964	29197	Retired 3/80. Held for disposition.
82B	July 1964	29198	Retired 1/80. Sold 8/80 to Precision National Corporation, Mt. Vernon, IL.
83B	July 1964	29199	Retired 6/79. Sold 11/79 to Naporano Iron & Metal Company, Newark, NJ.
84B	July 1964	29200	Retired 9/79. Held for disposition.
85B	July 1964	29201	Retired 10/79. Held for disposition.
86B	July 1964	29202	Retired 12/79. Sold 5/80 to Naporano Iron & Metal Company, Newark, NJ.
87B	July 1964	29203	Retired 9/79. Held for disposition.
88B	July 1964	29204	Retired 9/79. Held for disposition.
89B	July 1964	20205	Retired 9/79. Sold 8/80 to Hyman-Michaels Company, Madison, IL.
90B	August 1964	29206	Retired 4/80. Held for disposition.
91B	August 1964	29207	Retired 12/79. Sold 7/80 to Precision National Corporation, Mt. Vernon, IL.
92B	August 1964	29208	Retired 6/79. Sold 12/79 to Precision National Corporation, Mt. Vernon, IL.
93B	August 1964	29209	
94B	August 1964	29210	Retired 4/80. Held for disposition.
95B	September 1964	29211	Retired 6/79. Sold 4/80 to Precision National Corporation, Mt. Vernon, IL.
96B	September 1964	29212	Retired 6/79. Sold 4/80 to Precision National Corporation, Mt. Vernon, IL.
97B	September 1964	29213	Retired 6/79. Sold 12/79 to Precision National Corporation, Mt. Vernon, IL.
98B	September 1964	29214	Retired 9/79. Sold 8/80 to Hyman-Michaels Company, Madison, IL.

The squared-off DD35B ends stand defiantly proud at Council Bluffs, IA on 25 July 1978. These powerhouses boast 5000 horsepower from their twin 16 cylinder 567-D3A diesel engines. Only one cab-less unit remains active, and it is in long term storage along with eight sister cab DD35A's . . . their days being limited.

The front ("F") end of UP 81B faces west in this storage-line scene at Council Bluffs, IA on 11 September 1979. It was officially retired in March 1980 and has since given up much of its useable parts for inclusion in the store-keeper's supply bins. Originally, Electro-Motive had planned to produce the DD35's as only B-units. They would be cut-in between two smaller "control" units for a combined output in the 10,000-horsepower range. A total of 30 B-units were built during September 1963 through September 1964... Union Pacific bought 27 units and Southern Pacific purchased the other three.

Riding on jumbo-sized D-trucks, it is nearly thirty-five feet to the end from this vantage point! One of the major spotting features, other than just pure size, are the sanding boxes mounted above each truck assembly. Combined, they hold 46 cubic feet of sanding used in traction to control wheel-slip. Some of these sand boxes have been salvaged from retired units and applied to Union Pacific-built Electric Trailers to increase their capabilities in yard work.

Idling in the Las Vegas, NV yard, UP 87B awaits action on 19 September 1978. In the background is the Union Plaza which is owned by the corporation. These big units operated almost exclusively in the California Division in the late 1970's.—*Photo by Vic F. Reyna.*

Engine operating controls for the B-units are mounted on the gallery walls at the mid-section. This panel contains the #2 engine controls for UP 93B which has a modified removable electrical locker, a *Genisco* transition programmer and 6th notch power controls on the #2 engine. Note the modified rear having a DDA40X-styled access door. The #1 engine is a standard set-up with simplified controls. Council Bluffs, IA, 18 September 1980.

Modified end, housing the electrical test unit.

The world's largest single piece cast truck . . . produced by the Transportation Equipment Division, Rockwell International . . . rides under the massive DD35. Shown here is DD35B UP 72B, the first to be built which began service as EMD Demonstrator 5653 in November 1963. It was later purchased, secondhand, from EMD in June 1964. Retired June 1979, it was sold to Peaker Services, Inc., Brighton, MI in November 1979.

Almost out in the corn field, it is stored at Council Blufs, IA on 19 December 1979 . . . as retired. It was sold to Naporano Iron and Metal Company, Newark, NJ in May 1980. These giant-sized double-GP35's did yeoman service west of North Platte in taming the Rockies and into Southern California in assaulting the Sierras.

A three-quarter rear view of SD24M when it was assigned road number 3399. Awaiting its crew, the modified SD24 idles on the diesel service tracks at Council Bluffs, IA on 23 October 1974. While it was assigned to general road service, more frequently it did heavy transfer service in major yards in Kansas and Nebraska.

The left rear view shows the complex outboard plumbing arrangement. When the unit was initially re-engined and converted to constant speed in 1968, additional space was required to install the 3000-horsepower 16-645E3 diesel engine. When returned to standard throttle operation, it retained its 3000-horsepower capability and this "plumber's nightmare" stayed.

The small styled lettering on the car body was retained up through the repainting in 1978; however, it has carried all the variations under the cab window . . . pictured above: "We Can Handle It" . . . pictured below: the Union Pacific shield.

ELECTRO-MOTIVE'S SD24M ROSTER

UNIT	BUILDER DATE	BUILDER NUMBER	REMARKS
99	September 1959	25381	Originally UP 423. Converted to constant speed operations and renumbered UP 3100 8/68. Reverted to standard operation. Renumbered UP 3200 12/70. Renumbered 3399 3/72. Renumbered 3999 11/76. As it is basically the same unit renumbered, coverage for all numberings will be treated in this section.

Electro-Motive basically upgraded the earlier SD versions to produce their first turbocharged low-nosed units . . . dubbed SD24's. Satisfied with the demonstrations, Union Pacific purchased 30 cab and 45 cabless units in 1959 (later, they purchased the 4 demonstrators).

In an effort to maximize unit efficiency, UP 423 was selected in 1968 to have a 3000-horsepower 16 cylinder 645E3 diesel engine installed and be operated at a constant "high speed" or "idle." Speed would be controlled through excitation. The conversion was completed in August 1968 and the unit was renumbered to 3100.

The experiment in operating the engine at constant speed proved unsatisfactory and it was quickly revamped to standard throttle control. The 3000-horsepower engine remained installed.

To clear the way for newly purchased SD40 units, UP 3100 was renumbered to 3200 in December 1970, then to 3399 in March 1972, then to 3999 in November 1976 and to its current road number of 99 in November 1978.

Renumbered to UP3999 in November 1976 . . . its *fifth* road number, it awaits a westbound assignment in a trailing position in the power consist at Council Bluffs, IA on 29 January 1978. The basic reason for the unit's many renumberings was to clear the number for new SD40-type unit purchases. The distinct hump behind the cab is its major spotting feature. Only several dozen road units have the double rotating beacon installation . . . mostly early SD40's.

Renumbered UP 99 just weeks previously, its rests on the "run-around" track at Council Bluffs, IA on 11 December 1978. Shortly, it will go around the "balloon track" to the servicing area for supplies and be readied for movement to Kansas City, KS. The fairing in of the car body roof to the cab is clearly evident...the spotting feature that separates this SD24M from the standard model.

This late 1979 rear view shows off the typical SD24 back details. Note the new-styled lifting-pin lever handle which is being applied to older units. The 12, 21 and 27-point MU receptacles and standard mating hoses adorn the flat sheet plate pilot. This unit is at North Platte, NE for class repairs, and will shortly return to Kansas City, KS where it performs heavy drag jobs between other principal railroad yards and Union Pacific's Armstrong Yard.—*Photo by James W. Watson.*

The Highly Modified 3000-hp SD24M

In its local haunt...the west end of Armstrong Yard in Kansas City, KS on 18 May 1980...this 3000-horsepower locomotive can switch long strings of cars with ease. This hybrid unit is generally classified with the SD40's for class repairs and other maintenance considerations. This locomotive weighs in, fully loaded, at 399,480 pounds...carrying 3000 gallons of diesel fuel, 395 gallons of lubricating oil, 295 gallons of cooling water and 46 cubic feet of sand.

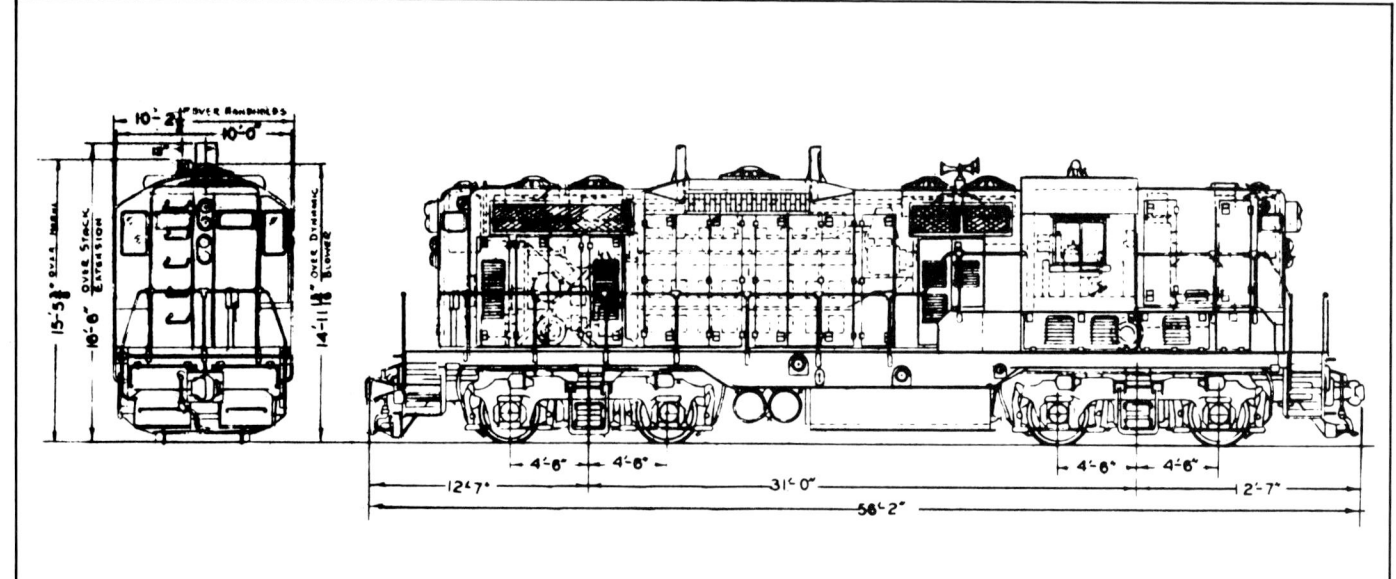

EMD GP7

GENERAL DATA
A.A.R. DESIGNATION	B-B
GEAR RATIO	62/15
WEIGHT LOADED	249,200 LBS.
LIGHT WEIGHT	232,655 LBS. APPROX.
MAXIMUM CURVATURE	WITH TRAIN
MAXIMUM CURVATURE	23° AS SINGLE UNIT
MAXIMUM SPEED	65 M.P.H.
MINIMUM CONT. SPEED	11.5 M.P.H.

SUPPLIES
FUEL	1600 GALS.
LUBE OIL	200 GALS.
COOLING WATER	215 GALS.
SAND	18 CU. FT.

DIESEL ENGINE
MODEL	SEE NOTE
TURBOCHARGER	NOT EQUIPPED
SPARK ARRESTER	EQUIPPED
AIR FILTER, BASIC:	
CARBODY	EQUIPPED
PRIMARY	IMPINGEMENT (PANEL)
ENINGE	IMPINGEMENT (PANEL)
FUEL HEATER	KELTY

NOTE:
DIESEL ENGINES:
UNITS 100-119 .... 16-567-B
UNITS 120-127 .... 16-567-BC

BRAKES
SCHEDULE	24RL F8 (80%) RELAY VALVE
AIR COMPRESSOR	WBO
BRAKE SHOES	HI FRICT. COMP.
SAFETY CONTROL	FOOT PEDAL

ELECTRICAL
MULTIPLE UNIT RECEPTACLES	12-21 & 27 PT
MAIN GENERATOR	D-12B
ALTERNATOR	D-14
TRACTION MOTORS, TYPE	D-27B
NUMBER OF TRACTION MOTORS	4
DYNAMIC BRAKES	FIELD LOOP
BATTERIES	64 V. 426 AMP. HRS.
HEADLIGHTS	TWIN SEALED BEAMS 200W EA.
AUXILIARY GENERATOR	10 KW
COOLING FANS	(4) 36" DIA.
CAB SIGNALS	NOT EQUIPPED
ROTATING WARNING LIGHTS	EQUIPPED
R.C.S.	NOT EQUIPPED

RUNNING GEAR
DRAFT GEAR	MS-485-5A
COUPLER	TYPE 'E'
JOURNALS	6½" x 12" HYATT R.B.
WHEELS	40" DIA.
TRUCKS	4 WHL., SWINGHANGER, CLASP BRKS.

MISCELLANEOUS
WHISTLE	LESLIE S-3 LRF
TOILET	EQUIPPED
FIRE EXTINGUISHERS	(3) 30 LB. ANSUL
WATER COOLER	EQUIPPED
FUEL FILLER	BUCKEYE
SPEED RECORDER	CP
PILOT SNOW PLOW	UNITS 120, 121, 123-125

With the long hood off, a comparison can be made with the general arrangement drawing above for engine components. It is at Omaha Shops, 19 September 1978, being stripped of all useable parts. Once all components or groupings have been removed, the hood will be reinstalled and the unit placed up for sale . . . "as is, where is."

It was purchased by Precision National Corporation, Mt. Vernon, IL in November 1978.

The long hood is the GP7's front . . . as evidenced by the out-sized pilot plow installation. Built in 1953, these units performed yeoman duties across the system during their 27-year life . . . now succumbing to more economical-to-operate modern road-switcher type locomotives. Council Bluffs, IA, 2 December 1977.

ELECTRO-MOTIVE'S GP7 ROSTER

UNIT	BUILDER DATE	BUILDER NUMBER	REMARKS
100	February 1953	17827	Originally UP 700:2, renumbered 11/53. Sold 4/79 to Bargains Galore, Portland, OR and shipped to Diesel Electric Service, St. Paul, MN.
101	February 1953	17828	Originally UP 701:2, renumbered 11/53. Sold 8/78 to Naporano Iron & Metal Company, Newark, NJ.
102	February 1953	17829	Originally UP 702:2, renumbered 11/53. Sold 10/77 to Precision National Corporation, Mt. Vernon, IL.
103	February 1953	17830	Originally UP 703:2, renumbered 11/53.
104	March 1953	17831	Originally UP 704:2, renumbered 11/53. Sold 10/77 to Precision National Corporation, Mt. Vernon, IL.
105	March 1953	17832	Originally UP 705:2, renumbered 11/53. Retired 10/79. Held for disposition.
106	March 1953	17833	Originally UP 706:2, renumbered 11/53. Sold 2/77 to Chrome Crankshaft Co., Chicago, IL.
107	March 1953	17834	Originally UP 707:2, renumbered 11/53.
108	March 1953	17835	Originally UP 708:2, renumbered 11/53. Sold 10/78 to Precision National Corporation, Mt. Vernon, IL.
109	March 1953	17836	Originally UP 709:2, renumbered 11/53. Sold 2/77 to Chrome Crankshaft Co., Chicago, IL.
110	July 1953	18569	Originally UP 710:2, renumbered 11/53. Sold 10/77 to Precision National Corporation, Mt. Vernon, IL.
111	July 1953	18570	Originally UP 711:2, renumbered 11/53. Retired 7/79. Sold 3/80 to General Electric, Hornell, NY.
112	July 1953	18571	Originally UP 712:2, renumbered 11/53.
113	August 1953	18572	Originally UP 713:2, renumbered 11/53. Sold 7/79 to Illinois Central Gulf and shipped to Paducah, KY.
114	August 1953	18573	Originally UP 714:2, renumbered 11/53. Sold 2/79 to Precision National Corporation, Mt. Vernon, IL.
115	August 1953	18574	Originally UP 715:2, renumbered 11/53. Sold 10/78 to Precision National Corporation, Mt. Vernon, IL.
116	August 1953	18575	Originally UP 716:2, renumbered 11/53. Sold 11/78 to Naporano Iron & Metal Company, Newark, NJ.
117	August 1953	18576	Originally UP 717:2, renumbered 11/53. Sold 7/79 to Illinois Central Gulf and shipped to Paducah, KY.
118	August 1953	18577	Originally UP 718:2, renumbered 11/53. Retired 3/80. Held for disposition.
119	September 1953	18578	Originally UP 719:2, renumbered 11/53. Sold 11/78 to Precision National Corporation, Mt. Vernon, IL.
120	October 1953	18711	Originally UP 720, renumbered 11/53. Retired 2/79. Sold 1/80 to Peaker Industries, Brighton, MN.
121	October 1953	18712	Originally UP 721, renumbered 11/53.
122	October 1953	18713	Originally UP 722, renumbered 11/53. Sold 11/78 to Precision National Corporation, Mt. Vernon, IL.
123	October 1953	18714	Originally UP 723, renumbered 11/53. Sold 11/78 to Illinois Central Gulf and shipped to Paducah, KY.
124	October 1953	18715	Originally UP 724, renumbered 11/53. Sold 10/77 to Precision National Corporation, Mt. Vernon, IL.
125	October 1953	18716	Originally UP 725, renumbered 11/53. Sold 10/77 to Precision National Corporation, Mt. Vernon, IL.
126	October 1953	18717	Originally UP 726, renumbered 11/53.
127	October 1953	18718	Originally UP 727, renumbered 11/53. Retired 6/80. Held for disposition.
128	October 1953	18719	Originally UP 728, renumbered 11/53. Sold 8/71 to Electro-Motive Division, LaGrange, IL.
129	October 1953	18720	Originally UP 729, renumbered 11/53. Sold 10/77 to Precision National Corporation, Mt. Vernon, IL.

Freshly painted UP 127 has just arrived from the west and idles on the "run around" tracks at Council Bluffs, IA on 15 April 1979. It was retired two months later and is being held for disposition. The long hood is the front, "F," on these "geeps," which started out on Union Pacific in the 700-Class.

The Class-unit, UP 100, pulls out of the diesel service lead at Council Bluffs, IA on 26 June 1978 with U50C UP 5039 in-trail enroute to Omaha Shops. The "geep" will deliver the big General Electric for stripping and later shipment to Erman Corporation in Turner, KS.

The GP7's started out as 700-Class units, delivered in 1953. They were quickly renumbered to the 100-Class that November.

The louvers serve as spotting features for the GP7 . . . with three sets located under the cab and two long sets under the forward mounted radiator.

A pair of GP7's present an "end" study at Council Bluffs, IA on 6 June 1973.

The front end, "F," is the long hood on the GP7 model . . . as shown by UP 117. The front number boards are mounted some 15 inches lower than the regular position, while on the short hood end, the boards are back at the standard height, as on UP 119.

Six units were equipped with the large branchline pilot plow. The rest of the GP7's have the flat sheet pilot as in both of these units. The stacked MU-receptacles are mounted above the walkway. Note the "double acting" auxiliary uncoupling lever handles . . . the original and the top lever.

UP 117 was sold to Illinois Central Gulf in July 1979, while UP 119 was sold to Precision National Corporation in November 1978.

Sporting the large branchline company-designed pilot snow plow, UP 120 awaits shipping instructions at Council Bluffs, IA on 6 April 1979. It was sold to Peaker Services, Inc., Brighton, MI in February 1979, who intends to remanufacture the unit. The louvering is closely identical to the opposite side's arrangement . . . and is one of the principal spotting features for this model. All GP7's were equipped with the small winterization cooling fan hatches . . . just above the radiator shutters.

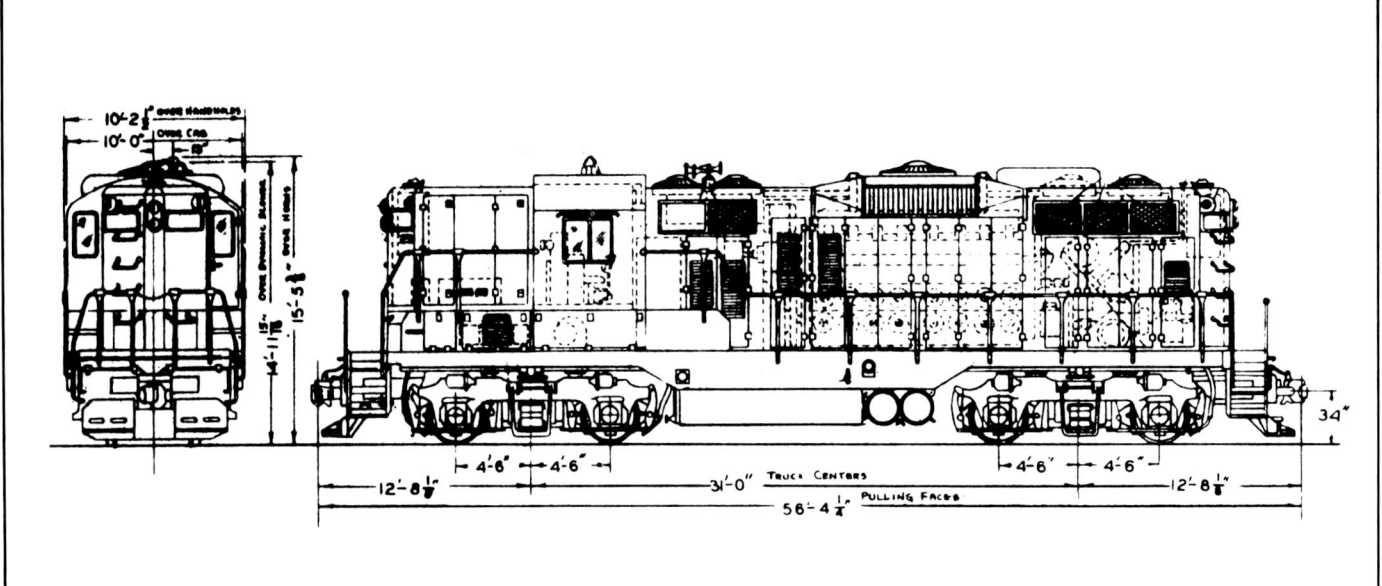

EMD GP9

GENERAL DATA
A.A.R. DESIGNATION	B-B
GEAR RATIO	62/15
WEIGHT LOADED	246,820 LBS.
LIGHT WEIGHT	232,276 LBS. APPROX.
MAXIMUM CURVATURE	13° FULL BUFF*
MAXIMUM CURVATURE	21° NORMAL OR PULL*
MAXIMUM SPEED	65 M.P.H.
MINIMUM CONT. SPEED	12 M.P.H.
MAXIMUM CURVATURE	39° AS SINGLE UNIT
CENTER OF GRAVITY	59.3" ABOVE RAIL (IN WORKING ORDER)

*WITH TRAIN

SUPPLIES
FUEL	1300 GALS.
LUBE OIL	200 GALS.
COOLING WATER	227 GALS.
SAND	18 CU. FT.

DIESEL ENGINE
MODEL	16-567-C
TURBOCHARGER	NOT EQUIPPED
SPARK ARRESTER	EQUIPPED
AIR FILTER, BASIC:	
CARBODY	EQUIPPED
PRIMARY	IMPINGEMENT (PANEL)
ENGINE	IMPINGEMENT OR ROTO-NAMIC
FUEL HEATER	KELTY

BRAKES
SCHEDULE	24RL F8 (80%) RELAY VALVE
AIR COMPRESSOR	WBO
BRAKE SHOES	HI FRICT. COMP.
SAFETY CONTROL	FOOT PEDAL

ELECTRICAL
MULTIPLE UNIT RECEPTACLES	12-21 & 27 PT
MAIN GENERATOR	D-12B
ALTERNATOR	D-14
TRACTION MOTORS, TYPE	D-47
NUMBER OF TRACTION MOTORS	4
DYNAMIC BRAKES	FIELD LOOP
BATTERIES	64 V. 426 AMP. HRS.
HEADLIGHTS	TWIN SEALED BEAMS 200W EA.
AUXILIARY GENERATOR	10 KW
COOLING FANS	(2) 48" 6-BLADE
CAB SIGNALS	NOT EQUIPPED
ROTATING WARNING LIGHTS	EQUIPPED
R.C.S.	NOT EQUIPPED

RUNNING GEAR
DRAFT GEAR	NC-496-1
COUPLER	TYPE 'E'
JOURNALS	6½" x 12" HYATT R.B.
WHEELS	40" DIA.
TRUCKS	4 WHL., SWINGHANGER, CLSP, BRKS.

MISCELLANEOUS
WHISTLE	LESLIE S-3 LRF
TOILET	EQUIPPED
FIRE EXTINGUISHERS	(3) 30 LB. ANSUL
WATER COOLER	EQUIPPED
FUEL FILLER	BUCKEYE
SPEED RECORDER	CP

Ready for action, UP 166 awaits assignment at Council Bluffs, IA on 31 October 1975. Its presence was noticed in eastern Nebraska as it performed branchline service and frequently was the "peddler" . . . setting-out and picking-up cars in all the towns on the First Subdivision. It was retired and sold to Rail Car Corporation, Colorado Springs, CO in June 1980.

Rounding the curve on the New Mainline at Omaha on 20 August 1980 is a pair of GP9's. Units numbered between 130 and 204 were delivered with dynamic brakes. It is not unusual to see Nebraska and Kansas Division locals operated by pairs or trios of GP9's . . . and in a number of cases, assigned to work a specific "zone." A number of these units have been sold . . . all quickly bought by dealers and other railroads.

Surely representing EMD's success story is the ubiquitous GP9. Union Pacific purchased two basic versions . . . with and without dynamic brake equipment. Initially delivered were non-dynamic equipped units (UP 205 through 244), built during January 1954.

The dynamic brake equipped units, UP 130 through 204, were delivered in February through April 1954. UP 204 was renumbered to UP 249 in August 1955 and assigned to jointly-owned [BN (NP) and UP] Camas Prairie Railroad in Idaho; the number UP 204 remains unassigned.

Sporting out-sized road numbers on the front hood and the company-designed branch-line snow plow, UP 149 idles on the diesel leads at Council Bluffs, IA on 6 August 1980.

The right rear truck assembly of UP 187, while at Council Bluffs, IA on 24 August 1980, clearly shows off the construction features of the ever-popular 4-wheel Blomberg-design truck. First introduced in 1939 under EMD road units, it has become the **standard** B-type truck used by Electro-Motive over the years.

Note the single row of louvers on the car body, under the radiator grilling . . . a distinguishing point between the GP9 and the GP7 which has a double row.

The left rear of UP 187, photographed the same day as above, allows a comparison of the rear construction features. As variations are wide spread among GP9's, it is best to show one unit when making left and right comparisons. The single row of louvers under the radiator are duplicated on the opposite side.

While the vertically stacked MU-receptacles are "first generation" styled equipment, the new-styled auxiliary uncoupling lever and removal of the foot boards mark compliance with current safety appliance standards established by AAR/FRA directives.

ELECTRO-MOTIVE'S GP9 ROSTER

UNIT	BUILDER DATE	BUILDER NUMBER	REMARKS
131	February 1954	19132	
132	February 1954	19133	
133	February 1954	19134	Retired 11/78. Accident 11/78 Pocatello, ID.
134	February 1954	19135	Retired 6/80. Held for disposition.
135	February 1954	19136	Sold 10/77 to Precision National Corporation, Mt. Vernon, IL.
136	February 1954	19137	
137	February 1954	19138	
138	February 1954	19139	
139	February 1954	19140	
141	February 1954	19142	Retired 5/79. Sold 7/80 to Naporano Iron & Metal Company, Newark, NJ.
142	February 1954	19143	Retired 3/80. Held for disposition.
143	February 1954	19144	
145	February 1954	19146	Sold 9/79 to Naporano Iron & Metal Company, Newark, NJ.
146	February 1954	19147	
147	February 1954	19148	Retired 8/78. Sold 2/79 to Precision National Corporation, Mt. Vernon, IL.
148	February 1954	19149	Retired 3/80. Held for disposition.
149	February 1954	19150	
150	February 1954	19151	
151	February 1954	19152	
152	February 1954	19153	
153	February 1954	19154	
154	February 1954	19155	
155	February 1954	19156	Retired 8/78. Sold 10/79 to Morrison-Knudsen Corporation, Boise, ID.
156	February 1954	19157	
157	February 1954	19158	
158	March 1954	19159	Retired 10/79. Sold 7/80 to Bargains Galore, Portland, OR and shipped to J Simon Sons, Tacoma, WA.
160	March 1954	19161	
161	March 1954	19162	Sold 11/78 to Naporano Iron & Metal Company, Newark, NJ.
162	March 1954	19163	Retired 2/79. Sold 9/79 to Precision National Corporation, Mt. Vernon, IL.
163	March 1954	19164	
164	March 1954	19165	Retired 6/80. Held for disposition.
165	March 1954	19166	
166	March 1954	19167	Retired 9/79. Sold 6/80 to Rail Car Corporation, Colorado Springs, CO.
167	March 1954	19168	
168	March 1954	19169	
170	March 1954	19171	
171	March 1954	19172	Retired 10/79. Sold 7/80 to Precision National Corporation, Mt. Vernon, IL.
173	March 1954	19174	
174	March 1954	19175	Retired 7/79. Held for disposition.
175	March 1954	19176	
176	March 1954	19177	Sold 3/77 to Precision National Corporation, Mt. Vernon, IL.
177	March 1954	19178	
179	March 1954	19180	Retired 12/78. Sold 7/79 to Illinois Central Gulf and shipped to Paducah, KY.
180	March 1954	19181	
182	March 1954	19183	Retired 6/80. Held for disposition.
184	April 1954	19185	Retired 3/80. Held for disposition.
186	April 1954	19187	Retired 10/79. Sold 7/80 to Precision National Corporation, Mt. Vernon, IL.
187	April 1954	19188	
188	April 1954	19189	
189	April 1954	19190	
191	April 1954	19192	Retired 8/80. Held for disposition.
192	April 1954	19193	
193	April 1954	19194	
194	April 1954	19195	Retired 5/79. Sold 9/79 to Precision National Corporation, Mt. Vernon, IL.
195	April 1954	19196	
196	April 1954	19197	Sold 10/77 to Precision National Corporation, Mt. Vernon, IL.
197	April 1954	19198	
200	April 1954	19201	Sold 6/80 to Rail Car Corporation, Colorado Springs, CO.
201	April 1954	19202	Sold 10/77 to Precision National Corporation, Mt. Vernon, IL.
202	April 1954	19203	
203	April 1954	19204	Retired 10/79. Sold 7/80 to Naporano Iron & Metal Company, Newark, NJ.

Working the Omaha North Yard assignment on 25 September 1977, UP 170 awaits its next chore outside the shop area. This view shows off the general construction features of the left side... noting, no louvered battery box doors and the single set of rear louvers.

The roofline detail is well presented by UP 174 working up the Summit at Omaha on 4 August 1978. The non-slip green area on top of the short hood shows the protected area for the hostler while filling the sand box. The larger winterization hatch protects the single large radiator fan.

This unit was retired in July 1979 and awaits disposition at this time. A review of the above roster shows the locomotive purge, started in 1978, in which the GP9 fleet suffered heavy losses. Some of the heavy chores have been taken over temporarily by the GP30 fleet.

The local Council Bluffs switching power idles between crews on 22 April 1980. Normally there are about six or seven units that tie-up here where they are resupplied and available for the next shift.

While Union Pacific did much engineering on the 300-Class GP9's, the early order remains pretty much "virgin." Compliance with factory modifications would be about the biggest changes, although some safety appliance change-outs were accomplished to meet AAR/FRA standards.

The large branch-line plows were designed and added by the company to UP 130-142, 145, 146, 151, 155, 157, 162, 167 and 169. The out-sized plow mounted on UP 141, shown at Council Bluffs, IA on 26 February 1979, has cleared many miles of Nebraska prairie snows over the years.

The roofline of UP 141 shows the typical arrangement of Union Pacific's GP9's. One major variation is the size of fans installed and another is the single or double fan winterization hatch installation. Horns have been positioned over the radiator fans to prevent winter freeze-ups; however, a number have been moved forward and mounted over the cab in compliance with new Union Pacific mechanical standards. Council Bluffs, IA, 4 April 1980.

What lies behind all the engine locker doors on the GP9...? This hood-off view shows the "guts" consisting of one large power plant that produces 1750 horsepower. The normal aspirating 16-cylinder 567C diesel engine mated to the main generator and alternator are mounted forward, while the air compressor and the cooling system accessory rack are mounted aft.

Being stripped at Omaha Shops on 29 June 1980, this unit has just been retired. All useable parts will be returned to the system's parts pool with the unit being placed up for sale... "as is, where is," after being "picked clean."

A trio of GP9B's are lined up at Council Bluffs, IA on 20 May 1974 awaiting power assignments. By the mid-1970's, the B-units had generally filtered back for service on the Nebraska Division. In several years, these units would be scrapped out and sold to Precision National Corporation: in order, UP 188B, 179B and 160B.

Sandwiched between two units, a normal position for a booster unit, UP 134B stands at Council Bluffs, IA on 21 March 1977. A number of these units picked up the mid-1970 markings using the slogan: "We Can Handle It." This left side view offers a good comparison to the right hand view just below... as to the basic similarities of construction. All GP9B's were equipped with dynamic brakes, evidenced by the housing blister atop at mid-section.

The right side view of UP 174B shows off the near classic lines of the ever popular "geep," sans cab and operating controls. This unit was sold to Precision National Corporation in October 1977 and subsequently scrapped. This view shows the small winterization hatch installed over the small forward fan atop the radiator area. Council Bluffs, IA, 23 March 1977.

Lined up, in funeral order, are units ready for disposition from the property. Headed up by UP 143B, these units will be sold and gone before the end of 1978. The 1976-1978 locomotive purge took a heavy toll on the GP9 fleet and decimated the B-units. UP 134B was rebuilt as a Santa Fe slug 124, having been sold earlier to Naporano Iron & Metal Company who brokered it to AT&SF. Council Bluffs, IA, 18 September 1978.

A pair of veterans run out their last days at Council Bluffs, IA on 14 April 1977. The rear view of UP 156B shows off the lines of an almost "pure" GP9B, uncluttered by modifications. The spotting features are the louvered doors... the single row on the door under the radiator grilling and the single set on the battery box drop-door. As these units had the smaller radiator fans, the small winterization hatch enclosed the forward fan.

This unit was sold to Precision National Corporation in October 1977. The U50C was sold to the Erman Corporation, Turner, KS in June 1978.

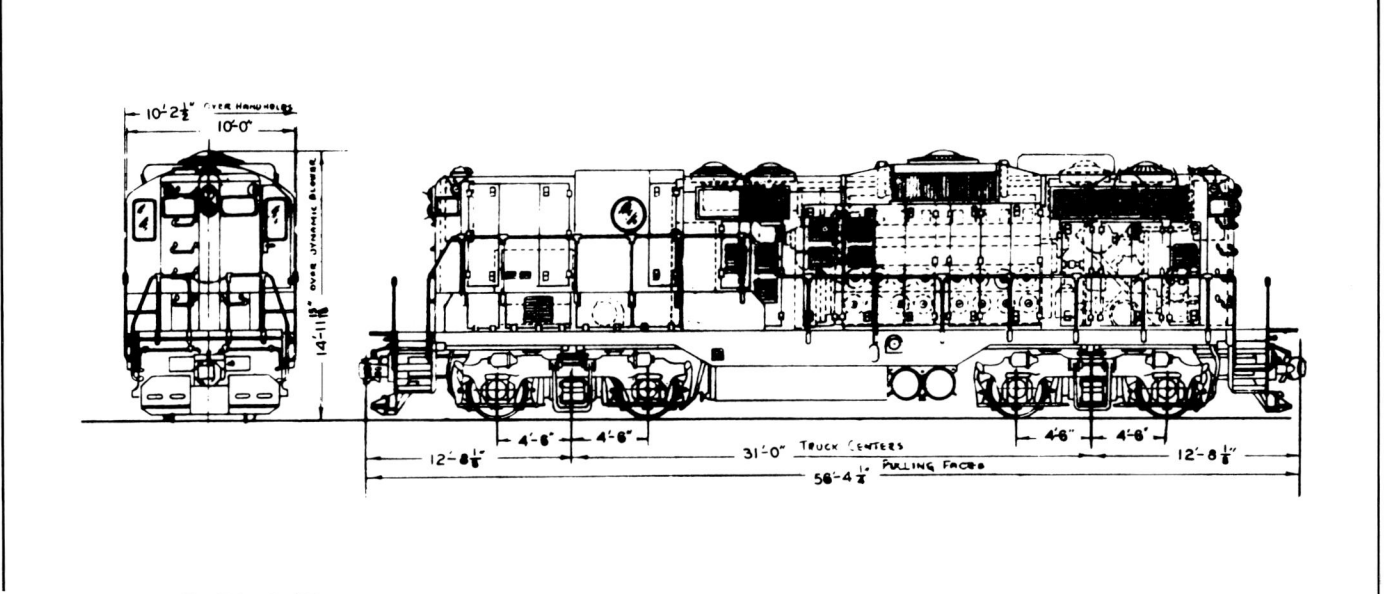

EMD GP9B

ELECTRO-MOTIVE'S GP9B ROSTER

UNIT	BUILDER DATE	BUILDER NUMBER	REMARKS
134B	February 1954	19210	Sold 11/78 to Naporano Iron & Metal Company, Newark, NJ.
138B	February 1954	19214	Sold 11/78 to Precision National Corporation, Mt. Vernon, IL.
143B	February 1954	19219	Sold 11/78 to Naporano Iron & Metal Company, Newark, NJ.
150B	February 1954	19226	Sold 3/77 to Precision National Corporation, Mt. Vernon, IL.
156B	February 1954	19232	Sold 10/77 to Precision National Corporation, Mt. Vernon, IL.
157B	February 1954	19233	Sold 11/78 to Precision National Corporation, Mt. Vernon, IL.
158B	February 1954	19234	Sold 11/78 to Precision National Corporation, Mt. Vernon, IL.
164B	March 1954	19240	Sold 9/78 to Precision National Corporation, Mt. Vernon, IL.
174B	March 1954	19250	Sold 10/77 to Precision National Corporation, Mt. Vernon, IL.
175B	March 1954	19251	Sold 3/77 to Precision National Corporation, Mt. Vernon, IL.
179B	March 1954	19255	Sold 10/77 to Precision National Corporation, Mt. Vernon, IL.
184B	April 1954	19260	Sold 9/78 to Precision National Corporation, Mt. Vernon, IL.
186B	April 1954	19262	Sold 11/78 to Illinois Central Gulf and shipped to Paducah, KY.
188B	April 1954	19264	Sold 2/77 to Precision National Corporation, Mt. Vernon, IL.
191B	April 1954	19267	Sold 3/77 to Precision National Corporation, Mt. Vernon, IL.
193B	April 1954	19269	Sold 2/77 to Precision National Corporation, Mt. Vernon, IL
194B	April 1954	19270	Sold 10/77 to Precision National Corporation, Mt. Vernon, IL.
197B	April 1954	19273	Sold 10/77 to Precision National Corporation, Mt. Vernon, IL.
204B	April 1954	19280	Sold 10/77 to Precision National Corporation, Mt. Vernon, IL.

Union Pacific has always been interested in cabless units. At Council Bluffs, IA on 26 September 1977, two such versions sat on parallel tracks. GP9B UP 186B shows off the uncluttered lines of a standard "geep" booster with the smaller sized fans. The face of SD24B UP 436B could be easily taken for a GP9 . . . except it is a six-axle, higher horsepower locomotive.

Union Pacific purchased a total of 125 GP9 cabless units. The only other B-unit purchases were made by Pennsylvania Railroad, who bought 40 units.

This "geep" was sold to Illinois Central Gulf and shipped in November 1978 to their Paducah (KY) Shops for inclusion in the GP11 rebuild program. It became ICG 8704.

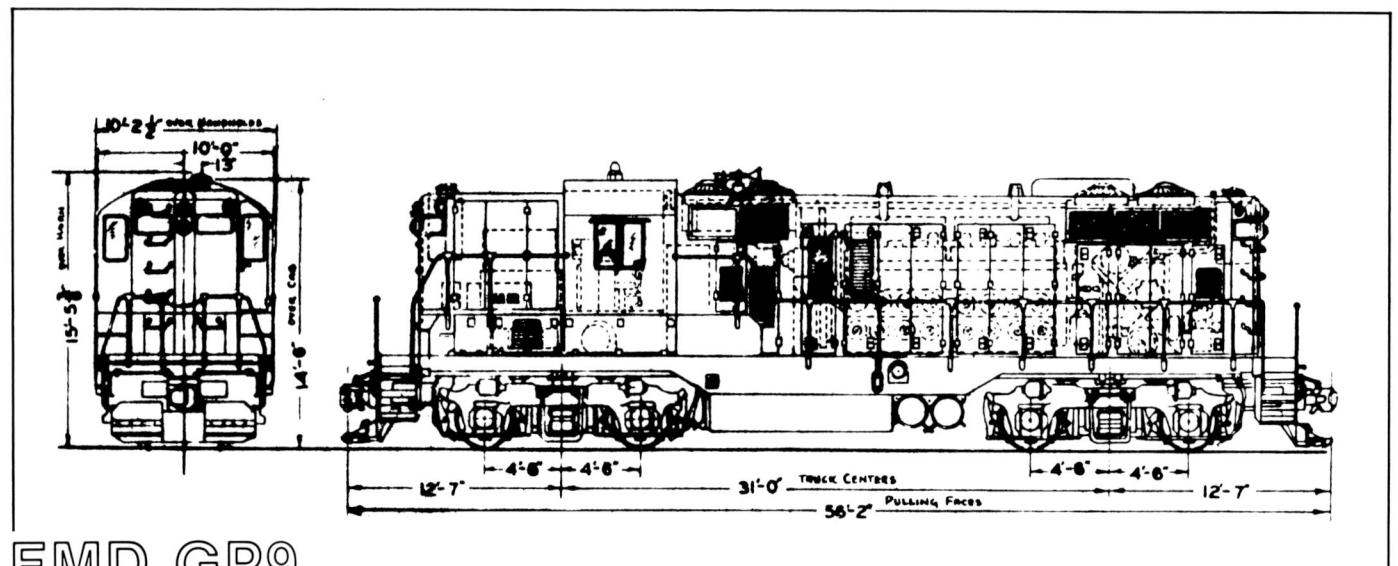

EMD GP9

GENERAL DATA
A.A.R. DESIGNATION	B-B
GEAR RATIO	62/15
WEIGHT LOADED	245,740 LBS.
LIGHT WEIGHT	231,891 LBS. APPROX.
MAXIMUM CURVATURE	WITH TRAIN
MAXIMUM CURVATURE	21° AS SINGLE UNIT
MAXIMUM SPEED	65 M.P.H.
MINIMUM CONT. SPEED	12 M.P.H.
CENTER OF GRAVITY	59.3" ABOVE RAIL (IN WORKING ORDER)

SUPPLIES
FUEL	1200 GALS.
LUBE OIL	200 GALS.
COOLING WATER	230 GALS.
SAND	18 CU. FT.

DIESEL ENGINE
MODEL	16-567-C
TURBOCHARGER	NOT EQUIPPED
SPARK ARRESTER	EQUIPPED
AIR FILTER, BASIC:	
CARBODY	EQUIPPED
PRIMARY	IMPINGEMENT PANEL
ENGINE	IMPINGEMENT OR ROTO-NAMIC
FUEL HEATER	KELTY

BRAKES
SCHEDULE	24RL F8 (80%) RELAY VALVE
AIR COMPRESSOR	WBO
BRAKE SHOES	HI FRIC. COMP
SAFETY CONTROL	FOOT PEDAL

ELECTRICAL
MULTIPLE UNIT RECEPTACLES	12-21 & 27 PT
MAIN GENERATOR	D-12B
ALTERNATOR	D-14
TRACTION MOTORS, TYPE	D-37B
NUMBER OF TRACTION MOTORS	4
DYNAMIC BRAKES	NOT EQUIPPED
BATTERIES	64 V. 426 AMP. HRS.
HEADLIGHTS	TWIN SEALED BEAMS 200W EA.
AUXILIARY GENERATOR	10 KW
COOLING FANS	(4) 36" FANS
CAB SIGNALS	(UNITS 234, 236 & 240) US&S 'E'
ROTATING WARNING LIGHTS	EQUIPPED
R.C.S.	NOT EQUIPPED

RUNNING GEAR
DRAFT GEAR	MS-485-5A
COUPLER	TYPE 'E'
JOURNALS	6½" x 12" HYATT R.B.
WHEELS	40" DIA.
TRUCKS	4 WHL., SWINGHANGER, CLSP. BRKS.

MISCELLANEOUS
WHISTLE	LESLIE S-3 LRF
TOILET	EQUIPPED
FIRE EXTINGUISHERS	(3) 30 LB. ANSUL
WATER COOLER	EQUIPPED
FUEL FILLER	BUCKEYE
SPEED RECORDER	CP
STAND BY WATER HEATERS	UNITS 217, 220, 223 & 225 ONLY

ELECTRO-MOTIVE'S GP9 ROSTER

UNIT	BUILDER DATE	BUILDER NUMBER	REMARKS
205	January 1954	19091	Retired 9/78. Sold 2/79 to Precision National Corporation, Mt. Vernon, IL.
206	January 1954	19092	Retired 8/78. Sold 1/79 to Precision National Corporation, Mt. Vernon, IL.
207	January 1954	19093	Sold 7/77 to Precision National Corporation, Mt. Vernon, IL.
209	January 1954	19095	
210	January 1954	19096	Sold 7/80 to Rail Car Corporation, Colorado Springs, CO.
211	January 1954	19097	
212	January 1954	19098	
213	January 1954	19099	Retired 12/79. Held for disposition.
215	January 1954	19101	
216	January 1954	19102	Retired 10/79. Sold 2/80 to Precision National Corporation, Mt. Vernon, IL.
217	January 1954	19103	
219	January 1954	19105	Retired 7/79. Sold 12/79 to Naporano Iron & Metal Company, Newark, NJ.
220	January 1954	19106	Retired 6/80. Held for disposition.
221	January 1954	19107	Retired 5/79. Sold 12/79 to Naporano Iron & Metal Company, Newark, NJ.
222	January 1954	19108	
223	January 1954	19109	Retired 8/80. Held for disposition.
224	January 1954	19110	Retired 2/79. Sold 10/79 to Morrison-Knudsen Corporation, Boise, ID.
225	January 1954	19111	Retired 5/79. Sold 12/79 to Naporano Iron & Metal Company, Newark, NJ.
226	January 1954	19112	
228	January 1954	19114	Retired 10/79. Held for disposition.
229	January 1954	19115	
230	January 1954	19116	Retired 5/79. Sold 1/80 to General Electric Corporation and shipped to Hornell, NY.
231	January 1954	19117	
232	January 1954	19118	
233	January 1954	19119	
236	January 1954	19122	
237	January 1954	19123	
238	January 1954	19124	Sold 11/78 to Precision National Corporation, Mt. Vernon, IL.
239	January 1954	19125	Sold 11/78 to Precision National Corporation, Mt. Vernon, IL.
240	January 1954	19126	
242	January 1954	19128	Sold 2/77 to Precision National Corporation, Mt. Vernon, IL.
243	January 1954	19129	Retired 8/80. Held for disposition.
244	January 1954	19130	Retired 12/79. Held for disposition.

A West Omaha "peddler" trundles back to town after a day's work of picking up and setting out cars in the various westside industrial tracts. This is mainline 2 near the 36th Street bridge . . . sometimes referred to as the new mainline or the Lane cutoff. UP 222 is normally assigned yard duties at Council Bluffs, IA. Omaha, NE, 18 March 1980.

Showing off the uncluttered lines of a non-dynamic brake-equipped GP9, UP 207 awaits its switching assignments at Council Bluffs, IA on 4 December 1975. A number of these units . . . 205-244, were assigned to flat yard switching duties.

This unit was sold to Precision National Corporation in February 1977 and shipped to Silvis, IL for rebuilding. It was released as Amtrak 766 in May 1977 and shipped east for service.

The popular 4-wheel Blomberg design truck rides under almost all Electro-Motive B-B locomotives. Sparkling in its fresh silvered paint, the front truck assembly of UP 209 offers close inspection. The large outside spring hanger dampens out the side-to-side and up-and-down movement . . . which has always been a challenge to problem-solving truck dynamics.

Note the single louvered battery box door . . . a spotting feature of the GP9. Adding a touch of class . . . the model plaque is attached to the step box on both sides.

Serviced and ready for the next switching crew, UP 211 idles on the service tracks at Council Bluffs, IA on 13 May 1979. This represents an "as delivered" look, except for the later style painting and lettering scheme. These "geeps" did not go through any extensive modification programs . . . they worked great—and continue to perform "as advertised."

The lack of the dynamic brake installation does not hamper their performance in turning in a day's work in the yard and limited transfer runs.

UP 216-226, above, sit on the switcher ready tracks at Council Bluffs, IA on 16 March 1975. Each has different painting and lettering schemes.

UP 222-223, below, show off their rear construction features on the switcher ready tracks at Council Bluffs, IA on 26 September 1975.

Sidelined on the storage tracks at Council Bluffs, IA on 11 May 1979, UP 230 has just been retired. It was later sold to General Electric in January 1980 and shipped to Hornell, NY for remanufacture as a commuter unit in the Pittsburgh, PA area. Fourteen of the forty units remain on the roster. This engineer's side view offers a comparison to the other views on these two pages; however, this block of locomotives retained most of their original manufactured appearance.

UP 250-299 were built and delivered in August and September 1954. This order was similar to earlier purchases of dynamic brake-equipped GP9's. Later, several received the company designed large branch-line snow plow (UP 264, 265 and 274). UP 261 has a larger 2400-gallon fuel tank; the standard fuel tank is 1200 gallons. Many of the "geeps" still retain their model identification plaque, attached to the front box step. UP 264 shown active at Council Bluffs, IA on 16 September 1980.

Equipped with a stand-by water heater, UP 249 started service as UP 204. It was renumbered UP 249 in August 1955 and assigned to the jointly owned Camas Prairie Railroad in Idaho. It was retired in August 1980. Council Bluffs, IA, 2 November 1980.

The roof-line of UP 283 from the cab rearward, shows the arrangement of the fans, location of the horns and the fairing-in of the dynamic brake blister. Council Bluffs, IA, 2 November 1980.

The "Omaha Triples" climbs the hill at Summit in Omaha, NE on 3 June 1979. UP 287, 209 and 272 pull up Mainline 3 with a delivery headed for South Omaha. These are all 1954-built GP9's... with UP 209 coming from the early 1954 order (UP 205-244) in January, which were not equipped with dynamic brakes; and the other two coming from the later order in September 1954.

An experiment in externally-mounted car body filters, two "geeps" had a number of square cut-outs removed from their engine locker doors. Snap-in filters shouldered into the square openings to permit a greater flow of clean air into the engine compartment. Shown at Council Bluffs, IA on 19 October 1980 is UP 283. The opposite side has the same basic arrangement of cut-outs. The other unit is UP 261, retired in December 1979.

UP 280 pulls a string of Rock Island returned locomotives at Council Bluffs, IA on 5 May 1980. In late April and early May, returned Rock Island locomotives and rolling stock leased from the Union Pacific filled every spare track in the area.

Idling in front of the St. Joseph Terminal diesel house on 1 September 1978, UP 295 is the local power for the day. Santa Fe and Union Pacific jointly own and operate the SJT which receives their locals at St. Joseph, MO and in-turn, makes the local set-outs and pickups, and deliveries to the Burlington Northern and Chicago & North Western. This rear view shows a "factory standard" well maintained GP9... wearing its 26 years quite nonchalantly.

245	April 1954	19552	Accident 6/77, Bosler, WY. Scrapped 12/77, Omaha Shops.
246	June 1954	19565	
247	June 1954	19566	
248	June 1954	19567	
249	April 1954	19205	Originally UP 204, renumbered 8/55. Retired 8/80. Held for disposition.
250	August 1954	19775	Sold 9/79 to Naporano Iron & Metal Company, Newark, NJ.
252	August 1954	19777	
253	August 1954	19778	Retired 1/80. Held for disposition.
255	August 1954	19780	Retired 6/80. Held for disposition.
256	August 1954	19781	
257	August 1954	19782	
258	August 1954	19783	Sold 9/79 to Precision National Corporation, Mt. Vernon, IL.
259	August 1954	19784	Sold 10/79 to Precision National Corporation, Mt. Vernon, IL.
260	August 1954	19785	
261	August 1954	19786	Retired 12/79. Held for disposition.
262	August 1954	19787	Retired 3/80. Held for disposition.
264	August 1954	19861	
265	August 1954	19862	
266	August 1954	19863	
267	August 1954	19864	Retired 8/80. Held for disposition.
269	September 1954	19866	
270	September 1954	19867	Accident 6/78 and scrapped 7/78, Pocatello Shops.
271	September 1954	19868	Retired 6/80. Held for disposition.
272	September 1954	19869	
273	September 1954	19870	Sold 2/79 to Bargains Galore, Portland, OR and shipped to Diesel Electric Service, St. Paul, MN.
275	September 1954	19872	
278	September 1954	19875	Sold 2/79 to Morrison-Knudsen Corporation, Boise, ID.
279	September 1954	19876	Retired 10/79. Sold 8/80 to Precision National Corporation, Mt. Vernon, IL.
280	September 1954	19877	
282	September 1954	19879	Sold 11/78 to Illinois Central Gulf and shipped to Paducah, KY.
283	September 1954	19880	Retired 6/80. Held for disposition.
284	September 1954	19881	
285	September 1954	19882	Retired 12/79. Sold 8/80 to Precision National Corporation, Mt. Vernon, IL.
286	September 1954	19883	Retired 5/79. Sold 1/80 to General Electric Corporation and shipped to Hornell, NY.
287	September 1954	19884	Retired 3/80. Held for disposition.
288	September 1954	19885	Retired 5/79. Sold 12/79 to Hyman-Michaels Company, Madison, IL.
289	September 1954	19886	Retired 8/78. Sold 4/79 to Naporano Iron & Metal Company, Newark, NJ.
291	September 1954	19888	
293	September 1954	19890	Retired 8/80. Held for disposition.
294	September 1954	19891	
295	September 1954	19892	
296	September 1954	19893	
297	September 1954	19894	Retired 10/79. Sold 5/80 to Naporano Iron & Metal Company, Newark, NJ.
298	September 1954	19895	
299	September 1954	19896	

NOTES:

A—UP 245-249 purchased for jointly operated (BN/UP) Camas Prairie Railroad. UP 293 replaced accident damaged UP 245 in 8/77.

B—UP 295-299 equipped with steam generators to support passenger operations. They were removed in 1972-1973 and 2400 gallon fuel tanks were installed.

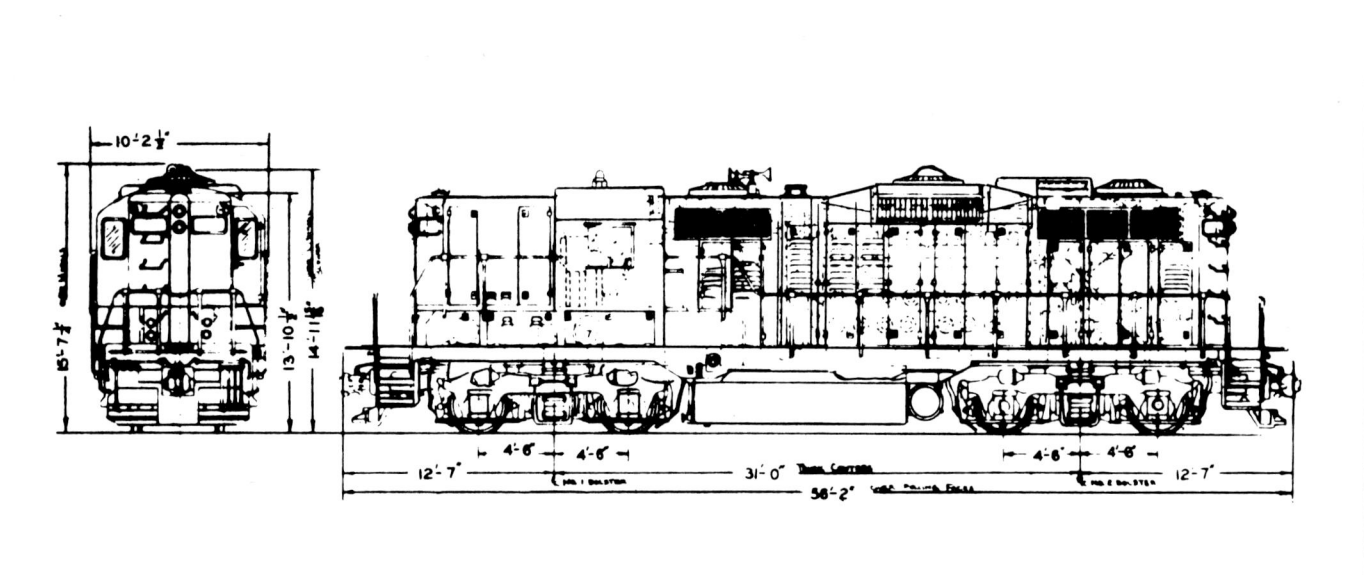

EMD GP9MA

GENERAL DATA

A.A.R. DESIGNATION	B-B
GEAR RATIO	62/15
WEIGHT LOADED	258,870 LBS.
LIGHT WEIGHT	236,406 APPROX.
MAXIMUM CURVATURE	13° FULL BUFF
MAXIMUM CURVATURE	21° NORMAL OR PULL
MAXIMUM SPEED	65 M.P.H.
MINIMUM CONT. SPEED	12 M.P.H.
MAXIMUM CURVATURE	39° AS SINGLE UNIT
CENTER OF GRAVITY	59.3" ABOVE RAIL (IN WORKING ORDER)

SUPPLIES

FUEL	2400 GALS.
LUBE OIL	200 GALS.
COOLING WATER	227 GALS.
SAND	18 CU. FT.

DIESEL ENGINE

MODEL	16-567-D2
TURBOCHARGER	EQUIPPED
SPARK ARRESTER	NOT REQUIRED
AIR FILTER, BASIC:	
CARBODY	EQUIPPED
PRIMARY	IMPINGEMENT (PANEL)
ENGINE	PANEL OIL BATH
FUEL HEATER	KELTY

NOTE:
CONVERTED TO TURBOCHARGED GP-9MA FROM GP-9A BY UPRR BEGINNING IN 1963.

BRAKES

SCHEDULE	24RL F8 (80%) RELAY VALVE
AIR COMPRESSOR	WBO
BRAKE SHOES	HI FRICT. COMP.
SAFETY CONTROL	FOOT PEDAL

ELECTRICAL

MULTIPLE UNIT RECEPTACLES	12-21 & 27 PT
MAIN GENERATOR	D-12B
ALTERNATOR	D-14
TRACTION MOTORS, TYPE	D-47
NUMBER OF TRACTION MOTORS	4
DYNAMIC BRAKES	FIELD LOOP
BATTERIES	64 V. 426 AMP. HRS.
HEADLIGHTS	TWIN SEALED BEAMS 200W EA.
AUXILIARY GENERATOR	10 KW
COOLING FANS	(2) 48" 6-BLADE
CAB SIGNALS	NOT EQUIPPED
ROTATING WARNING LIGHTS	EQUIPPED
R.C.S.	NOT EQUIPPED

RUNNING GEAR

DRAFT GEAR	NC-496-1
COUPLER	TYPE 'F'
JOURNALS	6½" x 12" HYATT R.B.
WHEELS	40" DIA.
TRUCKS	4 WHL., SWINGHANGER, CLSP. BRKS.

MISCELLANEOUS

WHISTLE	LESLIE S-3 LRF
TOILET	EQUIPPED
FIRE EXTINGUISHERS	(3) 30 LB. ANSUL
WATER COOLER	EQUIPPED
FUEL FILLER	BUCKEYE
SPEED RECORDER	CP

ELECTRO-MOTIVE'S GP9M ROSTER

UNIT	BUILDER DATE	BUILDER NUMBER	REMARKS
300[1]	July 1957	23656	Retired 9/78. Sold 9/79 to Precision National Corporation, Mt. Vernon, IL.
304[2]	July 1957	23660	Retired 9/78. Sold 12/79 to Precision National Corporation, Mt. Vernon, IL.
305[1]	July 1957	23661	
307[2]	July 1957	23663	
308[2]	July 1957	23664	Retired 5/79. Sold 10/79 to Morrison-Knudsen Corporation, Boise, ID.
311[1]	July 1957	23667	Retired 4/80. Sold 8/80 to Precision National Corporation, Mt. Vernon, IL.
313[1]	July 1957	23669	Retired 10/79. Sold 8/80 to Precision National Corporation, Mt. Vernon, IL.
316[2]	July 1957	23672	Retired 8/80. Held for disposition.
317[2]	July 1957	23673	Retired 10/79. Held for disposition.
320[1]	July 1957	23676	Retired 2/79. Sold 1/80 to Peaker Industries, Inc., Brighton, MN.
325[2]	September 1957	23681	Retired 9/79. Sold 7/80 to Naporano Iron & Metal Company, Newark, NJ.
326[2]	September 1957	23682	
328[2]	September 1957	23684	Retired 10/79. Held for disposition.
329[2]	September 1957	23685	
330[2]	September 1957	23686	Retired 1/80. Held for disposition.
332[2]	September 1957	23688	
334[2]	September 1957	23690	Retired 4/78. Sold 3/79 to Precision National Corporation, Mt. Vernon, IL.
335[2]	September 1957	23691	
339[2]	September 1957	23695	Retired 10/79. Sold 6/80 to Rail Car Corporation, Colorado Springs, CO.
340[2]	October 1957	23696	
343[2]	October 1957	23699	
344[2]	October 1957	23700	
347[2]	October 1957	23703	Retired 8/80. Held for disposition.
348[2]	October 1957	23704	Retired 4/78. Sold 3/79 to Precision National Corporation, Mt. Vernon, IL.

[1] *Converted to 2000hp turbocharged GP9M's by EMD in 1959.*

[2] *Converted to 2000hp turbocharged GP9M's by UP beginning in 1963.*

Freshly painted GP9MA points west at Council Bluffs, IA on 11 January 1976. Turbocharged experimentally by Union Pacific to 2000 horsepower in 1955, these units were considered "Omaha GP20's." The turbocharger-styled stack is visible just aft of the horns. The car body extension behind the cab is another spotting feature, as is the external plumbing running up both sides of the fuel tank.

One of the "Omaha GP20's"... it had been converted to turbocharged operation by the Union Pacific in a program started in 1963. This upgraded the 16-cylinder 567-D2 diesel engine to 2000-horsepower output... 250-horsepower more than the normal aspirating GP9's. There are no set groupings of those selected for the increased horsepower program, although they all came from the 300-Class units. Reference to the model roster will indicate those upgraded to GP9MA. UP 344 idles on the ready tracks at Council Bluffs, IA on 20 September 1978.

The left center section of UP 347 shows several modifications. The first and largest was the turbocharging program. The car body was extended, just aft of the cab, to permit installation of the turbocharger group. The two off-set louvered doors permit access to the various assemblies. The squared turbocharger stack is just aft of the horn group.

This unit was converted to burn residual fuel used by the large turbine fleet of the 1960's. While the plumbing has been removed, the attaching points are still visible on the large 2400-gallon fuel tank. The fuel was pumped from the forward wall of the fuel tank back along the left side to the rear compartment. There it was heated to operating temperature and routed forward to the engine for use.

UP 347's left side; Council Bluffs, IA, 10 May 1980.

Another turbocharged GP9, UP 330 idles at Council Bluffs, IA on 14 November 1979. Again, this unit was converted for Bunker-C fuel used by the turbines, as evidenced by the external plumbing running down the left side of the unit. While residual fuel was much cheaper, it required heating to moderate temperature before use. The heater assembly was located in the air compressor area at the rear of the car body. While disabled, the system remains intact.

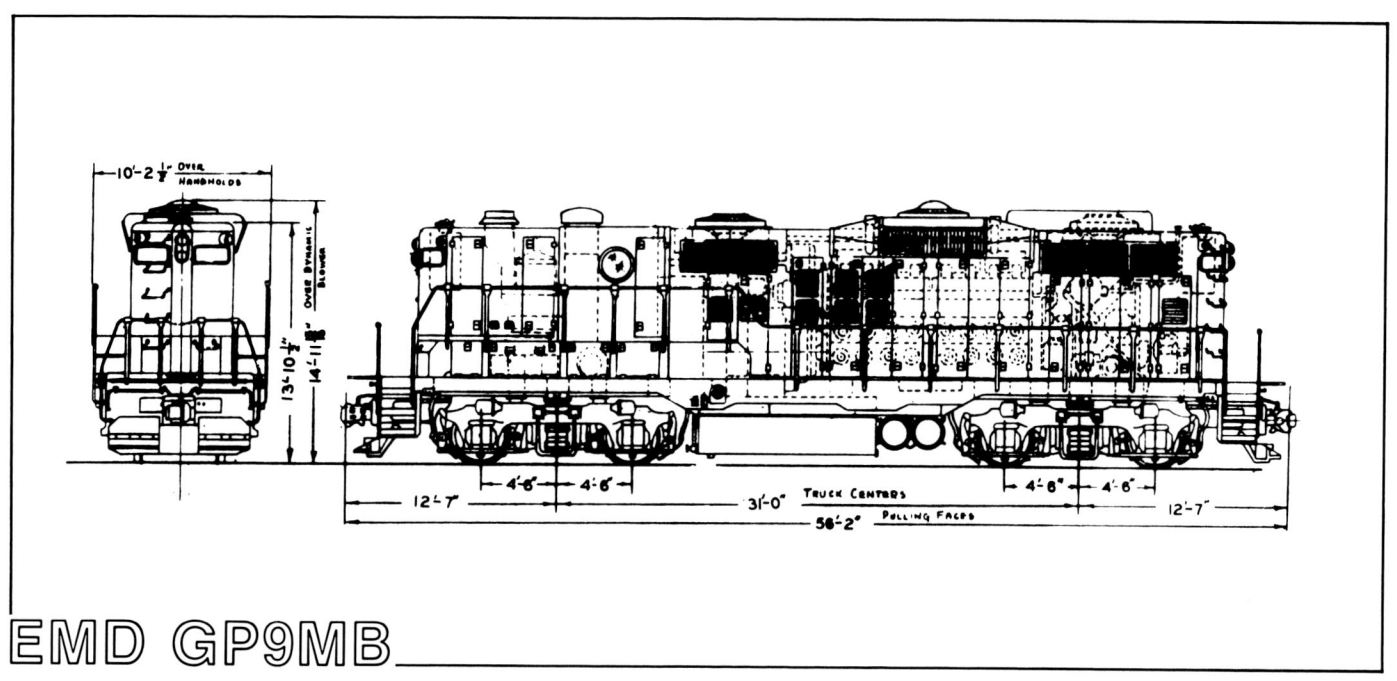

EMD GP9MB

THE GENERAL DATA HAS BEEN OMITTED. REFER TO DATA FURNISHED WITH THE GP9MB PRESENTATION.

ELECTRO-MOTIVE'S GP9BM ROSTER

UNIT	BUILDER DATE	BUILDER NUMBER	REMARKS
303B	September 1957	23709	Turbocharged to 2000hp by UP in 1963. Retired 5/79. Sold 12/79 to Bargains Galore, Portland, OR and shipped to Diesel Electric Service, St. Paul, MN.
307B	September 1957	23713	Turbocharged to 2000hp by UP in 1963. Sold 10/77 to Precision National Corporation, Mt. Vernon, IL.
308B	September 1957	23714	Turbocharged to 2000hp by EMD in 1959. Sold 3/77 to Precision National Corporation, Mt. Vernon, IL.
309B	September 1957	23715	Turbocharged to 2000hp by UP in 1963. Retired 9/78. Sold 9/79 to Precision National Corporation, Mt. Vernon, IL.
315B	September 1957	23721	Turbocharged to 2000hp by UP in 1963. Sold 3/77 to Precision National Corporation, Mt. Vernon, IL.
318B	September 1957	23724	Turbocharged to 2000hp by UP in 1963. Sold 11/78 to Illinois Central Gulf and shipped to Paducah, KY.
325B	September 1957	23731	Turbocharged to 2000hp by UP in 1963 Retired 5/79. Sold 12/79 to Naporano Iron & Metal Company, Newark, NJ.
333B	September 1957	23739	Turbocharged to 2000hp by UP in 1963. Sold 3/77 to Precision National Corporation, Mt. Vernon, IL.
334B	September 1957	23740	Turbocharged to 2000hp by UP in 1963. Retired 5/79. Sold 2/77 to Precision National Corporation, Mt. Vernon, IL.
335B	September 1957	23741	Turbocharged to 2000hp by UP in 1963. Sold 10/77 to Precision National Corporation, Mt. Vernon, IL.
336B	September 1957	23742	Turbocharged to 2000hp by UP in 1963. Sold 10/77 to Precision National Corporation, Mt. Vernon, IL.
337B	October 1957	23743	Turbocharged to 2000hp by UP in 1963. Sold 9/78 to Precision National Corporation, Mt. Vernon, IL.
339B	October 1957	23745	Turbocharged to 2000hp by UP in 1963. Retired 9/78. Sold Precision National Corporation, Mt. Vernon, IL.
340B	October 1957	23746	Turbocharged to 2000hp by UP in 1963. Sold 10/78 to Precision National Corporation, Mt. Vernon, IL.
344B	October 1957	23750	Turbocharged to 2000hp by UP in 1963. Sold 2/77 to Precision National Corporation, Mt. Vernon, IL.
348B	October 1957	23754	Turbocharged to 2000hp by UP in 1963. Retired 9/78. Sold 12/79 to Precision National Corporation, Mt. Vernon, IL.

In trail position, UP 325B awaits westbound action at Council Bluffs, IA on 25 March 1979. This is one of the steam generator equipped GP9MB's, identified by the generator exhaust stack and air-intake mounted atop the high short hood. The boiler is located inside the short hood. These units saw intermittent branchline passenger service in the 1960's, thus the heating capability.

This unit was retired in May 1979 and later sold to Naporano Iron & Metal Company in December 1979.

Union Pacific converted a number of their 300-Class GP9B units to 2000-horsepower turbocharged locomotives beginning in 1963. UP 303B, one such conversion, idles at Council Bluffs, IA on 19 June 1977. The same distinguishing features as the GP9MA's disclose the modification... the turbocharger stack and the extended car body housing the turbocharger group. Note that no horns are installed on B-units.

Seven GP9MB's have Vapor steam generators installed, as shown by UP 318B at Council Bluffs, IA, 1 January 1978. The others are 311B, 324B-326B, 343B, and 344B.

The rear view of UP 340B, photographed at Council Bluffs, IA on 21 August 1977, gives no clues to whether this unit is rated at 1750 or 2000 horsepower. Reference to the model roster will disclose it was turbocharged by Union Pacific in the mid-1960's.

The front end of GP9MB UP 348B shows off the construction features used to create the cabless "geep" version. The basic engine operating controls are located in the "windowed" compartment, the electrical locker arrangement is the same as with the cab version.

The Blomberg designed B-truck assembly shows off to good advantage in this view... at Council Bluffs, IA on 21 March 1977.

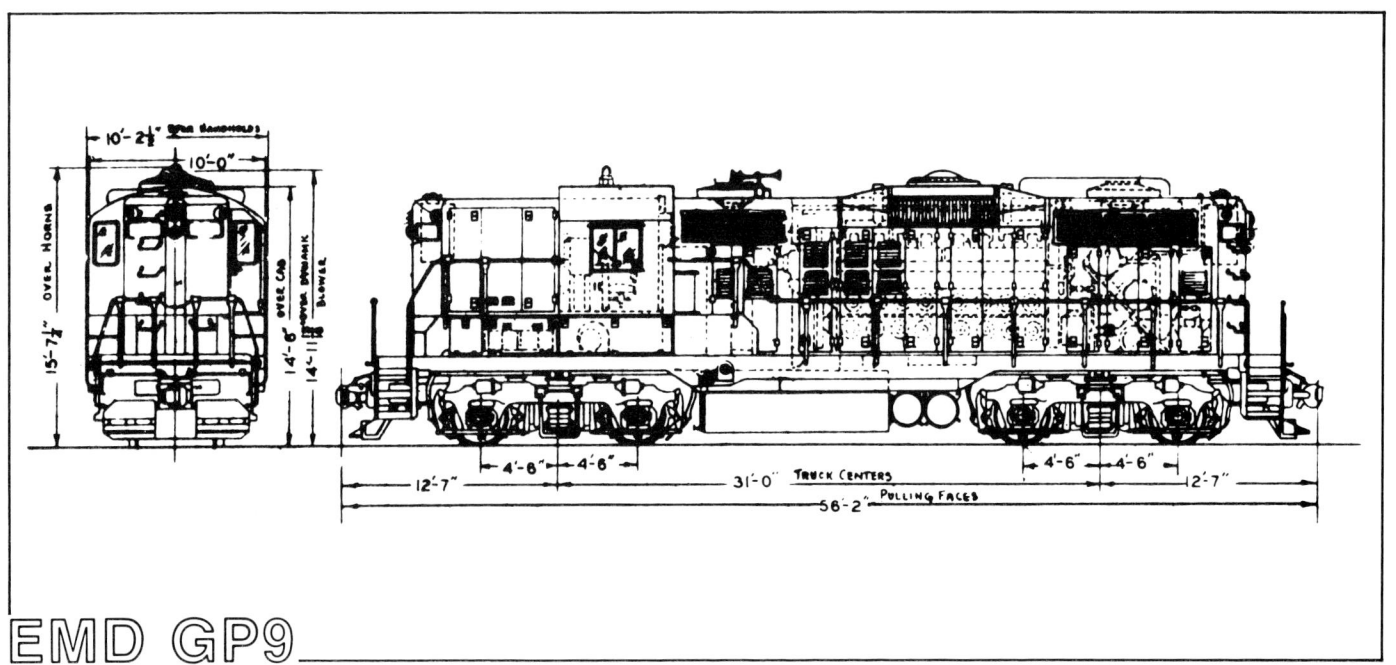

EMD GP9

THE GENERAL DATA HAS BEEN OMITTED.

ELECTRO-MOTIVE'S GP9 ROSTER

UNIT	BUILDER DATE	BUILDER NUMBER	REMARKS
302	July 1957	23658	Sold 11/78 to Illinois Central Gulf and shipped to Paducah, KY.
303	July 1957	23659	Retired 6/80. Held for disposition.
312	July 1957	23668	Retired 7/79. Sold 7/80 to Naporano Iron & Metal Company, Newark, NJ.
314	July 1957	23670	
315	July 1957	23671	Retired 6/80. Held for disposition.
318	July 1957	23674	
319	July 1957	23675	Retired 2/79. Sold 1/80 to Peaker Industries, Inc., Brighton, MN.
321	September 1957	23677	Retired 5/79. Sold 10/79 to Precision National Corporation, Mt. Vernon, IL.
324	September 1957	23680	Retired 8/80. Held for disposition.
327	September 1957	23683	
331	September 1957	23687	Sold 11/78 to Precision National Corporation, Mt. Vernon, IL.
336	September 1957	23692	
337	September 1957	23693	
338	September 1957	23694	
341	October 1957	23697	
345	October 1957	23701	
349	October 1957	23705	Retired 7/79. Sold 2/80 to Naporano Iron & Metal Company, Newark, NJ.

With just weeks until retirement, UP 321 sits at Council Bluffs, IA on 29 April 1980. Recently outshopped, it carries the late 1970's painting and lettering scheme for this model (the "geeps" cannot accept the large style lettering and numers on the car body such as used on larger units). Note the variation of the louver design on the battery box door on this unit and the one below.

Striking a classic pose, UP 303 points west at Council Bluffs, IA on 27 May 1979. It has just been recently retired . . . June 1980; however, it is being held for disposition. While Union Pacific has switched to six-axle units in their Electric Trailer conversion program, the possibility exists for converting several more "geep" bodies to slug service. Over the years, battery box doors get moved around . . . and this unit displays a different door arrangement than the one above.

The standard GP9 in the 300-Class built in the mid-1957's bears a commonality with its 1954 dynamic brake-equipped counterpart. A good example is UP 324 at Council Bluffs, IA on 18 October 1978. The modified skirt bares the 2400-gallon fuel tank . . . a feature pretty well followed on most late Union Pacific "geeps."

From this vantage point, the rear is about 25 feet away . . . a GP9 is 56 feet 2 inches long, as measured from the pulling face of the opposing couplers. Union Pacific has equipped its GP9's with either the single or double fan winterization protective hatch. The single fan kit (large) covers the large fan; the double fan kit (small) covers forward small fan. These covers are permanently installed and are equipped with a change-lever for either "summer" or "winter" operation . . . giving added full-season protection against dust or snow ingestion.

The dynamic brake blister protrudes from the center section of the car body which houses its grid resistors used to dissipate the power generated from the traction motors when in dynamic braking. Dynamic braking assists in train handling or in making a general reduction in train speed prior to using the air brakes.

UP 319 shown active at Council Bluffs, IA on 6 April 1979.

Facing west at Council Bluffs, IA on 6 April 1979, UP 318 awaits its crew for a local set-out and pick-up trip to North Platte, NE. The modified skirt over the fuel tank allowed the installation of the larger 2400-gallon tank. Several of the units still have special plumbing attached, as with UP 318, which permitted use of residual fuels (Bunker-C, used in the turbines). The fuel was routed down the side and into the aft compartment to a heater unit and brought up to temperature. At the right temperature, the fuel was then routed under the walkway to the engine compartment for use. After the retirement of the turbines, there no longer existed a requirement for Bunker-C fuel, and these units reverted back to using diesel fuel.

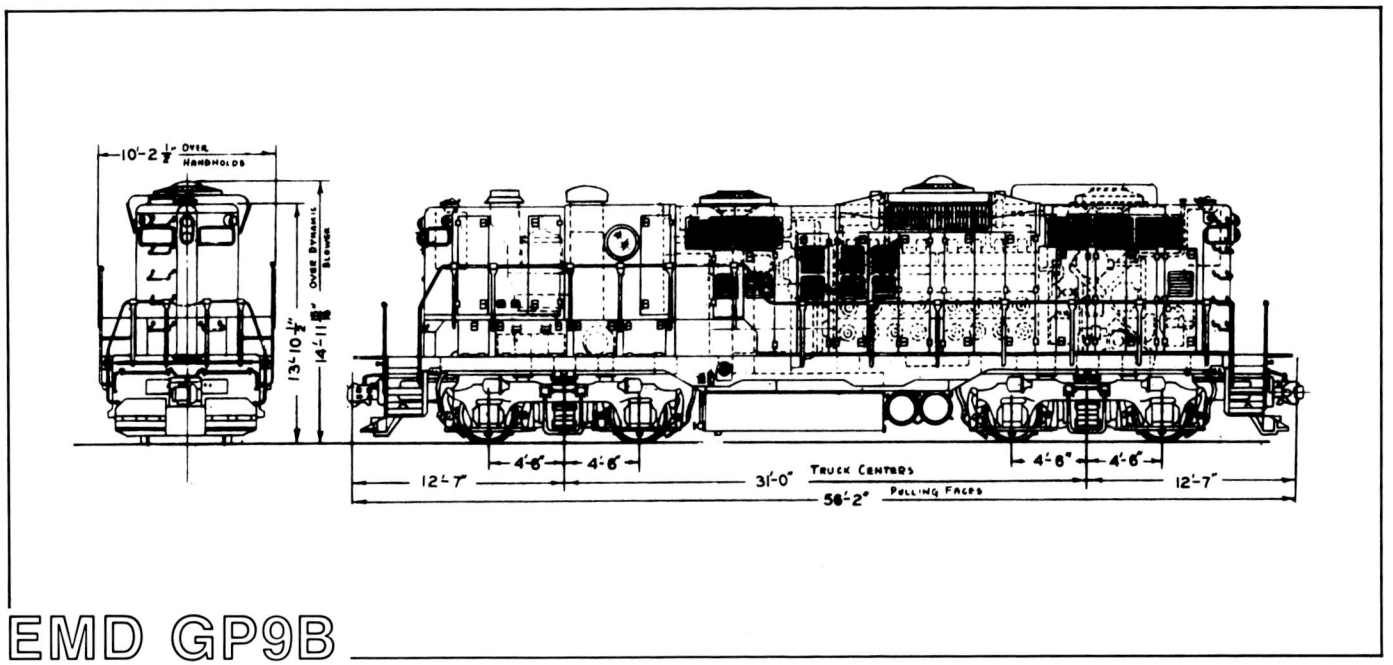

EMD GP9B

THE GENERAL DATA HAS BEEN OMITTED.

ELECTRO-MOTIVE'S GP9B ROSTER

UNIT	BUILDER DATE	BUILDER NUMBER	REMARKS	UNIT	BUILDER DATE	BUILDER NUMBER	REMARKS
312B	September 1957	23718	Sold 9/78 to Precision National Corporation, Mt. Vernon, IL.	338B	September 1957	23744	Sold 9/78 to Precision National Corporation, Mt. Vernon, IL.
329B	September 1957	23735	Sold 10/77 to Precision National Corporation, Mt. Vernon, IL.	347B	October 1957	23753	Retired 8/78. Held for disposition.

Hooked up and ready to go at Council Bluffs, IA on 14 August 1977 is UP 312B. This GP9B was modified in 1958 with the Air Research turbocharger unit to 2000-horsepower. Three other GP9B's received this firm's installation: UP 306B, 311B, and 348B. (The first turbocharged unit in the United States was UP 281, using the Air Research assembly, applied in September 1955 and released for testing that November.)

Pointing west, showing the left side, UP 312B provides a good reference to the view below.

A straight, never-modified, GP9B . . . UP 338B points east showing off its right side. The exhaust stack and air intake atop the short hood indicates a steam generator equipped unit. Fifteen GP9B's in the 300-Class were originally fitted out with heat capabilities . . . for branchline passenger service. Most of the steam equipment was deactivated in the late 1960's; however, the installation remained on-board. The later, larger sized overhead fans are obvious in their oversized housings. Council Bluffs, IA, 10 September 1977.

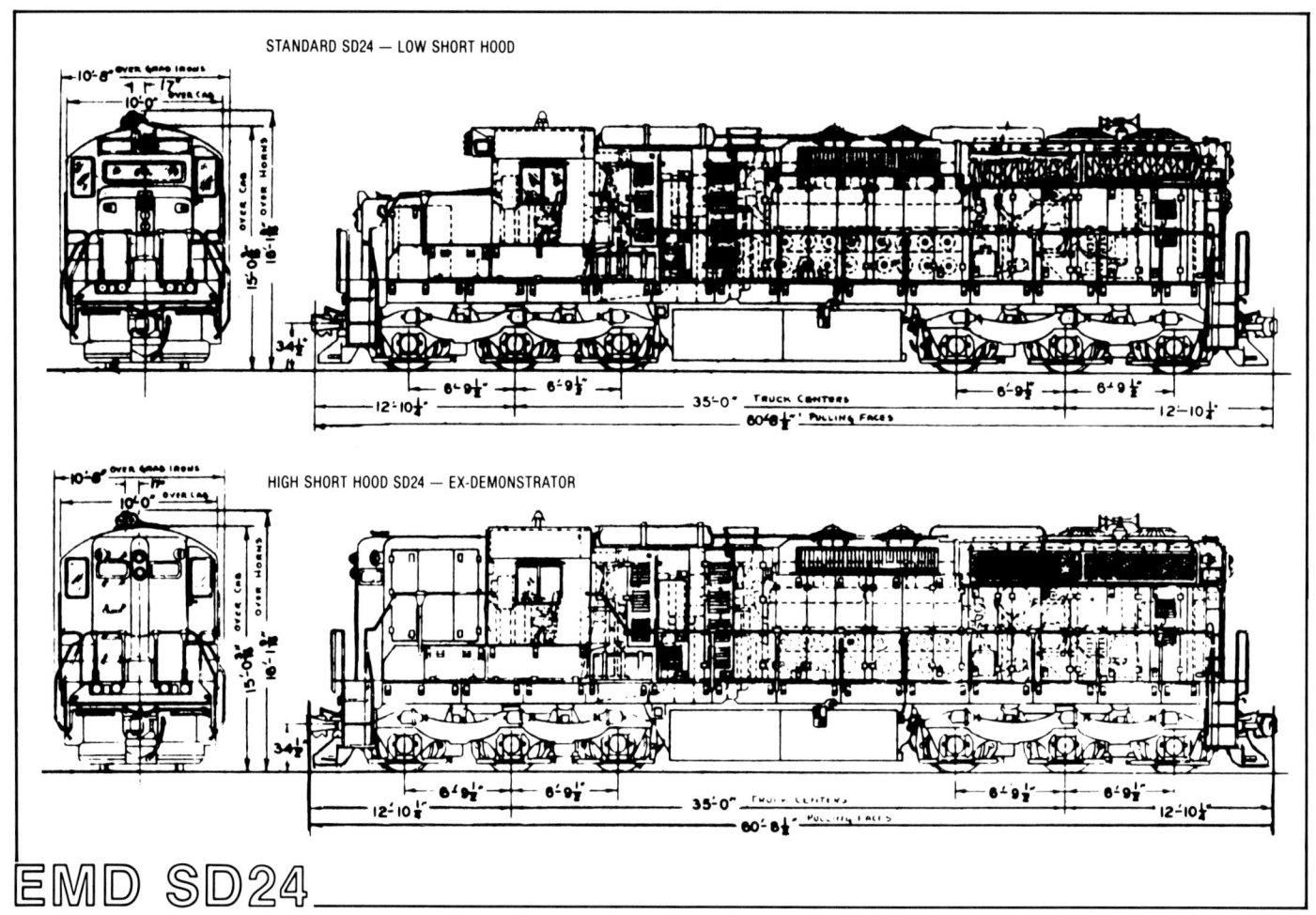

EMD SD24

GENERAL DATA
A.A.R. DESIGNATION	C-C
GEAR RATIO	62/15
WEIGHT LOADED	385,970 LBS.
LIGHT WEIGHT	355,947 LBS. APPROX.
MAXIMUM CURVATURE WITH TRAIN	
MAXIMUM CURVATURE	23° AS SINGLE UNIT
MAXIMUM SPEED	65 M.P.H.
MINIMUM CONT. SPEED	10 M.P.H.
CENTER OF GRAVITY	59.6 ABOVE RAIL (IN WORKING ORDER)

SUPPLIES
FUEL	3000 GALS.
LUBE OIL	220 GALS.
COOLING WATER	260 GALS.
SAND	46 CU. FT.

DIESEL ENGINE
MODEL	16-567 D
TURBOCHARGER	EQUIPPED
SPARK ARRESTER	NOT REQUIRED
AIR FILTER, BASIC:	
CARBODY	EQUIPPED
PRIMARY	IMPINGEMENT (PANEL)
ENGINE	OIL BATH PANEL
FUEL HEATER	KELTY

BRAKES
SCHEDULE	26 L
AIR COMPRESSOR	WBG
BRAKE SHOES	HI PHOS. CAST IRON
SAFETY CONTROL	FOOT PEDAL

ELECTRICAL
MULTIPLE UNIT RECEPTACLES	12-21 & 27 PT
MAIN GENERATOR	D-22 CT
ALTERNATOR	D-14
TRACTION MOTORS, TYPE	D-47
NUMBER OF TRACTION MOTORS	6
DYNAMIC BRAKES	POTENTIAL CONTROL
BATTERIES	64V. 426 AMP. HRS.
HEADLIGHTS	TWIN SEALED BEAMS 200W. EA.
AUXILIARY GENERATOR	10 KW.
COOLING FANS	(3) 48" 9-BLADE
CAB SIGNALS	US&S TYPE 'E'
ROTATING WARNING LIGHTS	EQUIPPED
R.C.S.	NOT EQUIPPED
RADIO C.C.S. ON UNITS 402 & 446	EQUIPPED
PACE SETTER CONTROL ON UNITS 409-412	

RUNNING GEAR
DRAFT GEAR	M-380A
COUPLER	(SEE NOTE)—TYPE 'F'*
JOURNALS	6½" x 12" HYATT R.B.
WHEELS	40" DIA.
TRUCKS	6 WHL., FLEXICOIL, CLSP. BRKS., HIGH CYL.

*UNITS 445-447 EQUIPPED WITH TYPE 'E' COUPLER

MISCELLANEOUS
WHISTLE	LESLIE S-3 LRF
TOILET	EQUIPPED
FIRE EXTINGUISHERS	(3) 30 LB. ANSUL
WATER COOLER	EQUIPPED
FUEL FILLER	BUCKEYE
SPEED RECORDER	CP

Coming in from the west is *Extra 409 East*, crossing the bridge spanning Green River, WY's namesake. It really is *green!* This is still in the heydays of the SD24 fleet when they operated over the entire system as head-end power. 6 May 1976.

EMD's "turbocharger equipped" SD24. The Union Pacific bought 30 A-units and 45 B-units, plus later purchasing the four EMD demonstrators, second-hand. The turbocharger stack is visible, just aft of the top-mounted air reservoirs behind the cab. Shown active at Council Bluffs, IA on 13 April 1980.

ELECTRO-MOTIVE'S SD24A ROSTER

UNIT	BUILDER DATE	BUILDER NUMBER	REMARKS
400	July 1959	25358	
401	July 1959	25359	
402	July 1959	25360	
403	July 1959	25361	
404	July 1959	25362	
405	July 1959	25363	
406	August 1959	25364	
407	August 1959	25365	Sold 10/77 to Precision National Corporation, Mt. Vernon, IL.
408	August 1959	25366	Sold 10/77 to Precision National Corporation, Mt. Vernon, IL.
409	August 1959	25367	
410	August 1959	25368	
411	August 1959	25369	Sold 10/77 to Precision National Corporation, Mt. Vernon, IL.
412	August 1959	25370	
413	August 1959	25371	
414	August 1959	25372	Retired 4/80. Held for disposition.
415	August 1959	25373	Sold 10/77 to Precision National Corporation, Mt. Vernon, IL.
416	September 1959	25374	Sold 10/77 to Precision National Corporation, Mt. Vernon, IL.
417	August 1959	25375	
418	September 1959	25376	Sold 10/77 to Precision National Corporation, Mt. Vernon, IL.
419	September 1959	25377	
420	September 1959	25378	
421	September 1959	25379	Sold 10/77 to Precision National Corporation, Mt. Vernon, IL.
422	September 1959	25380	
424	September 1959	25382	
425	October 1959	25383	
426	September 1959	25384	
427	September 1959	25385	Sold 10/77 to Precision National Corporation, Mt. Vernon, IL.
428	September 1959	25386	Retired 12/79. Held for disposition.
429	September 1959	25387	
445	August 1960	26034	EMD Demonstrator 7200. Bought second-hand 8/61. Retired 9/79. Held for possible slug conversion.
446	August 1960	26035	EMD Demonstrator 7201. Bought second-hand 8/61.
447	August 1960	26036	EMD Demonstrator 7202. Bought second-hand 8/61.
448	June 1958	24701	EMD Demonstrator 5579. Rebuilt to SD24 standards (1st EMD turbocharged unit) by EMD. Bought second-hand 9/62.

The sloped short hood of the SD24 points westward in this scene at Council Bluffs, IA on 22 May 1977. The smaller styled lettering along with the early 1970 slogan: "We Can Handle It," further helps date this view.

One of the major spotting features of the SD24 is obvious . . . the blower assembly bulge which juts from the central air system compartment just aft of the cab.

Also, part of the plumbing to the top-mounted air reservoirs cuts in front of the turbocharger stack located just aft of the "torpedo tubes."

Shown here in general service, it was selected to become the master unit for the "twelve motor" slug pair with S8 . . . ex-SD24B UP 444B, in January 1979. It is currently assigned to North Platte, NE, performing "hump yard" service.

Idling in the shadows of the "Everlasting Hills" at Ogden, UT on 21 November 1976, UP 410 awaits its next yard assignment. The plumbing from the compressor to the top-mounted air reservoirs is quite obvious in this view. During the mid-1970's, SD24's were assigned as heavy transfer switchers in most major yards across the system. Several were selected to become master units in the Electric Trailer conversion program. These units have earned their "keep" for the railroad.—*Photo by Kenneth M. Ardinger.*

Just up the tracks from Riverdale Yard—in the scene above, we find UP 425 "kicking" grain cars near the Southern Pacific facilities at Ogden several years later . . . 20 February 1979. The heavy yard usage is evident in this scene. The rugged Wahsatch Mountains form the backdrop.

A perfectly matched SD24 set rumbles across the "diamonds" of the Rock Island, Burlington Northern (ex-CB&Q) and the Milwaukee Road at Council Bluffs, IA on 18 May 1980. A quick comparison can be made between the A-unit and the B-unit. These units represent EMD's continued early development of turbocharged units during the early 1960's.

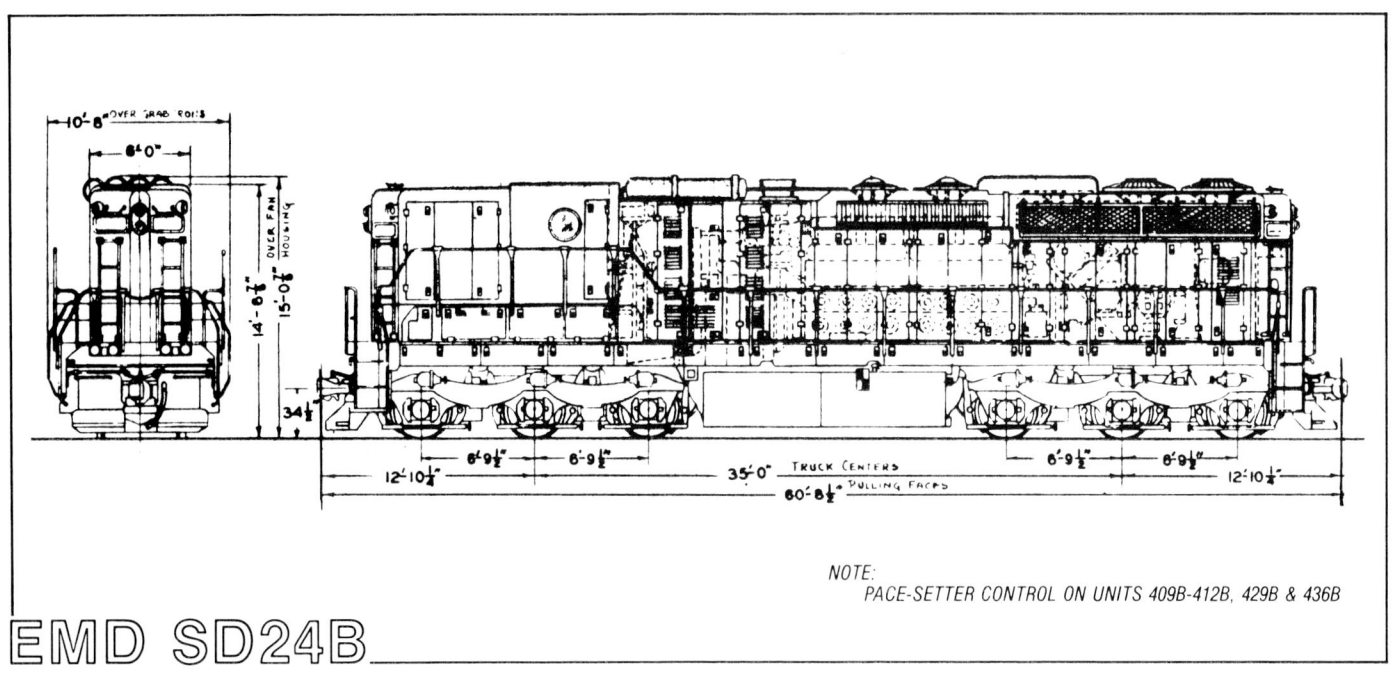

NOTE: PACE-SETTER CONTROL ON UNITS 409B-412B, 429B & 436B

EMD SD24B

REFER TO DATA PRESENTED WITH THE SD24 PRESENTATION.

ELECTRO-MOTIVE'S SD24B ROSTER

UNIT	BUILDER DATE	BUILDER NUMBER	REMARKS	UNIT	BUILDER DATE	BUILDER NUMBER	REMARKS
400B	July 1959	25388	Sold 10/77 to Precision National Corporation, Mt. Vernon, IL.	423B	August 1959	25411	Sold 10/77 to Precision National Corporation, Mt. Vernon, IL.
401B	July 1959	25389	Sold 8/78 to Naporano Iron & Metal Company, Newark, NJ.	424B	August 1959	25412	Sold 10/77 to Precision National Corporation, Mt. Vernon, IL.
402B	July 1959	25390	Sold 10/77 to Precision National Corporation, Mt. Vernon, IL.	425B	August 1959	25413	Sold 10/77 to Precision National Corporation, Mt. Vernon, IL.
403B	July 1959	25391	Sold 10/77 to Precision National Corporation, Mt. Vernon, IL.	426B	August 1959	25414	Sold 10/77 to Precision National Corporation, Mt. Vernon, IL.
404B	July 1959	25392	Sold 10/77 to Precision National Corporation, Mt. Vernon, IL.	427B	August 1959	25415	Sold 10/77 to Precision National Corporation, Mt. Vernon, IL.
405B	July 1959	25393	Sold 10/77 to Precision National Corporation, Mt. Vernon, IL.	428B	August 1959	25416	Retired 4/78. Sold 3/79 to Precision National Corporation, Mt. Vernon, IL.
406B	July 1959	25394	Rebuilt 1/78 to slug S7.	429B	August 1959	25417	Sold 10/77 to Precision National Corporation, Mt. Vernon, IL.
407B	August 1959	25395	Sold 10/77 to Precision National Corporation, Mt. Vernon, IL.	430B	August 1959	25418	Retired 7/79. Held for possible slug conversion.
408B	August 1959	25396					
409B	July 1959	25397	Sold 10/77 to Precision National Corporation, Mt. Vernon, IL.	431B	August 1959	25419	Retired 4/78. Sold 2/79 to Precision National Corporation, Mt. Vernon, IL.
410B	August 1959	25398	Sold 10/77 to Precision National Corporation, Mt. Vernon, IL.	432B	August 1959	25420	Sold 10/77 to Precision National Corporation, Mt. Vernon, IL.
411B	August 1959	25399	Retired 9/79. Held for possible slug conversion.	433B	August 1959	25421	Sold 10/77 to Precision National Corporation, Mt. Vernon, IL.
412B	August 1959	25400	Sold 10/77 to Precision National Corporation, Mt. Vernon, IL.	434B	September 1959	25422	Sold 10/77 to Precision National Corporation, Mt. Vernon, IL.
413B	August 1959	25401	Sold 10/77 to Precision National Corporation, Mt. Vernon, IL.	435B	September 1959	25423	Retired 4/78. Sold 2/79 to Precision National Corporation, Mt. Vernon IL.
414B	August 1959	25402	Sold 8/78 to Precision National Corporation, Mt. Vernon, IL.	436B	September 1959	25424	Sold 8/78 to Naporano Iron & Metal Company, Newark, NJ.
415B	August 1959	25403	Sold 10/77 to Precision National Corporation, Mt. Vernon, IL.	437B	September 1959	25425	Retired 4/78. Sold 12/79 to Naporano Iron & Metal Company, Newark, NJ.
416B	August 1959	25404	Sold 10/77 to Precision National Corporation, Mt. Vernon, IL.	438B	September 1959	25426	Sold 10/77 to Precision National Corporation, Mt. Vernon, IL.
417B	August 1959	25405	Sold 10/77 to Precision National Corporation, Mt. Vernon, IL.	439B	October 1959	25427	Sold 10/77 to Precision National Corporation, Mt. Vernon, IL.
418B	August 1959	25406	Sold 10/77 to Precision National Corporation, Mt. Vernon, IL.	440B	October 1959	25428	Sold 10/77 to Precision National Corporation, Mt. Vernon, IL.
419B	August 1959	25407	Sold 10/77 to Precision National Corporation, Mt. Vernon, IL.	441B	September 1959	25429	Sold 10/77 to Precision National Corporation, Mt. Vernon, IL.
420B	August 1959	25408	Sold 8/78 to Naporano Iron & Metal Company, Newark, NJ.	442B	September 1959	25430	Sold 10/77 to Precision National Corporation, Mt. Vernon, IL.
421B	August 1959	25409	Sold 10/77 to Precision National Corporation, Mt. Vernon, IL.	443B	September 1959	25431	Sold 10/77 to Precision National Corporation, Mt. Vernon, IL.
422B	August 1959	25410	Sold 10/77 to Precision National Corporation, Mt. Vernon, IL.	444B	September 1959	25432	Rebuilt 12/78 to slug S8.

The rear view of SD24B, UP 431B. This is the servicing pits at Council Bluffs, IA, once part of the old diesel house. Arriving eastbound units are brought around the "balloon" tracks and into this area for resupply . . . which has them headed correctly for westbound assignments.

Union Pacific was the only railroad to purchase the SD24B cabless boosters . . . 45 units numbered 400B through 444B. For all appearances, less the cab, these units have all the distinctive features of the cab units . . . dynamic brakes, turbocharger blower bulge on the left side and the top-mounted air reservoirs to name but a few. Shown active at Council Bluffs, IA on 25 March 1977.

A string of SD24B's sit outside the Omaha Shops on 17 March 1978. Note the company they are keeping . . . U50C's and an E-unit. It was around this time that critical equipment was removed from these units and reconditioned for the parts pool . . . the units placed up for sale—"as is, where is."

The right front of a cabless SD24 shows the mechanical features of the front end construction. The step-up platform provides the same plane as the floors in the cab units . . . thus reducing the re-engineering of providing the booster-styled unit by simply constructing the high short hood over the existing common structure. Shown active at Council Bluffs, IA on 11 April 1978.

Sitting on an out-of-service track at Council Bluffs, IA on 15 November 1977, UP 426B awaits shipment to Precision National Corporation at Mt. Vernon, IL. It was purchased one month earlier by PNC.

Note that the right side does not have the turbocharger blower bulge. The "chicken wire" barrier protects the radiator shutters on both the cabless and cab SD24's.

The front detail view shows the step-ups on either side of the car body. Classification light housings and placement are also EMD spotting features. Council Bluffs, IA, 25 April 1978.

FRONT END

ROOF DETAILS . . Looking forward

The roof line of UP 411B from the rear shows the radiator fans and compressor plumbing to the top-mounted air reservoirs. The turbocharger stack is just aft of the "torpedo tubes." Omaha, NE, 19 April 1980.

The front left details of UP 429B show the "half-moon" turbocharger blower bulge just aft of the step-ups. This unit was sold to Precision National Corporation in October 1977; however, it remained on property for a long period of time . . . this detail shot taken at Council Bluffs, IA on 8 May 1978.

PNC resold a number of SD24B's to Illinois Central Gulf for conversion into SD20's at their Paducah, KY shops.

Union Pacific converted UP 406B and 444B into electric trailers S7 and S8 respectively. Retained for possible future slug conversion are UP 411B and 430B.

AMERICAN LOCOMOTIVE C415 ROSTER

UNIT	BUILDER DATE	BUILDER NUMBER	REMARKS	UNIT	BUILDER DATE	BUILDER NUMBER	REMARKS
420	November 1966	3451-6	Stored unserviceable. For sale.	423	November 1966	3451-9	Stored unserviceable. For sale.
421	November 1966	3451-7	Stored unserviceable. For sale.	424	November 1966	3451-10	Stored unserviceable. For sale.
422	November 1966	3451-8	Stored unserviceable. For sale.				

NOTES:
A—Union Pacific financed the purchase of these locomotives which were numbered and lettered in the Rock Island standards.
B—These units retained the Rock Island numbering when returned to Union Pacific ownership in 5/80.

THE GENERAL ARRANGEMENT DIAGRAM HAS BEEN OMITTED.

ALCo's center cab switcher, C415's... came in three cab heights. The ones used on the Rock Island were of medium cab height. Union Pacific underwrote the purchase of the last five units, ex-RI 420-424. All five are stored, like RI 424, at Council Bluffs, IA on 3 May 1980. The model 251F engine is mounted in the long hood, while the auxiliary equipment is installed in the shorter hood. These were not numbered into the Union Pacific roster upon return.

Two views of RI 423 at Council Bluffs, IA on 8 October 1980 give some appreciation of the center cab design of ALCo's C415's. The front hood is longer, housing the engine, as seen on the left. The B-Type truck assembly is typical construction found under B-B ALCo locomotives. The visibility afforded to the crew is unexcelled.

These units were placed up for sale in April 1980... "as is, where is" at Silvis, IL. With no takers, the five ALCo's were brought to Council Bluffs, Ia and stored, awaiting an interested buyer.

Unwanted power returned from the now-defunct Rock Island awaits its fate in the deadline at Council Bluffs, IA on 8 October 1980. The ALCo C-415's were purchased by the Union Pacific and placed on long-term lease along with other locomotives . . . all painted and numbered in the Rock Island scheme.

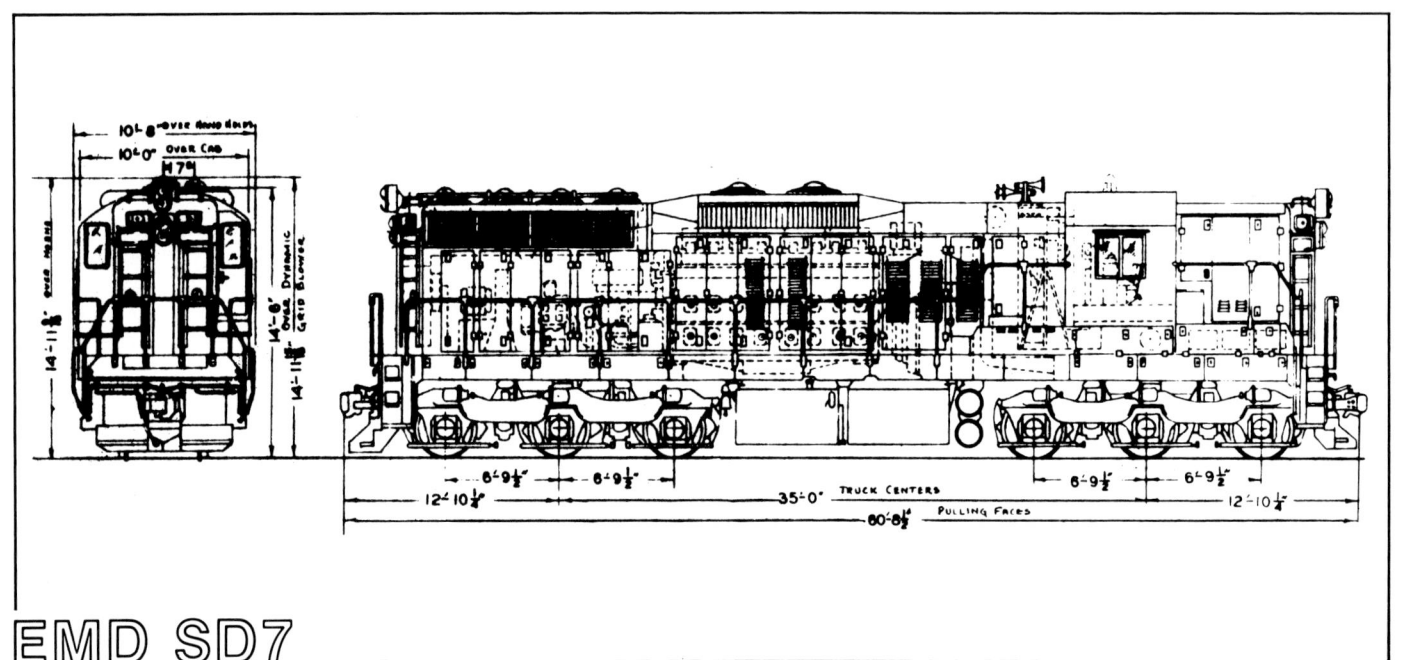

EMD SD7

GENERAL DATA
A.A.R. DESIGNATION	C-C
GEAR RATIO	62/15
WEIGHT LOADED	363,220 LBS.
LIGHT WEIGHT	337,282 LBS. APPROX.
MAXIMUM CURVATURE	WITH TRAIN
MAXIMUM CURVATURE	23° AS SINGLE UNIT
MAXIMUM SPEED	65 M.P.H.
MINIMUM CONT. SPEED	6 M.P.H.

SUPPLIES
FUEL	2400 GALS.
LUBE OIL	200 GALS.
COOLING WATER	260 GALS.
SAND	50 CU. FT.

DIESEL ENGINE
MODEL	16-567B
TURBOCHARGER	NOT EQUIPPED
SPARK ARRESTER	EQUIPPED
AIR FILTER, BASIC:	
CARBODY	EQUIPPED
PRIMARY	IMPINGEMENT (PANEL)
ENGINE	FARR (OIL BATH)
FUEL HEATER	KELTY

RUNNING GEAR
DRAFT GEAR	M-380A
COUPLER	TYPE 'E'
JOURNALS	6½" x 12" HYATT R.B.
WHEELS	40" DIA.
TRUCKS	6 WHL., FLEXICOIL, CLASP BRKS., HIGH CYLS.

ELECTRICAL
MULTIPLE UNIT RECEPTACLES	27 PT
MAIN GENERATOR	D-12
ALTERNATOR	D-14
TRACTION MOTORS, TYPE	D-37
NUMBER OF TRACTION MOTORS	6
DYNAMIC BRAKES	FIELD LOOP
BATTERIES	64 V. 426 AMP. HRS.
HEADLIGHTS	TWIN SEALED BEAMS 200W EA.
AUXILIARY GENERATOR	10 KW
COOLING FANS	(4) 36" DIA.
CAB SIGNALS	NOT EQUIPPED
ROTATING WARNING LIGHTS	EQUIPPED
R.C.S.	NOT EQUIPPED

NOTE:
UP 454 & 456 EQUIPPED W/RADIO SPEED HUMP CONTROL FOR NORTH PLATTE YARD.

BRAKES
SCHEDULE	24RL B TYPE RELAY
AIR COMPRESSOR	WBG
BRAKE SHOES	HI FRICT. COMP.
SAFETY CONTROL	FOOT PEDAL

MISCELLANEOUS
WHISTLE	LESLIE S-3 LRF
TOILET	EQUIPPED
FIRE EXTINGUISHERS	(3) 30 LB. ANSUL
WATER COOLER	EQUIPPED
FUEL FILLER	BUCKEYE
SPEED RECORDER	CP

ELECTRO-MOTIVE'S SD7 ROSTER

UNIT	BUILDER DATE	BUILDER NUMBER	REMARKS
450	June 1953	18284	Originally UP 775, renumbered 2/63. Retired 9/79. Held for possible slug conversion.
451	June 1953	18285	Originally UP 776, renumbered 12/62. Retired 9/79. Held for possible slug conversion.
452	June 1953	18286	Originally UP 777, renumbered 2/63. Retired 7/79. Held for possible slug conversion.
453	June 1953	18287	Originally UP 778, renumbered 12/62. Retired 10/79. Held for possible slug conversion.
454	June 1953	18288	
455	June 1953	18289	Retired 3/80. Held for possible slug conversion.
456	June 1953	18290	Sold 1/79 to Precision National Corporation, Mt. Vernon, IL.
457	June 1953	18293	Sold 4/79 to Naporano Iron & Metal Company, Newark, NJ.
458	June 1953	18291	
459	June 1953	18292	

The SD7 front end will certainly not win any beauty contest! This unit is equipped with radio speed hump control for use in North Platte yards. Originally numbered UP 799, it was renumbered to its current slot in January 1963. Council Bluffs, IA, 20 April 1978.

Originally numbered UP 775-784, they were renumbered UP 450-459 between December 1962 and February 1963. Bedecked with running lights, UP 453 sits out the day on the freighthouse tracks at Salt Lake City, UT, 24 April 1976. In the background sits a stored gas-electric turbine. Not an overly popular "between generation" model, EMD produced 188 units during 1952-1953.

Riding on C-type trucks, the SD7 weighs 363,220 pounds fully loaded with 2400 gallons of diesel fuel, 200 gallons of lubricating oil, 260 gallons of cooling water and 50 cubic feet of sand.

UP 454, 458 and 459—the last remaining active SD7's on Union Pacific's locomotive roster—serve as "master units" in the electric trailer (slug) mating assignments.

UP 450, formerly UP 775, sports the "We Can Handle It" cab slogan applied during the early 1970's. Council Bluffs, IA, 4 September 1980.

In pristine appearance, UP 451 will soon be heading out west. One of the SD7's spotting features is the location of the classification lights . . . well in from the sides and almost centered over the number boards. Louvered inspection doors run the length of the left side . . . while solid doors appear on the right side. The top-mounted set of twin seal beam headlights has been removed, leaving the mounting plate pointing skyward . . . empty. This unit was retired in September 1979 and is being held for possible conversion to an electric trailer (slug) . . . along with UP 450, 452, 453 and 455. Shown active at Council Bluffs, IA on 13 November 1977.

Just months from being sold, UP 456 sits on the deadline storage tracks at Council Bluffs, IA, 18 September 1978. On 1 January 1979, Precision National Corporation will purchase this unit. The left side has the louvered doors running the length of the locomotive. The twin exhaust stacks stick up.

Roof details of UP 450, looking forward from the cab, show the twin exhaust stacks, the fans and dynamic brake blister. The lifting eyes facilitate shop removal of major car body assemblies. Council Bluffs, IA, 12 August 1979.

The front end of the SD7 appears powerful with the radiator housing extending outward. Roof-mounting ladders are installed on the left and right sides on both the front and rear ends. Note the older lift-pin lever handle, as compared to the now standard handle applied to UP 452, on the right.

Active on the diesel service lead, Council Bluffs, IA, 20 April 1978.

Sitting in the deadline storage at Council Bluffs, IA on 24 February 1980, it is being held for possible conversion to electric trailer (slug) service. A better view of the roof details is possible . . . with the twin exhaust stacks straddling dynamic brake section and the slightly extended radiator housing.

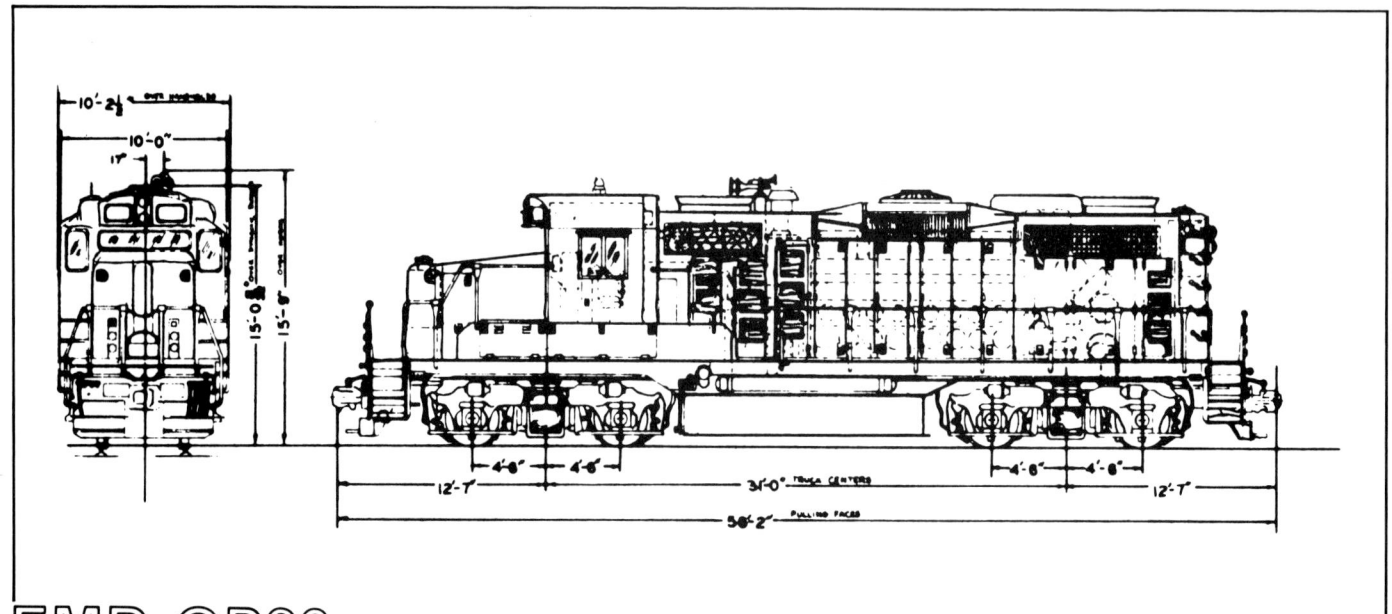

EMD GP20

GENERAL DATA
A.A.R. DESIGNATION	B-B
GEAR RATIO	62/15
WEIGHT LOADED	258,170 LBS.
LIGHT WEIGHT	235,916 LBS. APPROX.
MAXIMUM CURVATURE	13° FULL BUFF*
MAXIMUM CURVATURE	21° NORMAL OR PULL*
MAXIMUM SPEED	65 M.P.H.
MINIMUM CONT. SPEED	14 M.P.H.
MAXIMUM CURVATURE	39° AS SINGLE UNIT
CENTER OF GRAVITY	59.6" ABOVE RAIL (IN WORKING ORDER)

*WITH TRAIN

SUPPLIES
FUEL	2350 GALS.
LUBE OIL	220 GALS.
COOLING WATER	227 GALS.
SAND	18 CU. FT.

DIESEL ENGINE
MODEL	16-567-D2
TURBOCHARGER	EQUIPPED
SPARK ARRESTER	NOT REQUIRED
AIR FILTER, BASIC:	
CARBODY	EQUIPPED
PRIMARY	IMPINGEMENT (PANEL)
ENGINE	PANEL OIL BATH
FUEL HEATER	KELTY

BRAKES
SCHEDULE	26 L
AIR COMPRESSOR	WBO
BRAKE SHOES	HI FRICT. COMP.
SAFETY CONTROL	FOOT PEDAL

ELECTRICAL
MULTIPLE UNIT RECEPTACLES	12-21 & 27 PT
MAIN GENERATOR	D-22 BT
ALTERNATOR	D-14
TRACTION MOTORS, TYPE	D-47B-1
NUMBER OF TRACTION MOTORS	4
DYNAMIC BRAKES	FIELD LOOP
BATTERIES	64 V. 426 AMP. HRS.
HEADLIGHTS	TWIN SEALED BEAMS 200W EA.
AUXILIARY GENERATOR	10 KW
COOLING FANS	(1) 36" & (2) 48" 8-BLADE
CAB SIGNALS	US&S TYPE 'E'
ROTATING WARNING LIGHTS	EQUIPPED
R.C.S.	NOT EQUIPPED

RUNNING GEAR
DRAFT GEAR	NC-496-1
COUPLER	TYPE 'F'
JOURNALS	6½" x 12" HYATT R.B.
WHEELS	40" DIA.
TRUCKS	4 WHL., SWINGHANGER, CLSP. BRKS.

MISCELLANEOUS
WHISTLE	LESLIE S-3 LRF
TOILET	EQUIPPED
FIRE EXTINGUISHERS	(3) 30 LB. ANSUL
WATER COOLER	EQUIPPED
FUEL FILLER	BUCKEYE
SPEED RECORDER	CP

Pulling eastward through the old passenger terminal area of Omaha and towards the Missouri River and Council Bluffs, IA is UP 491 leading a Milwaukee GP40. This down on view pretty well shows the construction features of EMD's initial attempts at turbocharging . . . the forward-mounted fan, the squared-off turbocharger stack, and the bulging car body just aft of the cab housing the turbocharger group. The technology amassed by Union Pacific's experimentation with their "Omaha GP20's" in the mid-1950's spawned this 2000-horsepower locomotive's production.

The westbound grain train is headed up with older equipment on 22 August 1975... GP20-SD24B-GP20. Awaiting its air-check at Council Bluffs, IA, it delivers its consist to Kansas City for further movement to a Texas seaport for export. The switching plant in the background has since been razed.

In company with a brand new General Electric C30-7 UP 2507, UP 491 points west at Council Bluffs, IA on 5 September 1980. The dwindling fleet of GP20's has seen them relegated to Priority III units . . . which limits mechanical expenditures. Normal chores are local assignments. Purchased in 1960, these units were originally numbered in the 700-Class for about 2 years prior to being renumbered into their current series.

The rear roof line is broken up with a winterization hatch covering one fan, the other remaining exposed. The air intake grills provide filtered air to the engine locker.

All production models were equipped with dynamic brakes, except for 15 units built for the New York Central. In many respects, the GP20's rear construction features are similar to that of the GP9's.

These units weigh-in, fully loaded, at 258,170 pounds . . . with 2,350 gallons of diesel fuel, 220 gallons of lubrication oil, 227 gallons of cooling water and 18 cubic feet of sand.

Shown active at the diesel servicing area, Council Bluffs, IA, on 29 August 1980.

Sharing space on the diesel service leads at Council Bluffs, IA on 29 August 1980 is brand new General Electric C30-7 UP 2502 and GP20 UP 496.

There is just about twenty years of technology separating these two road units. The GP20 represents EMD primitive turbocharging spurred on by Union Pacific's experimentation during the late 1950's with the "Omaha GP20's" . . . while the General Electric C30-7 embodies all the "space-age" advancements in engine and electrical/electronics designs.

The turbocharger stack is just forward of the dynamic brake blister and behind the forward mounted fan. The 16-cylinder 567-D2 diesel engine turns out 2000 horsepower.

ELECTRO-MOTIVE'S GP20 ROSTER

UNIT	BUILDER DATE	BUILDER NUMBER	REMARKS
470	July 1960	26045	Originally UP 700, renumbered 1/63. Sold 10/77 to Precision National Corporation, Mt. Vernon, IL.
471	July 1960	26046	Originally UP 701, renumbered 12/62. Sold 10-77 to Precision National Corporation, Mt. Vernon, IL.
472	July 1960	26047	Originally UP 702, renumbered 12/62. Sold 11/78 to Precision National Corporation, Mt. Vernon, IL.
473	July 1960	26048	Originally UP 703, renumbered 12/62. Sold 3/79 to Naporano Iron & Metal Company, Newark, NJ.
474	July 1960	26049	Originally UP 704, renumbered 12/62.
475	July 1960	26050	Originally UP 705, renumbered 1/63. Retired 3/80. Held for disposition.
476	July 1960	26051	Originally UP 706, renumbered 12/62.
477	July 1960	26052	Originally UP 707, renumbered 12/62. Retired 5/79. Sold 1/80 to Peaker Industries, Brighton, MN.
478	July 1960	26053	Originally UP 708, renumbered 12/62. Sold 10/77 to Precision National Corporation, Mt. Vernon, IL.
479	July 1960	26054	Originally UP 709, renumbered 1/63. Sold 10/77 to Precision National Corporation, Mt. Vernon, IL.
480	July 1960	26055	Originally UP 710, renumbered 1/63. Sold 10/79 to Precision National Corporation, Mt. Vernon, IL.
481	July 1960	26056	Originally UP 711, renumbered 12/62.
482	July 1960	26057	Originally UP 712, renumbered 12/62. Sold 10/77 to Precision National Corporation, Mt. Vernon, IL.
483	July 1960	26058	Originally UP 713, renumbered 12/63. Sold 4/79 to Bargains Galore, Portland, OR and shipped to Diesel Electric Service, St. Paul, MN.
484	July 1960	26059	Originally UP 714, renumbered 1/63. Retired 3/80. Held for disposition.
485	August 1960	26060	Originally UP 715, renumbered 1/63. Retired and scrapped at Omaha Shops 10/78.
486	August 1960	26061	Originally UP 716, renumbered 12/62.
487	August 1960	26062	Originally UP 717, renumbered 12/62.
488	July 1960	26063	Originally UP 718, renumbered 12/62. Sold 10/77 to Precision National Corporation, Mt. Vernon, IL.
489	July 1960	26064	Originally UP 719, renumbered 12/62. Retired 9/78. Sold 2/80 to Naporano Iron & Metal Company, Newark, NJ.
490	July 1960	26065	Originally UP 720, renumbered 12/62. Retired 4/80. Held for disposition.
491	July 1960	26066	Originally UP 721, renumbered 12/62.
492	July 1960	26067	Originally UP 722, renumbered 12/63. Retired 10/79. Held for disposition.
493	August 1960	26068	Originally UP 723, renumbered 1/63. Retired 12/79. Held for disposition.
494	August 1960	26069	Originally UP 724, renumbered 12/62.
495	August 1960	26070	Originally UP 725, renumbered 12/62.
496	August 1960	26071	Originally UP 726, renumbered 1/63. Retired 10/79. Held for disposition.
497	August 1960	26072	Originally UP 727, renumbered 12/62. Sold 10/77 to Precision National Corporation, Mt. Vernon, IL.
498	August 1960	26073	Originally UP 728, renumbered 12/62. Retired 5/79. Sold 10/79 to Morrison-Knudsen, Boise, ID.
499	September 1960	26074	Originally UP 729, renumbered 12/62. Sold 1/79 to Precision National Corporation, Mt. Vernon, IL.

An engineer's-side top view of GP20 UP 484 shows off the sloping short hood along with some of the top-mounted turbocharging components. The top of the short hood is painted with light green non-reflective skid-proof paint. The rounded cab roofline is a holdover from GP9 mechanical features . . . which will give way to EMD's angular-styled roofs on follow-on construction.

Note the foot boards, an item since removed . . . and the older-styled auxiliary uncoupling lever—upgraded safety appliances to comply with AAR/FRA standards. The high-mounted, stacked MU-receptacles are also signs of "first generation" diesel operations . . . providing capabilities for 12-, 21- and 27-point plug-ins. The wire VHF whip antenna is top-mounted, just aft of the twin headlight assembly.

Shown on the "run-around" track at Council Bluffs, IA on 9 May 1978.

Pointing west, it awaits its assignment on the leads at Council Bluffs, IA on 29 March 1977. UP 488 keeps company with several other interesting units . . . UP 5025, a U50C sold in June 1978 to Erman Corporation, Turner, KS; and, UP 197B, a GP9B sold to Precision National Corporation, Mt. Vernon, IL in October 1977.

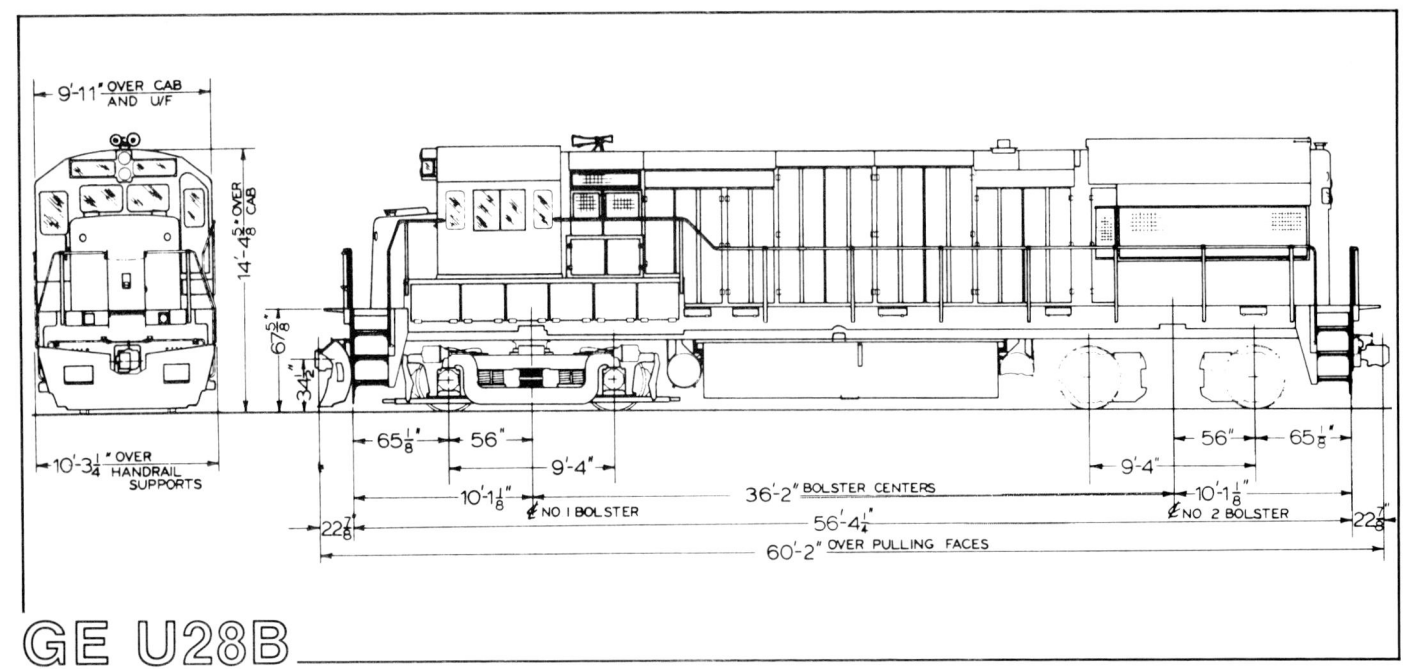

GE U28B

GENERAL DATA
A.A.R. DESIGNATION	B-B
GEAR RATIO	79/24
WEIGHT LOADED	265,800 LBS.
LIGHT WEIGHT	241,188 LBS.
MAXIMUM CURVATURE	WITH TRAIN
MAXIMUM CURVATURE	39° AS SINGLE UNIT
MAXIMUM SPEED	65 M.P.H.
MINIMUM CONT. SPEED	18.4 M.P.H.
CENTER OF GRAVITY	

SUPPLIES
FUEL	2900 GALS.
LUBE OIL	380 GALS.
COOLING WATER	300 GALS.
SAND	48 CU. FT.

DIESEL ENGINE
MODEL	7FDL16C2
TURBOCHARGER	EQUIPPED
SPARK ARRESTER	NOT EQUIPPED
AIR FILTER, BASIC:	
CARBODY	NONE
PRIMARY	DONALDSON CENTRIFUGAL
ENGINE	AIR MAZE PANEL BATH
FUEL HEATER	

BRAKES
SCHEDULE	26 L
AIR COMPRESSOR	WBO
BRAKE SHOES	CAST IRON
SAFETY CONTROL	

ELECTRICAL
MULTIPLE UNIT RECEPTACLES	27 PT
MAIN GENERATOR	GT 598
ALTERNATOR	NONE
TRACTION MOTORS, TYPE	GE 752
NUMBER OF TRACTION MOTORS	4
DYNAMIC BRAKES	NOT EQUIPPED
BATTERIES	64 VOLT
HEADLIGHTS	TWIN SEALED BEAM 200W EA.
AUXILIARY GENERATOR	GY27E
COOLING FANS	MECHANICAL
CAB SIGNALS	NOT EQUIPPED
WARNING LIGHTS	EQUIPPED
R.C.S.	NOT EQUIPPED

RUNNING GEAR
DRAFT GEAR	
COUPLER	TYPE 'E'
JOURNALS	6½" x 12" TIMKEN SC CLASS GG
WHEELS	40" DIA.
TRUCKS	4 WHL. EQUALIZER, CLSP. BRKS.

MISCELLANEOUS
WHISTLE	NATHAN P135-R24
TOILET	DRY HOPPER
FIRE EXTINGUISHERS	
WATER COOLER	
FUEL FILLER	SNYDER
SPEED RECORDER	

GENERAL ELECTRIC U28B ROSTER

UNIT	BUILDER DATE	BUILDER NUMBER	REMARKS
500	October 1966	36156	Stored unserviceable. (RI 262)
501	October 1966	36157	Stored unserviceable. (RI 263)
502	October 1966	36158	Repainted as UP 4-15-80.
503	November 1966	36159	Repainted as UP 5-14-80.
504	November 1966	36160	Stored unserviceable. (RI 266)
505	November 1966	36161	Stored unserviceable. (RI 267)
506	November 1966	36162	Repainted as UP 5-15-80.
507	November 1966	36163	Repainted as UP 5-19-80.
508	November 1966	36164	Stored unserviceable. (RI 270)
509	December 1966	36165	Stored unserviceable. (RI 271)
510	December 1966	36166	Repainted as UP 4-17-80.
511	December 1966	36167	Stored unserviceable. (RI 273)
512	December 1966	36168	Repainted as UP 4-16-80.
513	December 1966	36169	Stored unserviceable. (RI 275)
514	December 1966	36170	Stored unserviceable. (RI 276)
515	December 1966	36171	Repainted as UP 5-22-80.
516	December 1966	36172	Repainted as UP 5-21-80.
517	December 1966	36173	Repainted as UP 5-16-80.
518	December 1966	36174	Repainted as UP 4-27-80.
519	December 1966	36175	Repainted as UP 4-13-80.

Having been qualified "serviceable," this ex-Rock Island U28B is about to receive a new livery . . . Union Pacific-style. This is the North Platte locomotive paint shop which does nearly all unit painting. After all painting and lettering was complete in late April 1980, it was added to the long line of stored units at North Platte, NE.—*Photo by James W. Watson.*

Just arrived from the west, two ex-Rock Island units await the hostler at Council Bluffs, IA on 4 April 1980. While appearing pretty "ratty," this unit made a number of runs between North Platte and Council Bluffs until sidelined for electrical problems. It was declared unserviceable in May and awaits retirement and disposition. These units bear a closer resemblance to the follow-on U30B than the U25B which spawned the "U-boat" line . . . however, all bear the similar "family looks." In reverting back to Union Pacific ownership, the shops applied white numbers on black boards; but, UP 508 received the reverse arrangements.

Assigned to the "Joe Local," ex-Rock Island U28B has its old markings roughly marked out and only the new number boards give one the idea of proper ownership.

UP 518 worked the Marysville, KS to St. Joseph, MO "turn" until recalled to North Platte for shopping and a repainting into Union Pacific colors.

It is now stored with other ex-Rock Island locomotives stored serviceable at North Platte, NE.

Shown ready for action at Marysville, KS on 9 April 1980.— Photo by James W. Watson.

The "Joe Local" is headed-up by ex-Rock Island U28B numbered into Union Pacific's scheme as UP 512. This unit was used between Marysville, KS and St. Joseph, MO until it was repainted and placed into storage at North Platte, NE. The only positive identification are the number boards . . . all other markings have been obliterated. Marysville, KS, 9 April 1980.—Photo by James W. Watson.

Fresh from the paint shops, ex-Rock Island U28B takes on a new look as in Union Pacific livery as UP 510 at North Platte on 28 June 1980. These units were given a "fine tooth comb" inspection at North Platte Shops and those found serviceable were fully qualified mechanically and electrically prior to being painted. Most went immediately to the storage line; however, several did operate in Union Pacific colors for a short period of time on the Nebraska and Kansas Divisions before joining the others.

Freshly-painted ex-Rock Island U28B shows off its natural owner's scheme as UP 507 at North Platte, NE on 14 June 1980. A total of 11 U28B's are stored serviceable at this large railroad center: 502, 503, 506, 507, 510, 512, 514, 516-519. Many of these units operated in the roughed-out paint scheme when first delivered back to Union Pacific; however, once painted, few were seen on the high iron.—*Photo by James W. Watson.*

Another line-up shot of stored serviceable units at North Platte, NE on 14 June 1980. In addition to the long string of ex-Rock Island units on the right, there are 73 locomotives in the general view: GP30's, SDP35's, U30C's, GP40's, SD40-2's, and DDA40X's. The general downturn in traffic due to the slumping economy has sidelined a high number of road units. Based on in-coming new units, the fate of the returned ex-Rock Island equipment is uncertain.—*Photo by James W. Watson.*

The long yellow line . . . These are shopped ex-Rock Island units in Union Pacific's paint scheme that went into storage at North Platte, NE, after release from the shops. There are 21 units . . . U28B's and GP40's . . . in this row on 14 June 1980. In other parts of the mechanical shop and still stored at Council Bluffs, IA are the balance of the returned units . . . some operational but most unserviceable. Disposition instructions are still under consideration.—*Photo by James W. Watson.*

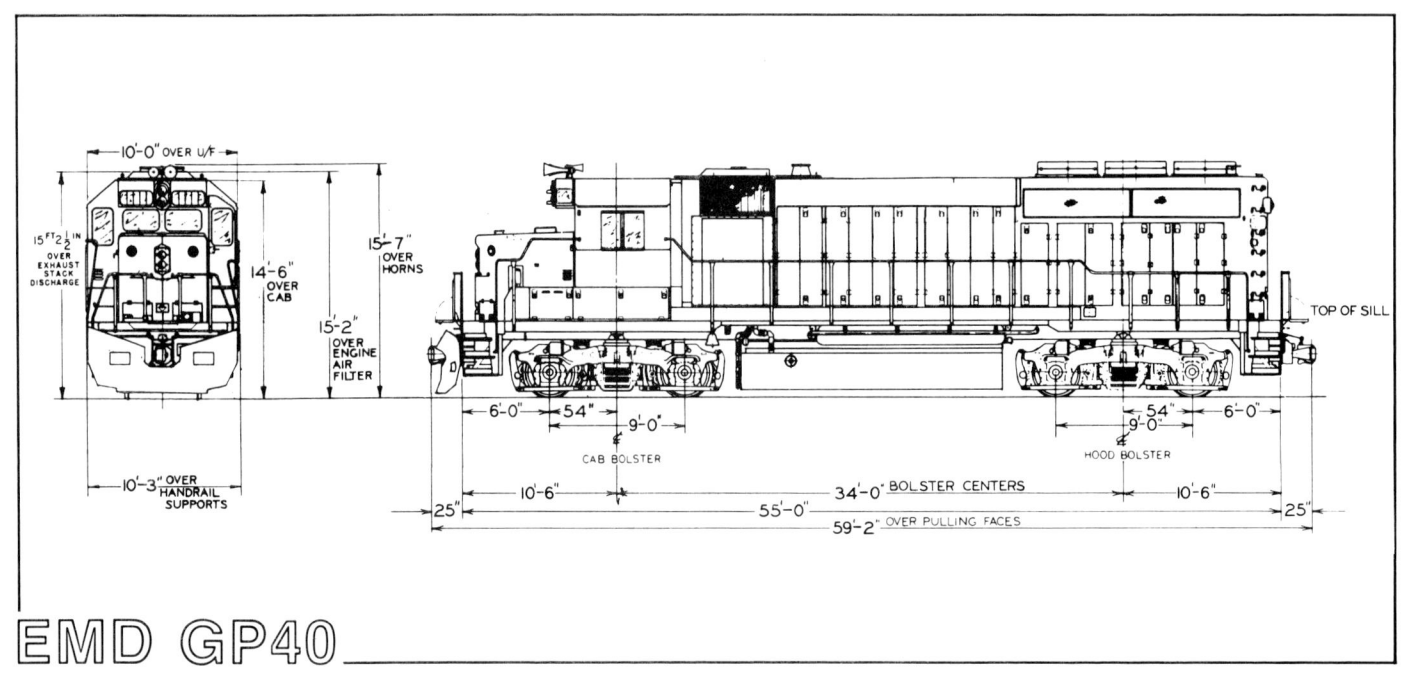

EMD GP40

THE GENERAL DATA HAS BEEN OMITTED.

ELECTRO-MOTIVE'S GP40 ROSTER

UNIT	BUILDER DATE	BUILDER NUMBER	REMARKS
600	September 1966	32232	Ex-RI 340. Repainted to Union Pacific scheme 19 April 1980.
601	September 1966	32233	Ex-RI 341. Stored unserviceable.
602	September 1966	32234	Ex-RI 342. Stored unserviceable.
603	September 1966	32235	Ex-RI 343. Renumbered 7 April 1980.
604	September 1966	32236	Ex-RI 344. Repainted to Union Pacific scheme 8 April 1980.
605	September 1966	32237	Ex-RI 345. Stored unserviceable.
606	September 1966	32238	Ex-RI 346. Renumbered 3 April 1980.
607	September 1966	32239	Ex-RI 347. Stored unserviceable.
608	September 1966	32240	Ex-RI 348. Repainted to Union Pacific scheme 11 April 1980.
609	September 1966	32241	Ex-RI 349. Stored unserviceable.
610	September 1966	32242	Ex-RI 350. Repainted to Union Pacific scheme 6 April 1980.
611	September 1966	32243	Ex-RI 351. Repainted to Union Pacific scheme 2 April 1980.
612	September 1966	32244	Ex-RI 352. Stored unserviceable.
613	September 1966	32245	Ex-RI 353. Stored unserviceable.
614	September 1966	32246	Ex-RI 354. Repainted to Union Pacific scheme 3 April 1980.
615	September 1966	32247	Ex-RI 355. Repainted to Union Pacific scheme 13 April 1980.
616	October 1966	32248	Ex-RI 356. Repainted to Union Pacific scheme 7 April 1980.
617	October 1966	32249	Ex-RI 357. Stored unserviceable.
618	October 1966	32250	Ex-RI 358. Stored unserviceable.
619	October 1966	32251	Ex-RI 359. Stored unserviceable.
620	December 1966	32588	Ex-RI 362. Stored unserviceable.
621	December 1966	32589	Ex-RI 363. Stored unserviceable.
622	December 1966	32590	Ex-RI 364. Renumbered 7 April 1980.
623	December 1966	32591	Ex-RI 365. Stored unserviceable.
624	December 1966	32592	Ex-RI 366. Stored unserviceable.
625	December 1966	32593	Ex-RI 367. Stored unserviceable.
626	December 1966	32594	Ex-RI 368. Repainted to Union Pacific scheme 8 April 1980.
627	December 1966	32595	Ex-RI 369. Stored unserviceable.
628	December 1966	32597	Ex-RI 371. Repainted to Union Pacific scheme 12 April 1980.
629	December 1966	32598	Ex-RI 372. Renumbered 1 April 1980.
630	December 1966	32599	Ex-RI 373. Stored unserviceable.
631	March 1970	36386	Ex-RI 4700. Stored unserviceable.
632	March 1970	36387	Ex-RI 4701. Renumbered 2 April 1980.
633	March 1970	36388	Ex-RI 4702. Stored unserviceable.
634	March 1970	36389	Ex-RI 4703. Stored unserviceable.
635	March 1970	36390	Ex-RI 4704. Renumbered 3 April 1980.
636	March 1970	36391	Ex-RI 4705. Stored unserviceable.
637	March 1970	36392	Ex-RI 4706. Repainted to Union Pacific scheme 14 April 1980.
638	March 1970	36393	Ex-RI 4707. Stored unserviceable.
639	March 1970	36394	Ex-RI 4708. Renumbered 1 April 1980.
640	March 1970	36395	Ex-RI 4709. Stored unserviceable.
641	April 1970	36396	Ex-RI 4710. Stored unserviceable.
642	April 1970	36397	Ex-RI 4711. Stored unserviceable.
643	April 1970	36398	Ex-RI 4712. Renumbered 1 April 1980.
644	April 1970	36399	Ex-RI 4713. Stored unserviceable.
645	April 1970	36400	Ex-RI 4714. Repainted to Union Pacific scheme 5 April 1980.
646	April 1970	36401	Ex-RI 4715. Repainted to Union Pacific scheme 10 April 1980.
647	April 1970	36402	Ex-RI 4716. Renumbered 5 april 1980.
648	April 1970	36403	Ex-RI 4717. Stored unserviceable.
649	April 1970	36404	Ex-RI 4718. Stored unserviceable.
650	April 1970	36405	Ex-RI 4719. Stored unserviceable.

NOTES:

A—These units were returned to Union Pacific ownership in 4/80.

Quickly marked, UP 635 mingles with an assortment of power at Council Bluffs, IA on 15 April 1980. The returned ex-Rock Island leased locomotives were in poor mechanical condition. The Electro-Motive units have fared much better than the General Electric "U-boats"; however, all 15 operational GP40's have been stored at North Platte. There are 26 unserviceable GP40's stored awaiting repairs.

Freshly painted in Union Pacific's scheme is ex-Rock Island 356, a GP40. While purchased new by the Union Pacific, these units were leased to the Rock Island and were painted and lettered into their scheme. When returned in April through June, 1980, serviceable units were repainted while the balance were stored.

This repainted GP40 from Rock Island to Union Pacific colors looks almost natural at Council Bluffs, IA on 28 September 1980. This is an ex-RI 4700-Class unit which Union Pacific had purchased new and leased directly to the Rock Island in the early 1970's. Union Pacific quickly repossessed these units during April-June 1980 and sent them to North Platte for mechanical inspection. Those that were found mechanically sound were repainted into the Union Pacific scheme and placed into service.

The rear detail of a GP40 from the ex-RI 350-Class, UP 616 sports a fresh Union Pacific image at Council Bluffs, IA on 20 September 1980.

The cab and front trucks of newly-painted UP 611 provide a detail study of the GP40. These units have been operating on the Kansas Division; however, have worked into Council Bluffs, IA on occasion . . . since out-shopped at North Platte. Council Bluffs, IA, 19 September 1980.

The interim paint scheme on the Rock Island locomotives returned to Union Pacific was a hasty blocking out of all previous markings and the addition of Union Pacific road numbers in the number boards and under the cab windows. Determination of operational capabilities dictated whether the unit would be painted or simply placed in the deadline. UP 632 shown at the diesel servicing area at Council Bluffs, IA on 19 April 1980.

The North Platte paint shop was quite busy converting all serviceable ex-Rock Island equipment into the Union Pacific scheme during May through June 1980. The units were completely inspected and those requiring maintenance at or below a level established by the Union Pacific were repaired and then repainted. Freshly painted UP 645 shown active at Council Bluffs, IA on 22 April 1980.

Due to the down-turn in freight traffic, freshly out-shopped GP40's sit on an out-of-service track at North Platte, NE on 21 May 1980. Those units found serviceable from the ones returned by lessee Rock Island were quickly given Union Pacific's image. Such was the case with rolling equipment, too! The storage lines have remained pretty much as shown here. *Photo by Richard Stephenson.*

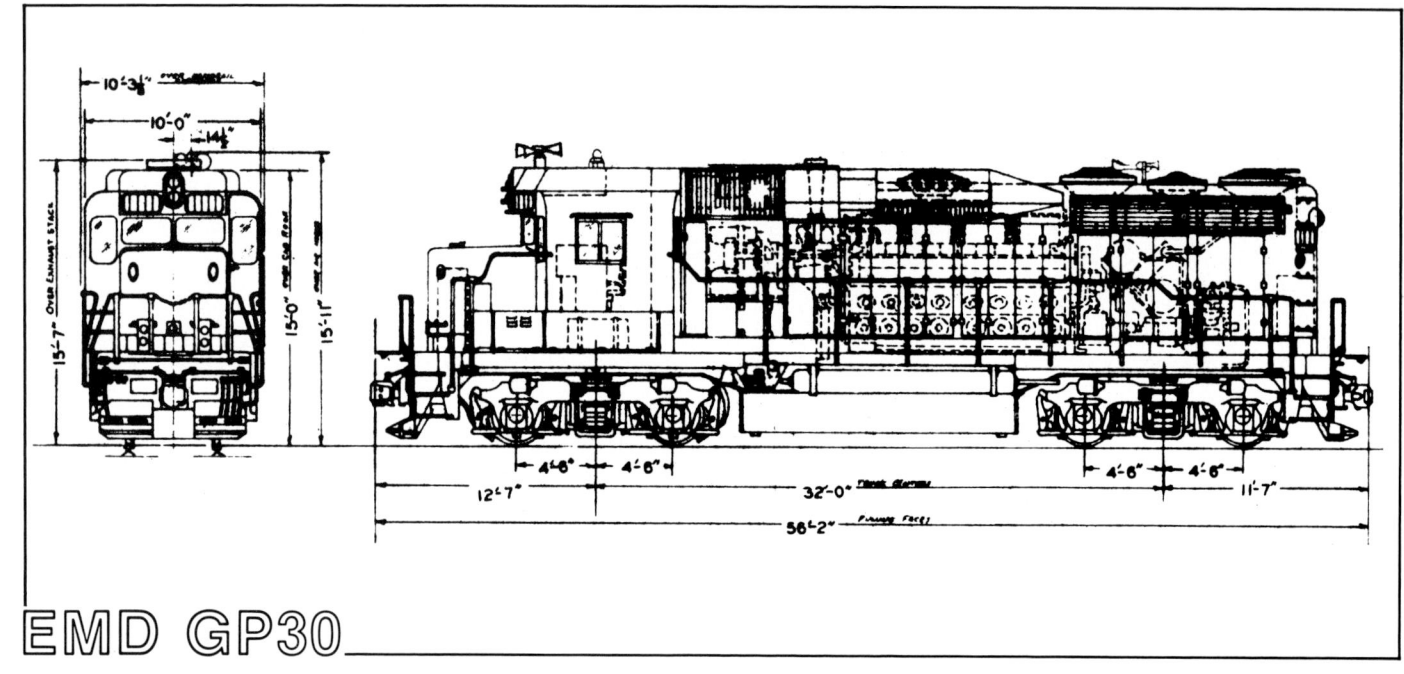

EMD GP30

GENERAL DATA
A.A.R. DESIGNATION	B-B
GEAR RATIO	62/15
WEIGHT LOADED	262,600 LBS.
LIGHT WEIGHT	235,746 LBS. APPROX.
MAXIMUM CURVATURE	WITH TRAIN
MAXIMUM CURVATURE	21° AS SINGLE UNIT
MAXIMUM SPEED	65 M.P.H.
MINIMUM CONT. SPEED	12 M.P.H.
CENTER OF GRAVITY	63.5" ABOVE RAIL (IN WORKING ORDER)

SUPPLIES
FUEL	2600 GALS.
LUBE OIL	220 GALS.
COOLING WATER	227 GALS.
SAND	46 CU. FT.

DIESEL ENGINE
MODEL	16-567-D3
TURBOCHARGER	EQUIPPED
SPARK ARRESTER	NOT REQUIRED
AIR FILTER, BASIC:	
CARBODY	NOT EQUIPPED
PRIMARY	DYNAVANE
ENGINE	ROTO-NAMIC
FUEL HEATER	KELTY

BRAKES
SCHEDULE	26 L J8 (80%) RELAY VALVE
AIR COMPRESSOR	WBG
BRAKE SHOES	HI FRICT. COMP
SAFETY CONTROL	FOOT PEDAL

ELECTRICAL
MULTIPLE UNIT RECEPTACLES	12-21 & 27 PT
MAIN GENERATOR	D-22
ALTERNATOR	D-14
TRACTION MOTORS, TYPE	D-57
NUMBER OF TRACTION MOTORS	4
DYNAMIC BRAKES	POTENTIAL CONTROL
BATTERIES	64 V. 426 AMP. HRS.
HEADLIGHTS	TWIN SEALED BEAMS 200W EA.
AUXILIARY GENERATOR	10 KW
COOLING FANS	(1) 36" & (2) 48" FANS
CAB SIGNALS	US&S TYPE 'E'
ROTATING WARNING LIGHTS	EQUIPPED
R.C.S.	NOT EQUIPPED

RUNNING GEAR
DRAFT GEAR	M-381
COUPLER	TYPE 'E'
JOURNALS	6½" x 12" HYATT R.B.
WHEELS	40" DIA.
TRUCKS	4 WHL., SWINGHANGER, CLSP, BRKS.

MISCELLANEOUS
WHISTLE	LESLIE S-3 LRF
TOILET	EQUIPPED
FIRE EXTINGUISHERS	(3) 30 LB. ANSUL
WATER COOLER	EQUIPPED
FUEL FILLER	BUCKEYE
SPEED RECORDER	CP

ELECTRO-MOTIVE'S GP30 ROSTER

UNIT	BUILDER DATE	BUILDER NUMBER	UNIT	BUILDER DATE	BUILDER NUMBER	UNIT	BUILDER DATE	BUILDER NUMBER
700:4	February 1963	28160	712:3	February 1963	28192	724:3	March 1963	28204
701:4	February 1963	28161	713:3	March 63	28193	725:3	April 1963	28205
702:4	February 1963	28162	714:3	March 1963	28194	726:3	April 1963	28206
703:4	February 1963	28163	715:3	March 1963	28195	727:3	April 1963	28207
704:4	February 1963	28164	716:3	March 1963	28196	728:3	April 1963	28208
705:4	February 1963	28165	717:3	March 1963	28197	729:3	May 1963	28209
706:4	February 1963	28166	718:3	March 1963	28198	730:3	April 1963	28210
707:4	February 1963	28167	719:3[2]	March 1963	28199	731:3	April 1963	28211
708:3	February 1963	28168	720:3	March 1963	28200	732:3	April 1963	28212
709:3	February 1963	28169	721:3	March 1963	28201	733:3	April 1963	28213
710:3	February 1963	28190	722:3	March 1963	28202	734:3	April 1963	20214
711:3	March 1963	28191	723:3	April 1963	28203	735:3[3]	June 1963	28351

[1]UP 700-734 built with parts from trade-in F3/7A's and B's.
[2]Rebuilt to GP30M with 2500hp in 1974.
[3]Built with parts from trade-in F9AM 516.

A westbound C&NW's Iowa Power "Sgt. Bluffs" coal empty is headed up with Union Pacific power leading. It is bitter cold as the consist clears the Missouri River bridge that links the Council Bluffs, IA yard to the Omaha, NE TOFC/COFC yard. Mainline 1 action . . . 31 January 1980.

UP 704 faces west at Council Bluffs, IA on 14 August 1977.

The distinctive face of the GP30 as it faces west at Green River, WY on 24 April 1976.

A rear view shows off the connecting hoses and MU-cable. Council Bluffs, IA, 7 April 1978.

UP 700-707 are the fourth units to carry these road numbers; UP 708-729 are the third units to carry these road numbers. All but UP 735 were built with parts from F3/7A and B-units traded-in. The large top blister covering the dynamic brake resistors is the major spotting feature of the GP30. UP 700 is shown active at North Platte, NE, 1 September 1979.

The overhead view of UP 725 accents the large dynamic brake housing and the large-small-large radiator fan arrangement. Omaha, NE, 10 December 1978.

The local power assignment at St. Joseph, MO on 1 September 1978 was a GP30 and two GP9B's . . . idling in front of the St. Joseph Terminal diesel house.

Having just arrived from the west is a GP30A and B set . . . UP 709 and 701B. While not equipped with a pilot snow plow, the GP30's seem to "bull" their way across the Nebraska Division during the winter months. Again, the large roof-work identifies the GP30. Recently, the units have been assigned to major yards to handle transfers and general yard switching.

An interesting construction feature is the 10-inch difference in the cab's length. The distance of the wall aft of the engineer's window is 21 inches, while on the fireman's side the same wall is 31 inches! The extra length allows tandem seating for the fireman and head brakeman.

Shown on the "run around" track at Council Bluffs, IA on 8 December 1978.

85

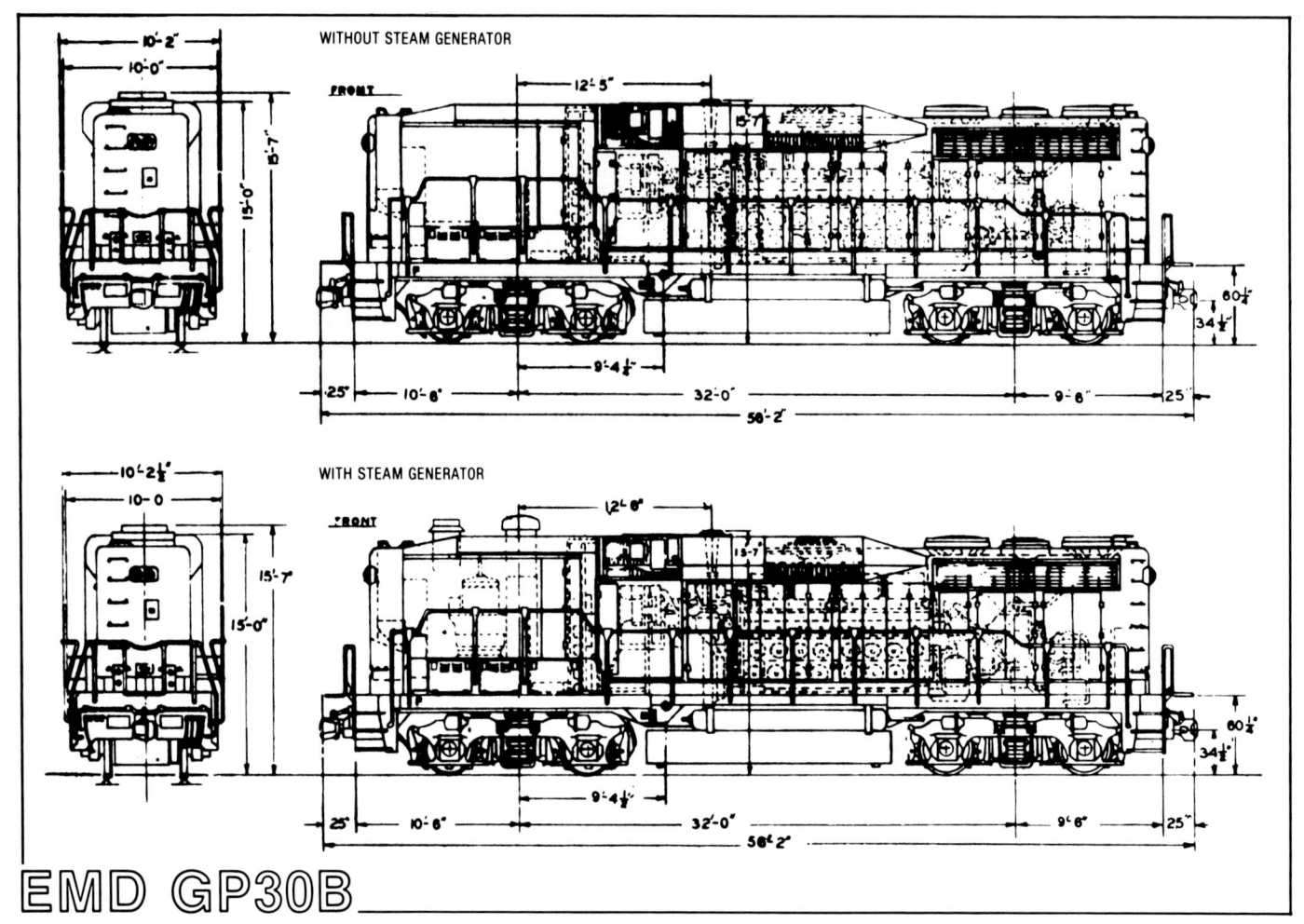

EMD GP30B

GENERAL DATA
A.A.R. DESIGNATION	B-B
GEAR RATIO	62/15
WEIGHT LOADED	258,800 LBS.
LIGHT WEIGHT	231,946 LBS. APPROX.
MAXIMUM CURVATURE	WITH TRAIN
MAXIMUM CURVATURE	23° AS SINGLE UNIT
MAXIMUM SPEED	65 M.P.H.
MINIMUM CONT. SPEED	12 M.P.H.
CENTER OF GRAVITY	63.5" ABOVE RAIL (IN WORKING ORDER)

SUPPLIES
FUEL	2600 GALS.
LUBE OIL	220 GALS.
COOLING WATER	227 GALS.
SAND	46 CU. FT.

DIESEL ENGINE
MODEL	16-567-D3
TURBOCHARGER	EQUIPPED
SPARK ARRESTER	NOT REQUIRED
AIR FILTER, BASIC:	
CARBODY	NOT EQUIPPED
PRIMARY	DYNAVANE
ENGINE	ROTO-NAMIC
FUEL HEATER	KELTY

BRAKES
SCHEDULE	26 L J18 (80%) RELAY VALVE
AIR COMPRESSOR	WBG
BRAKE SHOES	HI FRICT. COMP.
SAFETY CONTROL	NOT EQUIPPED

ELECTRICAL
MULTIPLE UNIT RECEPTACLES	12-21 & 27 PT
MAIN GENERATOR	D-32
ALTERNATOR	D-14
TRACTION MOTORS, TYPE	D-57
NUMBER OF TRACTION MOTORS	4
DYNAMIC BRAKES*	POTENTIAL CONTROL
BATTERIES	64 V. 426 AMP. HRS.
HEADLIGHTS	TWIN SEALED BEAMS 200W EA.
AUXILIARY GENERATOR	10 KW
COOLING FANS	(1) 36" 10-BLADE & (2) 48" 6-BLADE
CAB SIGNALS	NOT EQUIPPED
ROTATING WARNING LIGHTS	NOT EQUIPPED
R.C.S.	NOT EQUIPPED

*EXTENDED RANGE

RUNNING GEAR
DRAFT GEAR	M-381
COUPLER	TYPE 'E'
JOURNALS	6½" x 12" HYATT R.B.
WHEELS	40" DIA.
TRUCKS	4 WHL., SWINGHANGER, CLASP BRKS.

MISCELLANEOUS
WHISTLE	NOT EQUIPPED
TOILET	NOT EQUIPPED
FIRE EXTINGUISHERS	(4) 30 LB. ANSUL
WATER COOLER	NOT EQUIPPED
FUEL FILLER	BUCKEYE
SPEED RECORDER	NOT EQUIPPED
STEAM GENERATOR	VAPOR OK-4625*

*INSTALLED ON UP727B-739B.

Pulling in a westbound consist, steam generator equipped UP 738B whisks through the turnouts on mainline 3 in Omaha's Summit yards on 22 July 1978. While the steam generator equipment remains on-board, all GP30B's so configured have had the equipment deactivated. Note the lack of horns on the B-unit, while the GP30A, in front, has its horns in the original rear-position.

Only forty GP30B's were produced with *all* going to the Union Pacific. The cabless unit provided some cost savings in not having the expensive operating controls installed. These units were capable of multiple unit operations by having the 12, 21 and 27 point receptacles for proper mating with other units.

UP 719B was involved in an accident at North Platte, NE and retired in August 1980. It will be scrapped on property in late 1980.

Shown active at Council Bluffs, IA, 17 April 1980.

The major spotting feature of the GP30 model is the large top blister covering the dynamic brake resistors coupled with the centralized air system. This construction feature is more clearly seen in this top front view. Council Bluffs, IA, 9 April 1979.

The rear details of the GP30B and the A are identical, except UP 727B-734B which have steam generators for passenger service. Here, with UP 734B, the water filler cover is obvious on the side of a deeper walkway which houses the plumbing requirements. This group of GP30B's are the only GP30 units that housed steam generators! Council Bluffs, IA, 5 June 1979.

ELECTRO-MOTIVE'S GP30B ROSTER

UNIT	BUILDER DATE	BUILDER NUMBER	UNIT	BUILDER DATE	BUILDER NUMBER	UNIT	BUILDER DATE	BUILDER NUMBER
700B:2	April 1963	28215	714B	May 1963	28229	727B[3]	June 1963	28242
701B	May 1963	28216	715B	May 1963	28230	728B[3]	June 1963	28243
702B:2	June 1963	28217	716B	May 1963	28231	729B[3]	June 1963	28244
703B:2	April 1963	28218	717B	June 1963	28232	730B[3]	July 1963	28245
704B:2	May 1963	28219	718B	June 1963	28233	731B[3]	July 1963	28246
705B:2	May 1963	28220	719B[2]	June 1963	28234	732B[3]	July 1963	28247
706B:2	May 1963	28221	720B	June 1963	28235	733B[3]	July 1963	28248
707B	May 1963	28222	721B	June 1963	28236	734B[3]	July 1963	28249
708B	May 1963	28223	722B	June 1963	28237	735B[3]	July 1963	28250
709B	May 1963	28224	723B	June 1963	28238	736B[3]	July 1963	28251
711B	May 1963	28226	724B	June 1963	28239	737B[3]	July 1963	28252
712B[1]	May 1963	28227	725B	June 1963	28240	738B[3]	July 1963	28253
713B	May 1963	28228	726B	June 1963	28241	739B[3]	July 1963	28254

[1] Accident Speer, WY 6/77. Scrapped 8/77 at Omaha Shops.
[2] Accident North Platte, NE 8/80. Pending retirement.

[3] Equipped with steam generators for standby passenger service, currently non-operable.

The Union Pacific was the only railroad to purchase the GP30B units, buying 40 of them. Eight of these units . . . UP 727B-734B . . . have steam generators installed for passenger service. These units can be quickly spotted by the air intake and smoke stack mounted on the top front end of the cabless unit. The area normally occupied by the cab is given over to the steam generator and its controls. All generators have been deactivated.

The water fill is through the intake mounted in the walkway on the right rear of the unit.

The front sanding box filler is centered above the twin 200-watt seal beam headlight housing . . . while the rear sanding box is mounted at the top rear of the carbody. The total sand requirement, fully serviced, is 46 cubic feet of dry sand.

Council Bluffs, IA, 10 September 1978.

UP 730B offers another view of the steam generator stack and cabless front end arrangement. The ratchet-type hand brake is let-in on the left front of the car body. The multiple unit receptacle has 12, 21 and 27 point connections providing full compatibility with any locomotive lash-up. Council Bluffs, IA, 1 August 1979.

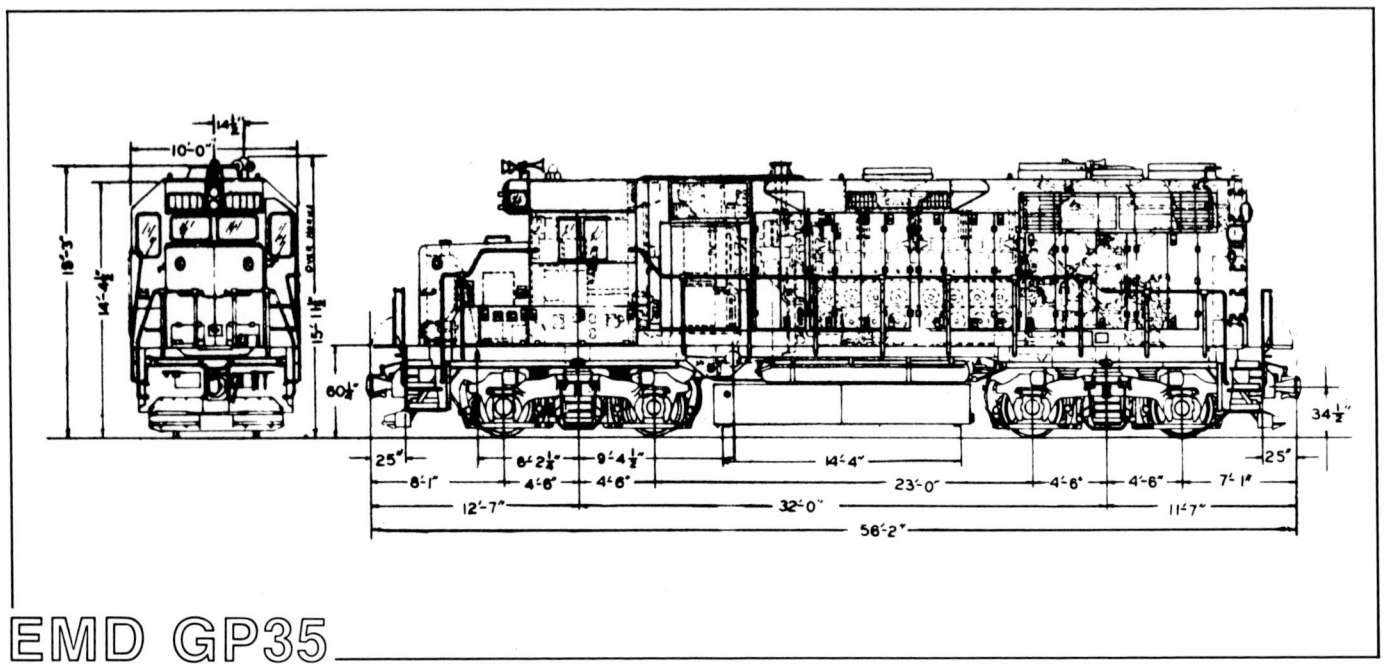

EMD GP35

GENERAL DATA

A.A.R. DESIGNATION	B-B
GEAR RATIO	62/15
WEIGHT LOADED	261,290 LBS.
LIGHT WEIGHT	234,464 LBS. APPROX.
MAXIMUM CURVATURE	WITH TRAIN
MAXIMUM CURVATURE	21° AS SINGLE UNIT
MAXIMUM SPEED	65 M.P.H.
MINIMUM CONT. SPEED	12 M.P.H.
CENTER OF GRAVITY	64.7 ABOVE RAIL (IN WORKING ORDER)

SUPPLIES

FUEL	2600 GALS.
LUBE OIL	243 GALS.
COOLING WATER	275 GALS.
SAND	40 CU. FT.

DIESEL ENGINE

MODEL	16-567-D3A
TURBOCHARGER	EQUIPPED
SPARK ARRESTER	NOT REQUIRED
AIR FILTER, BASIC:	
CARBODY	NOT EQUIPPED
PRIMARY	DYNAVANE
ENGINE	DYNAVANE
FUEL HEATER	KELTY

BRAKES

SCHEDULE	26 L
AIR COMPRESSOR	WBG
BRAKE SHOES	HI FRICT. COMP.
SAFETY CONTROL	FOOT PEDAL

ELECTRICAL

MULTIPLE UNIT RECEPTACLES	12-21 & 27 PT
MAIN GENERATOR	D-32
ALTERNATOR	D-32
TRACTION MOTORS, TYPE	D-67B1
NUMBER OF TRACTION MOTORS	4
DYNAMIC BRAKES*	POTENTIAL CONTROL
BATTERIES	64 V. 246 AMP. HRS.
HEADLIGHTS	TWIN SEALED BEAMS 200W EA.
AUXILIARY GENERATOR	10 KW
COOLING FANS	(2) 48" DIA. & (1) 36" DIA.
CAB SIGNALS	US&S TYPE 'E'
ROTATING WARNING LIGHTS	EQUIPPED
R.C.S.	NOT EQUIPPED

*EXTENDED RANGE

RUNNING GEAR

DRAFT GEAR	M-381
COUPLER	TYPE 'E'
JOURNALS	6½" x 12" HYATT R.B.
WHEELS	40" DIA.
TRUCKS	4 WHL., SWINGHANGER, CLASP. BRKS.

MISCELLANEOUS

WHISTLE	LESLIE S-3 LRF
TOILET	EQUIPPED
FIRE EXTINGUISHERS	(3) 30 LB. ANSUL
WATER COOLER	EQUIPPED
FUEL FILLER	BUCKEYE
SPEED RECORDER	CP

ELECTRO-MOTIVE'S GP35 ROSTER

UNIT	BUILDER DATE	BUILDER NUMBER	UNIT	BUILDER DATE	BUILDER NUMBER	UNIT	BUILDER DATE	BUILDER NUMBER
740	May 1964	29168	748	June 1964	29176	756	July 1964	29184
741	May 1964	29169	749	June 1964	29177	757	July 1964	29185
742	May 1964	29170	750	June 1964	29178	758	July 1964	29186
743	May 1964	29171	751	June 1964	29179	759	July 1964	29187
744	May 1964	29172	752	June 1964	29180	760	July 1964	29188
745	May 1964	29173	753	June 1964	29181	761	July 1964	29189
746	May 1964	29174	754	June 1964	29182	762[1]	August 1963	28319
747	May 1964	29175	755	June 1964	29183	763[2]	November 1963	28352

[1] Purchased secondhand 5/64. EMD demonstrator unit #5652.
[2] Purchased secondhand 5/64. EMD demonstrator unit #5654.

Rounding the last turn in Omaha on 28 September 1979, Extra 756 East, with trailing Rock Island units, will be on straight tracks heading towards the Missouri River bridge and its destination . . . Council Bluffs, IA. The GP35's have served as "pilot" units for the last half dozen years on the eastern end of the Nebraska Division.

Striking a builder pose at Council Bluffs, IA on 1 August 1975, UP 747 has the first generation slogan applied proclaiming: "Dependable Transportation." The major spotting features on this "clean body" unit is the turbocharger stack and radiator fan arrangement of one large-one small-one large fan. There were about 1,250 GP35's built between late 1963 and early 1966 . . . with a variety of options offered such as high short hoods, without dynamic brakes, larger fuel tanks, and steam generators . . . however, Union Pacific opted for the most standard version, as seen here.

The major construction spotting features of most units are found at the front or rear of the unit . . . and presented here is such a view. The lead unit . . . UP 748, still has the "economy" type lettering which has no black edging, while trailing unit . . . UP 743, sports a "new image" paint job. The freshly painted trucks permits a better study of their construction. The slant-roof fairs into the car body just forward of the centralized air system. Shown on the diesel service lead at Council Bluffs, IA on 13 June 1976.

The beveled short hood points west at Council Bluffs, IA on 10 June 1979.
Union Pacific bought the EMD GP35 demonstrators in May 1964 that toured with the DD35B's, which were painted in red and white demonstrator scheme. The GP35 demos, 5652 and 5654, were numbered UP 762 and 763.
These units have stayed on the Nebraska Division during most of their later career. They serve as "pilot units" for off-line power consists and westbound C&NW trains entering the system at Fremont, NE.
These units have not been equipped with pilot snow plows even though they operate in snow-prone territory.

A pair of GP35's head west on Mainline 3 at Omaha's Summit on 30 March 1978. Two styles of cab markings are obvious . . . the later style "shield" applied to the lead unit, UP 742, while trailing UP 749 has the early 1970's "We Can Handle It" slogan applied. The angular, slant roof cab shows off to good advantage as does the centralized air system which is located just aft of the cab.

The rigors of Nebraska winters are evident! The howling prairie winds, sometimes at near-gale force, snow-pack the unprotected units as they traverse the open land. The engine heat melts some of the snow which almost instantly turns to ice at the running board level. Council Bluffs, IA, 28 January 1979.

An on-coming overhead view allows comparison with the view at the top showing the "going away" perspective of the GP35 roof details. These units were built with parts from trade-in F3/F7A and B-units. The major spotting feature "top-side" is the small fan located between the two large sized radiator fans and the turbocharger stack just aft of the centralized air system. The GP35's have the wire whip antenna mounted on the cab roof. This is Mainline 2 in Omaha, with a westbounder on 7 October 1978.

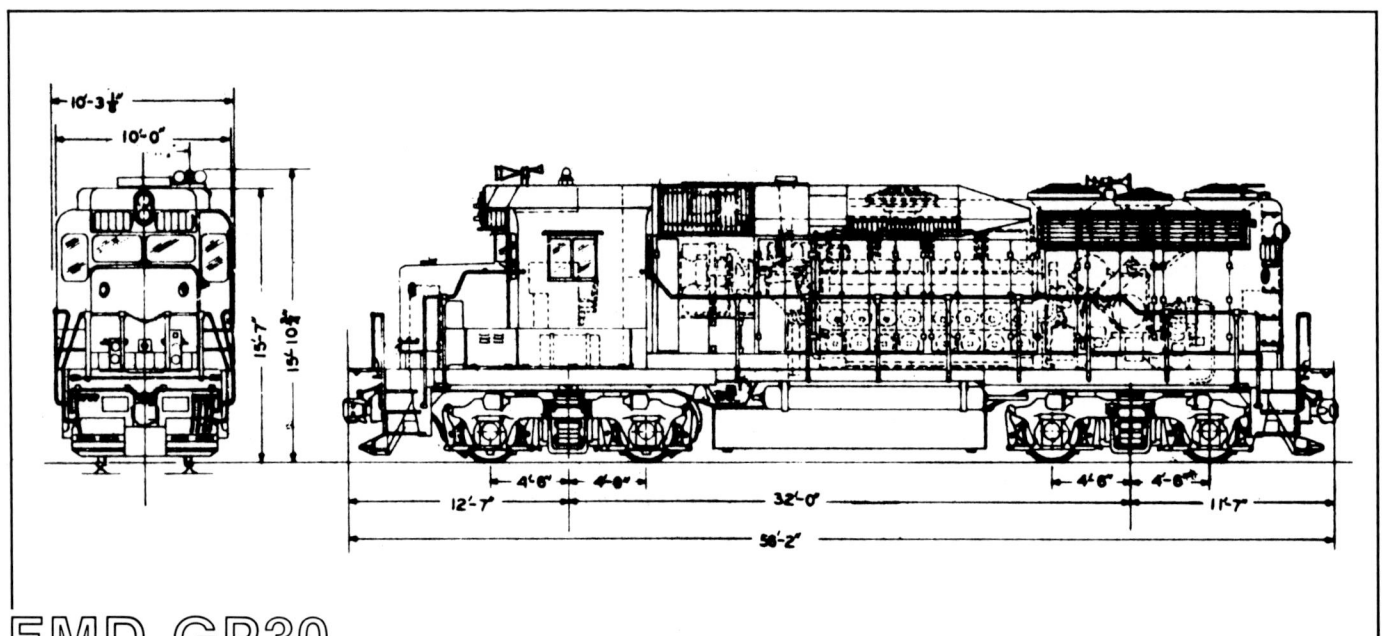

EMD GP30

GENERAL DATA
A.A.R. DESIGNATION	B-B
GEAR RATIO	62/15
WEIGHT LOADED	259,900 LBS.
LIGHT WEIGHT	233,046 LBS. APPROX.
MAXIMUM CURVATURE	WITH TRAIN
MAXIMUM CURVATURE	21° AS SINGLE UNIT
MAXIMUM SPEED	71 M.P.H.
MINIMUM CONT. SPEED	12 M.P.H.
CENTER OF GRAVITY	63.5" ABOVE RAIL (IN WORKING ORDER)

SUPPLIES
FUEL	2600 GALS.
LUBE OIL	220 GALS.
COOLING WATER	227 GALS.
SAND	46 CU. FT.

DIESEL ENGINE
MODEL	16-567-D3
TURBOCHARGER	EQUIPPED
SPARK ARRESTER	NOT REQUIRED
AIR FILTER, BASIC:	
CARBODY	NOT EQUIPPED
PRIMARY	DYNAVANE
ENGINE	ROTO-NAMIC
FUEL HEATER	KELTY

RUNNING GEAR
DRAFT GEAR	M-380A
COUPLER	TYPE 'F'
JOURNALS	6⅞" x 12" HYATT R.B.
WHEELS	40" DIA.
TRUCKS	4 WHL., SWINGHANGER, CLSP. BRKS.

ELECTRICAL
MULTIPLE UNIT RECEPTACLES	12-21 & 27 PT
MAIN GENERATOR	D-22
ALTERNATOR	D-14
TRACTION MOTORS, TYPE	D-57
NUMBER OF TRACTION MOTORS	4
DYNAMIC BRAKES	FLD. LOOP & POTL. CONT.*
BATTERIES	64 V. 426 AMP. HRS.
HEADLIGHTS	TWIN SEALED BEAMS 200W EA.
AUXILIARY GENERATOR	10 KW
COOLING FANS	(1) 36" & (2) 48" FANS
CAB SIGNALS	SEE NOTE
ROTATING WARNING LIGHTS	EQUIPPED
R.C.S.	NOT EQUIPPED

*EXTENDED RANGE
NOTE:
  C.C.S. US&S TYPE 'E' UNITS: 800-819, 821, 824, 825, 833 & 875
       US&S TYPE 'EL' UNITS: 820, 823, 826-832, & 834-874 & 822

BRAKES
SCHEDULE	26 L
AIR COMPRESSOR	WBG
BRAKE SHOES	HI FRICT. COMP.
SAFETY CONTROL	FOOT PEDAL

MISCELLANEOUS
WHISTLE	LESLIE S-3 LRF
TOILET	EQUIPPED
FIRE EXTINGUISHERS	(3) 30 LB. ANSUL
WATER COOLER	EQUIPPED
FUEL FILLER	BUCKEYE
SPEED RECORDER	CP
PILOT SNOW PLOW	UNITS 800-803

Working a "special," UP 870 idles at Las Vegas, NV on 15 May 1980, with a string of passenger equipment. This consist was brought to town behind steamer UP 8444 in conjunction with Las Vegas Day celebrations. Sporting fresh paint, the GP30 compliments the "spic 'n span" line-up . . . soon to be heading back east to home territory.—Photo by Martin Bosynak.

Sawing over to Mainline 2, Extra 819 West approaches the Missouri River bridge as it departs Council Bluffs, IA on 3 May 1979. Finding a matched GP30A and B-unit set on the head-end in 1979 is unusual. This local "peddler" will pick-up and set-out cars along its way to North Platte.

ELECTRO-MOTIVE'S GP30 ROSTER

UNIT	BUILDER DATE	BUILDER NUMBER	UNIT	BUILDER DATE	BUILDER NUMBER	UNIT	BUILDER DATE	BUILDER NUMBER
800	July 1962	27509	825	August 1962	27534	850	September 1962	27559
801	July 1962	27510	826	September 1962	27535	851	September 1962	27560
802	July 1962	27511	827	August 1962	27536	852	September 1962	27561
803	July 1962	27512	828	September 1962	27537	853	October 1962	27562
804[2]	July 1962	27513	829	September 1962	27538	854	October 1962	27563
805	July 1962	27514	830	August 1962	27539	855	October 1962	27564
806	July 1962	27515	831	September 1962	27540	856	October 1962	27565
807[2]	July 1962	27516	832	September 1962	27541	858	October 1962	27567
808	July 1962	27517	833	August 1962	27542	859	October 1962	27568
809[2]	July 1962	27518	834	September 1962	27543	860	October 1962	27569
810	July 1962	27519	835[2]	September 1962	27544	861	September 1962	27570
811	July 1962	27520	836	September 1962	27545	862	October 1962	27571
812	July 1962	27521	837	September 1962	27546	863	October 1962	27572
813[2]	July 1962	27522	838	September 1962	27547	865	October 1962	27574
814	July 1962	27523	839	September 1962	27548	866	October 1962	27575
815[2]	July 1962	27524	840	September 1962	27549	867	October 1962	27576
816	August 1962	27525	841	September 1962	27550	868	October 1962	27577
817[2]	July 1962	27526	842	September 1962	27551	869	October 1962	27578
818	July 1962	27527	843	September 1962	27552	870	October 1962	27579
819	July 1962	27528	844	September 1962	27553	871	October 1962	27580
820[2]	September 1962	27529	845	September 1962	27554	872	October 1962	27581
821	August 1962	27530	846	September 1962	27555	873	October 1962	27582
822	August 1962	27531	847	September 1962	27556	874	October 1962	27583
823	August 1962	27532	848	September 1962	27557	875[1]	August 1961	26613
824	August 1962	27533	849	September 1962	27558			

[1] EMD GP22 demonstrator #5929, built 6/61; rebuilt as GP30 demonstrator #1962, 8/61. Purchased second-hand 9/62.

[2] Leased to Kennecott Copper Corporation's Utah Mines Division, Bingham, UT, 9/75 to 11/78.

On local assignment at Lincoln, NE, a pair of GP30's idle in view of the Nebraska State Capitol. Its "Football Saturday," 5 October 1980, and not much moves in Lincoln when Nebraska's **Cornhuskers** are on the gridiron! The newest lettering scheme is shown, which omits the road number under the cab window.

A down-on view gives a better perspective of the varying cab roof lines of the GP30. The centralized air system is just aft of the cab. The horns have been moved forward in accordance with recent Union Pacific mechanical directives and mounted just aft of the wire whip antenna.

The fireman's cab wall is most interesting. The tandem seating arrangement for the fireman and head brakeman requires 10 inches of additional cab space... thus, the wall behind the window is constructed 31 inches long to satisfy the seating requirements (10 inches longer than the opposite engineer's wall).

On the "run-around" track, Council Bluffs, IA, 1 September 1980.

Heading west with U50C UP 5019, UP 812 awaits its crew on the diesel service tracks at Council Bluffs, IA on 6 July 1976. The first generation slogan—"Dependable Transportation" pretty well spells out the life-style of the GP30's: dependable! It should be pointed out that the 800-Class GP30's were deliverd a year earlier than the 700-Class.

The rear view of UP 858 shows the footboards still attached to the rear pilot plate . . . since removed. The cut-outs provided protection to the hose glad-hands when stowed. The arrangement of the safety appliances have become pretty much standardized as evidenced in this view. Council Bluffs, IA, 15 October 1977.

Sporting the mid-1970's slogan—"We Can Handle It," UP 838 shows off a different view of the GP30's major spotting feature . . . the pronounced roof line. Flared back from the cab's number boards, the roof-work incorporates the centralized air system and the dynamic brake blister . . . better than 2/3 of the roof line. Note the angle of the engineer's door as it fits the curved roof. The distance of the wall behind the engineer's window to the door is 21 inches . . . 10 inches shorter than on the fireman's side. Council Bluffs, IA, 15 August 1977.

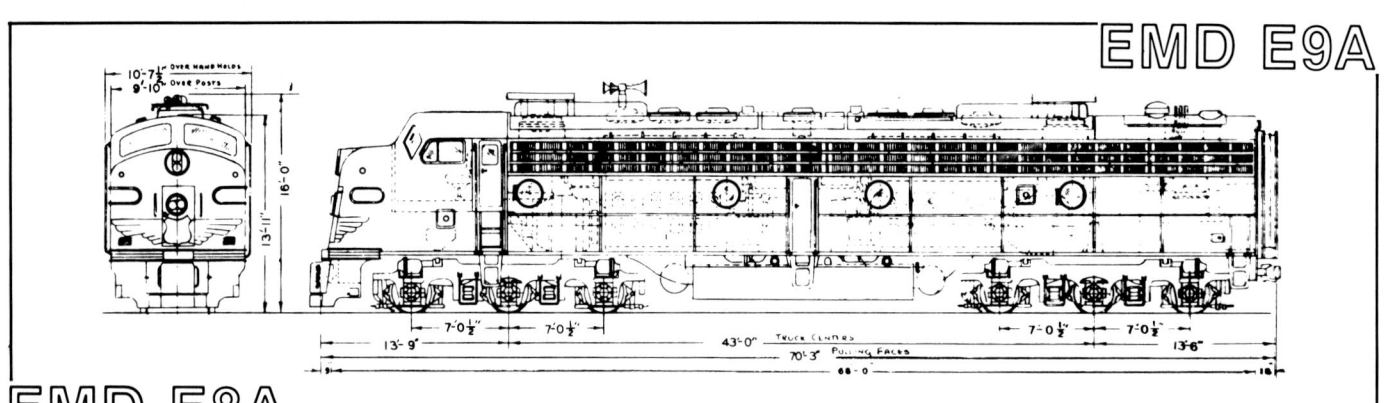

EMD E-8A

GENERAL DATA
A.A.R. DESIGNATION	A1A-A1A
GEAR RATIO	55/22
WEIGHT LOADED	340,300 LBS.
LIGHT WEIGHT	309,161 LBS. APPROX.
MAXIMUM CURVATURE	WITH TRAIN
MAXIMUM CURVATURE	21° AS SINGLE UNIT
MAXIMUM SPEED	98 M.P.H.
MINIMUM CONT. SPEED	30 M.P.H.
WEIGHT ON DRIVERS	228,906 LBS.

SUPPLIES
FUEL	1700 GALS.
LUBE OIL	330 GALS.
COOLING WATER	436 GALS.
SAND	16 CU. FT.
BOILER WATER	1350 GALS.

DIESEL ENGINE
MODEL	(2) 12-567-B
TURBOCHARGER	NOT EQUIPPED
SPARK ARRESTER	EQUIPPED
AIR FILTER, BASIC:	
CARBODY	EQUIPPED
PRIMARY	IMPINGEMENT (CARBODY)
ENGINE	IMPINGEMENT
FUEL HEATER	KELTY

ELECTRICAL
MULTIPLE UNIT RECEPTACLES	12-21 PT*
MAIN GENERATOR	(2) D-15-B
ALTERNATOR	(2) D-16
TRACTION MOTORS, TYPE	D-27-B
NUMBER OF TRACTION MOTORS	4
DYNAMIC BRAKES	FIELD LOOP
BATTERIES	32 CELL 64V. 426 AMP. HRS.
HEADLIGHTS	TWIN SEALED BEAMS 200W. EA.
AUXILIARY GENERATOR	10 KW.
COOLING FANS	(8) 36" FANS
CAB SIGNALS	US&S TYPE 'E'
ROTATING WARNING LIGHTS	EQUIPPED
R.C.S.	NOT EQUIPPED

ON REAR END ONLY

RUNNING GEAR
DRAFT GEAR	M-380A
COUPLER	TYPE 'H'
JOURNALS	6½" x 12" HYATT R.B.
WHEELS	36" DIA.
TRUCKS	6 WHL., SWINGHANGER, CLASP BRAKES, HIGH CYLS.

BRAKES
SCHEDULE	24RL F-6 (60%) RELAY VALVE
AIR COMPRESSOR	(2) ABO
BRAKE SHOES	HI PHOS. CAST IRON
SAFETY CONTROL	FOOT PEDAL

MISCELLANEOUS
WHISTLE	LESLIE S-3 LRF & S-25
TOILET	EQUIPPED
FIRE EXTINGUISHERS	(6) 30 LB. ANSUL
WATER COOLER	EQUIPPED
FUEL FILLER	BUCKEYE
SPEED RECORDER	CP
STEAM GENERATOR	(1) OK-4740

EMD E-9A

GENERAL DATA
A.A.R. DESIGNATION	A1A-A1A
GEAR RATIO	55/22
WEIGHT LOADED	344,184 LBS.*
LIGHT WEIGHT	313,045 LBS. APPROX.*
MAXIMUM CURVATURE	WITH TRAIN
MAXIMUM CURVATURE	21° AS SINGLE UNIT
MAXIMUM SPEED	98 M.P.H.
MINIMUM CONT. SPEED	31.5 M.P.H.
WEIGHT ON DRIVERS	231,558 LBS. APPROX.

UNIT 955 HAS 1200 GAL. FUEL TANK, WEIGHS 336,260 LBS. LOADED

SUPPLIES
FUEL	1700 GALS.
LUBE OIL	330 GALS.
COOLING WATER	436 GALS.
SAND	18 CU. FT.
BOILER WATER	1350 GALS.

DIESEL ENGINE
MODEL	(2) 12-567-C
TURBOCHARGER	NOT REQUIRED
SPARK ARRESTER	EQUIPPED
AIR FILTER, BASIC:	
CARBODY	EQUIPPED
PRIMARY	IMPINGEMENT (CARBODY PANELS)
ENGINE	IMPINGEMENT OR ROTO-NAMIC
FUEL HEATER	KELTY

ELECTRICAL
MULTIPLE UNIT RECEPTACLES	12-21 PT*
MAIN GENERATOR	(2) D-15B
ALTERNATOR	(2) D-4D
TRACTION MOTORS, TYPE	D-37-B
NUMBER OF TRACTION MOTORS	4
DYNAMIC BRAKES	FIELD LOOP
BATTERIES	32 CELL 64V. 426 AMP. HRS.
HEADLIGHTS	TWIN SEALED BEAMS 200W. EA.
AUXILIARY GENERATOR	(2) 10 KW.
COOLING FANS	(8) 36" FANS
CAB SIGNALS	US&S TYPE 'E'
ROTATING WARNING LIGHTS	EQUIPPED
R.C.S.	NOT EQUIPPED

ON REAR END ONLY

RUNNING GEAR
DRAFT GEAR	M-380A
COUPLER	TYPE 'H'
JOURNALS	6½" NOMINAL DIA. HYATT R.B.
WHEELS	36" DIA.
TRUCKS	6 WHL., EQUALIZER, SWINGHANGER, CLASP BRKS., HIGH CYL.

BRAKES
SCHEDULE	24RL J6 (60%) RELAY VALVE
AIR COMPRESSOR	(2) ABO
BRAKE SHOES	HI PHOS. CAST IRON
SAFETY CONTROL	FOOT PEDAL

MISCELLANEOUS
WHISTLE	LESLIE S-2M & S-25**
TOILET	EQUIPPED
FIRE EXTINGUISHERS	(6) 30 LB. ANSUL
WATER COOLER	EQUIPPED
FUEL FILLER	BUCKEYE
SPEED RECORDER	CP
STEAM GENERATOR	(1) OK4740 74D06
**UNIT 954	LESLIE S-3 LRF & S-25

One-half of the retained passenger locomotives stands in front of the Omaha Shops on 5 July 1977 . . . being ready for another special movement. In addition to pulling Union Pacific's "yellow machine," the A-units have been used to protect Amtrak's *San Francisco Zephyr* between Ogden, UT and Denver. CO while on UP rails.

ELECTRO-MOTIVE'S E8A ROSTER

UNIT	BUILDER DATE	BUILDER NUMBER	REMARKS
928	July 1950	10779	Retired 8/80. Held for disposition.

ELECTRO-MOTIVE'S E9A ROSTER

UNIT	BUILDER DATE	BUILDER NUMBER	REMARKS	UNIT	BUILDER DATE	BUILDER NUMBER	REMARKS
951	June 1955	20488	Retired 8/80. Held for disposition.	960	October 1955	20497	Retired 8/80. Held for disposition.
954	July 1955	20491	Retired 8/80. Held for disposition.				

Idling at Portland, OR on 4 August 1978, the single remaining E8A on the Union Pacific shows off its classic lines. This model began the standardization of Union Pacific's passenger power, with a total of 18 A-units entering the fleet during the early 1950's.—*Photo by Vic F. Reyna.*

The arriving Junior Old Timers Special slides down the grade into Omaha on 12 May 1979 with UP 968B, 929 and 1406 as trailing power. The SDP35's seldom worked in conjunction with the "covered wagons," but served to protect the run on this occasion. In fact, on the westbound trip the steam generating SDP35 served on the point. UP 951 was repainted to standard Union Pacific scheme in July 1978 after having served continuously in the red-white-blue "Preamble Express" scheme applied four years earlier.

The faces of the retained E-unit fleet on the opposite page are highlighted by the "Preamble Express" shown at Council Bluffs, IA on 4 May 1977. The basic paint was freshened up several times over its four year period in this patriotic scheme.

The "covered wagons" operate the company specials and other civic oriented passenger trips. All were photographed at Council Bluffs, IA. UP 928: 6 May 1977; UP 951: 6 May 1977; UP 954: 14 July 1975; UP 960: 27 June 1977.

The A and B-units were stored in June and retired by August 1980. Two have been retained for display purposes and are shown here being routed to North Platte paint shops for refurbishing. The E8A was completely stripped, becoming a "shell," while the E9A UP 951 is a completely functioning unit. The E8A will be donated to a museum for display. The E9A will enter Union Pacific's permanent locomotive collection stored at Cheyenne, WY. They are shown being shipped out at Council Bluffs, IA on 26 October 1980.

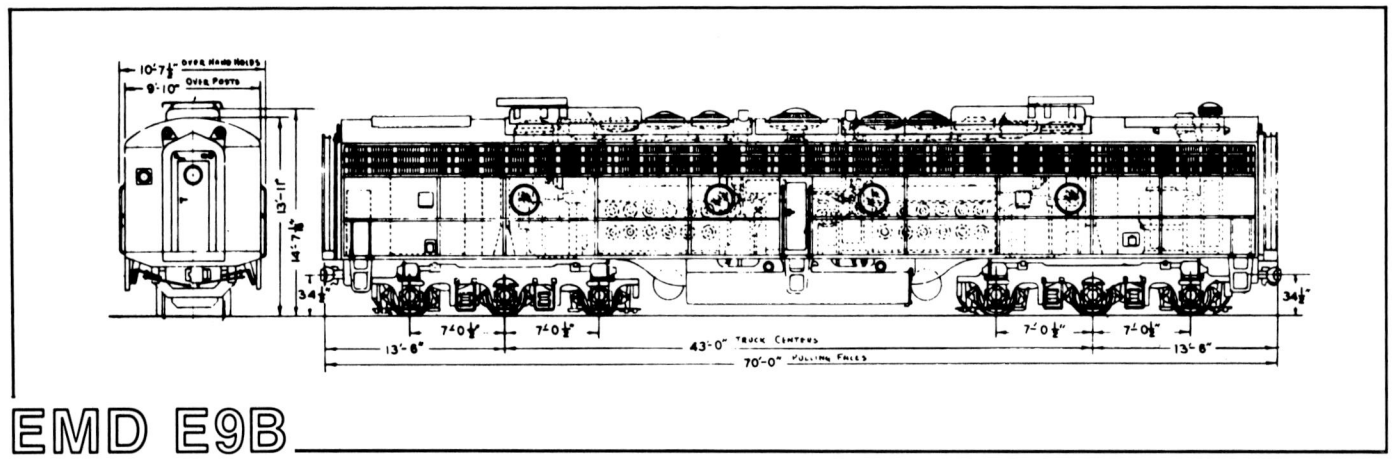

EMD E9B

GENERAL DATA
A.A.R. DESIGNATION	A1A-A1A
GEAR RATIO	55/22
WEIGHT LOADED	340,490 LBS.*
LIGHT WEIGHT	302,791 LBS. APPROX.*
MAXIMUM CURVATURE	WITH TRAIN
MAXIMUM CURVATURE	21° AS SINGLE UNIT
MAXIMUM SPEED	98 M.P.H.
MINIMUM CONT. SPEED	31.5 M.P.H.
WEIGHT ON DRIVERS	232,660 LBS. APPROX.

*UNITS 968B & 973B HAVE 1700 GAL. FUEL TANKS & WEIGH 347,000 LBS. LOADED & 305,701 LBS. LIGHT WEIGHT.

WEIGHT ON DRIVERS	229,642 LBS. APPROX.

SUPPLIES
FUEL	1200 GALS.
LUBE OIL	330 GALS.
COOLING WATER	436 GALS.
SAND	18 CU. FT.
BOILER WATER	2550 GALS.

DIESEL ENGINE
MODEL	(2) 12-567-C
TURBOCHARGER	NOT EQUIPPED
SPARK ARRESTER	EQUIPPED
AIR FILTER, BASIC:	
CARBODY	EQUIPPED
PRIMARY	IMPINGEMENT (CARBODY)
ENGINE	IMPINGEMENT OR ROTO-NAMIC
FUEL HEATER	KELTY

BRAKES
SCHEDULE	24-RL F-6 (60%) RELAY VALVE
AIR COMPRESSOR	(2) ABO
BRAKE SHOES	HI PHOS. CAST IRON
SAFETY CONTROL	NONE

ELECTRICAL
MULTIPLE UNIT RECEPTACLES	12-21 PT
MAIN GENERATOR	(2) D-15-B
ALTERNATOR	(2) D-16
TRACTION MOTORS, TYPE	D-37-B
NUMBER OF TRACTION MOTORS	4
DYNAMIC BRAKES	FIELD LOOP
BATTERIES	32 CELL 64 V. 426 AMP. HRS.
HEADLIGHTS	NOT EQUIPPED
AUXILIARY GENERATOR	(2) 10 KW
COOLING FANS	(8) 36" FANS
CAB SIGNALS	NOT EQUIPPED
ROTATING WARNING LIGHTS	EQUIPPED
R.C.S.	NOT EQUIPPED

RUNNING GEAR
DRAFT GEAR	M-380A
COUPLER	TYPE 'H'
JOURNALS	6½" NOM. DIA.-HYATT R.B.
WHEELS	36" DIA.
TRUCKS	6 WHL., EQUALIZER, SWINGHANGER CLASP BRKS., HIGH CYLS.

MISCELLANEOUS
WHISTLE	NOT EQUIPPED
TOILET	NOT EQUIPPED
FIRE EXTINGUISHERS	(6) 30 LB. ANSUL
WATER COOLER	NOT EQUIPPED
FUEL FILLER	BUCKEYE
SPEED RECORDER	NOT EQUIPPED
STEAM GENERATOR	(1) OK-4740

ELECTRO-MOTIVE'S E9B ROSTER

UNIT	BUILDER DATE	BUILDER NUMBER	REMARKS	UNIT	BUILDER DATE	BUILDER NUMBER	REMARKS
968B	October 1955	20508	Retired 8/80. Held for disposition.	973B:2	October 1955	20513	Retired 8/80. Held for disposition.
969B:2	October 1955	20509	Retired 8/80. Held for disposition.	974B:2	October 1955	20514	Retired 8/80. Held for disposition.

Lined up, "elephant-style," UP 974B and 969B await action at Council Bluffs, IA on 30 September 1976. Now all retired and being stripped for useable parts, these B-units will be remembered as part of Union Pacific's "yellow machines" that headed up their crack passenger trains. There were a total of 34 E8B's during the passenger heyday . . . and the four, pictured on the right, were retained for special company operations after Amtrak took over passenger service.

UP 968B at Council Bluffs, IA on 3 January 1976.

UP 969B at Council Bluffs, IA on 27 February 1977.

UP973B at Omaha, NE on 16 September 1979.

UP 974B at Council Bluffs, IA on 28 November 1978.

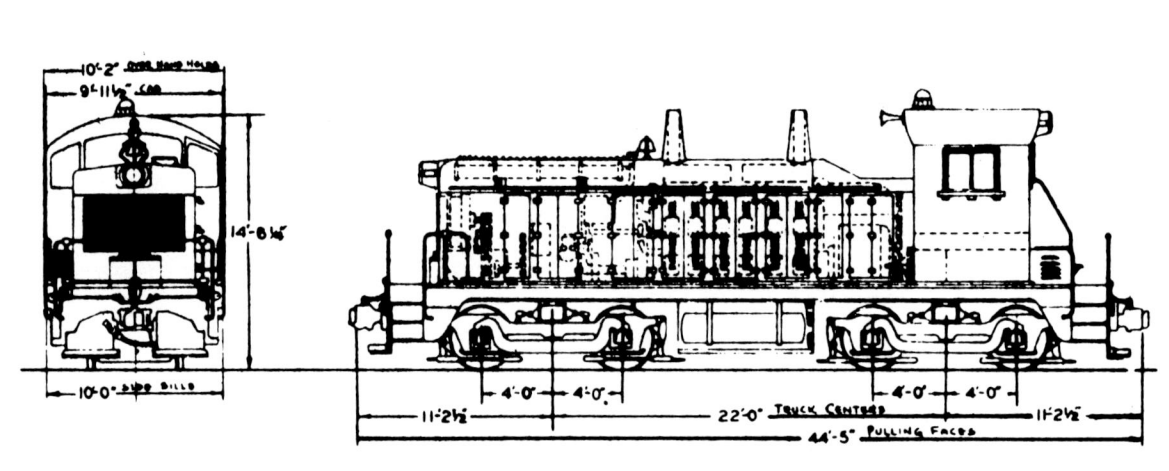

THE GENERAL DATA HAS BEEN OMITTED.

EMD NW2

ELECTRO-MOTIVE'S NW2 ROSTER

UNIT	BUILDER DATE	BUILDER NUMBER	REMARKS
1003	May 1940	1002	Sold 6/77 to Chrome Crankshaft Company, Chicago, IL.
1004	May 1940	1003	Sold 10/78 to Precision National Corporation, Mt. Vernon, IL.
1005	May 1940	1004	Sold 3/78 to Precision National Corporation, Mt. Vernon, IL.
1006	June 1940	1005	Retired 5/79. Sold 12/79 to Bargains Galore, Portland, OR and shipped to Diesel Electric Service, St. Paul, MN.
1007	June 1940	1006	
1008	June 1940	1007	Sold 3/78 to Precision National Corporation, Mt. Vernon, IL.
1011	July 1940	1124	Donated 8/78 to State of Utah.
1012	July 1940	1125	Retired 2/79. Sold 12/79 to Hyman-Michaels Company, Madison, IL.
1013	August 1940	1126	Retired 2/79. Sold 10/79 to Hyman-Michaels Company, Madison, IL.
1017	February 1941	1246	Retired 10/79. Sold 1/80 to Bargains Galore, Portland, OR and shipped to Diesel Electric Service, St. Paul, MN.
1018	February 1941	1247	Sold 11/78 to Chrome Crankshaft Company, Chicago, IL.
1019	February 1941	1248	Retired 9/78. Sold 1/80 to Bargains Galore, Portland, OR and shipped to Diesel Electric Service, St. Paul, MN.
1022	March 1941	1251	Sold 12/78 to Joseph Simon & Sons, Tacoma, WA.
1023	April 1941	1252	Sold 6/77 to Chrome Crankshaft Company, Chicago, IL.
1024	April 1941	1253	
1025	October 1941	1686	Retired 9/79. Sold 7/80 to Bargains Galore, Portland, OR and shipped to Joseph Simon & Sons, Tacoma, WA.
1026	October 1941	1687	
1027	May 1942	1688	Retired 4/80. Held for disposition.
1030	June 1942	1691	
1031	June 1942	1692	Retired 6/80. Held for disposition.
1032	June 1942	1693	
1034	July 1942	1695	Sold 2/77 to Chrome Crankshaft Company, Chicago, IL.
1036:2	May 1946	3422	Sold 2/77 to Chrome Crankshaft Company, Chicago, IL.
1037:2	May 1946	3423	
1039:2	June 1946	3425	
1040:2	June 1946	3426	
1041:2	June 1946	3427	Retired 5/79. Sold 1/80 to Peaker Industries, Inc., Brighton, MN.
1042:2	July 1946	3428	
1043:2	July 1946	3429	
1044:2	July 1946	3430	
1047:2	July 1946	3433	Retired 9/78. Sold 2/80 to Precision National Corporation, Mt. Vernon, IL.
1049:2	July 1946	3435	
1050:2	July 1946	3436	Retired 10/79. Held for disposition.
1051:2	February 1947	4697	
1052:2	February 1947	4698	Sold 3/78 to Precision National Corporation, Mt. Vernon, IL.
1054:2	February 1947	4700	
1055:2	February 1947	4701	
1056:2	February 1947	4702	Sold 11/78 to Chrome Crankshaft Company, Madison, IL.
1058:2	March 1947	4704	Sold 6/77 to Chrome Crankshaft Company, Madison, IL.
1059:2	March 1947	4705	
1061:2	March 1947	4707	
1062:2	April 1947	4708	
1063:2	May 1947	4709	Sold 7/80 to Precision National Corporation, Mt. Vernon, IL.
1064:2	May 1947	4710	
1065:2	May 1947	4711	Sold 3/78 to Precision National Corporation, Mt. Vernon, IL.
1068:2	May 1947	4714	Sold 11/78 to Chrome Crankshaft Company, Chicago, IL.
1069:2	June 1947	4715	Sold 11/78 to Chrome Crankshaft Company, Chicago, IL.
1071:2	June 1947	4717	Sold 6/77 to Chrome Crankshaft Company, Chicago, IL.
1072:2	June 1947	4718	Sold 3/78 to Precision National Corporation, Mt. Vernon, IL.
1074:2	June 1947	4720	Sold 3/78 to Precision National Corporation, Mt. Vernon, IL.
1075:2	June 1947	4721	Retired 2/79. Sold 11/79 to Peaker Industries, Inc., Brighton, MN.
1076	March 1948	6336	Retired 12/79. Held for disposition.
1077	March 1948	6337	
1078	March 1948	6338	Retired 9/79. Sold 7/80 to Precision National Corporation, Mt. Vernon, IL.
1080	April 1948	6340	
1081	April 1948	6341	
1082	April 1948	6342	Retired 4/80. Held for disposition.
1083	April 1948	6343	
1085	May 1948	6345	
1086	May 1948	6346	
1087	June 1948	6347	Retired 10/79. Held for disposition.
1088	June 1948	6348	Sold 3/78 to Precision National Corporation, Mt. Vernon, IL.
1090	July 1948	6350	Retired 3/80. Held for disposition.
1091	August 1948	6351	
1092	August 1948	6352	
1093	September 1948	6353	Retired 5/79. Sold 8/80 to Hyman-Michaels, Madison, IL.
1094	September 1948	6354	
1095	September 1948	6355	

Representing the "after WWII" group of NW2's, this 32-year-old switcher is still showing a relative monthly availability of 85.9 percent in 1980! The fleet has dwindled down to about two dozen units; however, many of the units sold are still in useful service on other railroads or industrial sites. It idles in the late afternoon sun at Council Bluffs, IA on 25 March 1979.

One of the post-WWII models, UP 1047 was purchased in 1946 and sold to Naporano Iron & Metal Company, Newark, NJ in February 1980. In its 34 years of service on the system, this representative NW2 posted high daily availability . . . the hallmark of this model.
Council Bluffs, IA, 1 December 1979.

The crew-end of the NW2 provides good operating visibility and climatic protection for the switching crew who ride either inside or on the back "porch."
The canvas awning is usually replaced with a winterization window installation on the engineer's side when the first snowflakes fall.
UP 1075, the last of the 1947 order, is shown at Council Bluffs, IA on 21 June 1979. It was retired four months earlier and sold to Peaker Services, Inc., Brighton, MN in November 1979.

Another cab-end view of a NW2 shows the high amount of visibility afforded the engineer and his switching crew.
This is a pre-WWII model, built in August 1940. It had been retired less than a month when this photograph was taken at Council Bluffs, IA on 15 March 1979. It was sold to Hyman-Michaels Company, Madison, IL in October 1979.
Most of the switchers were equipped with the "cabbage-style" stack spark arresters . . . a big deterrent in starting grass fires during the hot summer months.

The first post-WWII NW2 received by Union Pacific was UP 1036, built in May 1946. Shown waiting for its switching crew at Council Bluffs, IA, 19 September 1975 . . . it would be sold to Chrome Crankshaft in February 1977 just short of its 31st birthday!

It appears from the stack markings that the "cabbage-style" spark arresters had been previously installed. The engineer's winterization window indicates the unit has been prepared for cold weather operations.

Lacking the radiator "window shade," UP 1069 pokes its face eastward at Council Bluffs, IA on 19 October 1978. Note the non-standard equipment box.

A pair of switchers faces each other at Council Bluffs, IA on 3 July 1977. The rear of UP 1023 still has footboards attached to the pilot sheet. Sold a month earlier, it is being shipped to Chrome Crankshaft.

This overhead view restates the whole construction story of NW2's . . . the half-length radiator grill, two centered exhaust stacks, the car body pinching back to cab along with the sloping hood and no sanding box on the front platform—all major distinguishing features. Council Bluffs, IA, 1 August 1979.

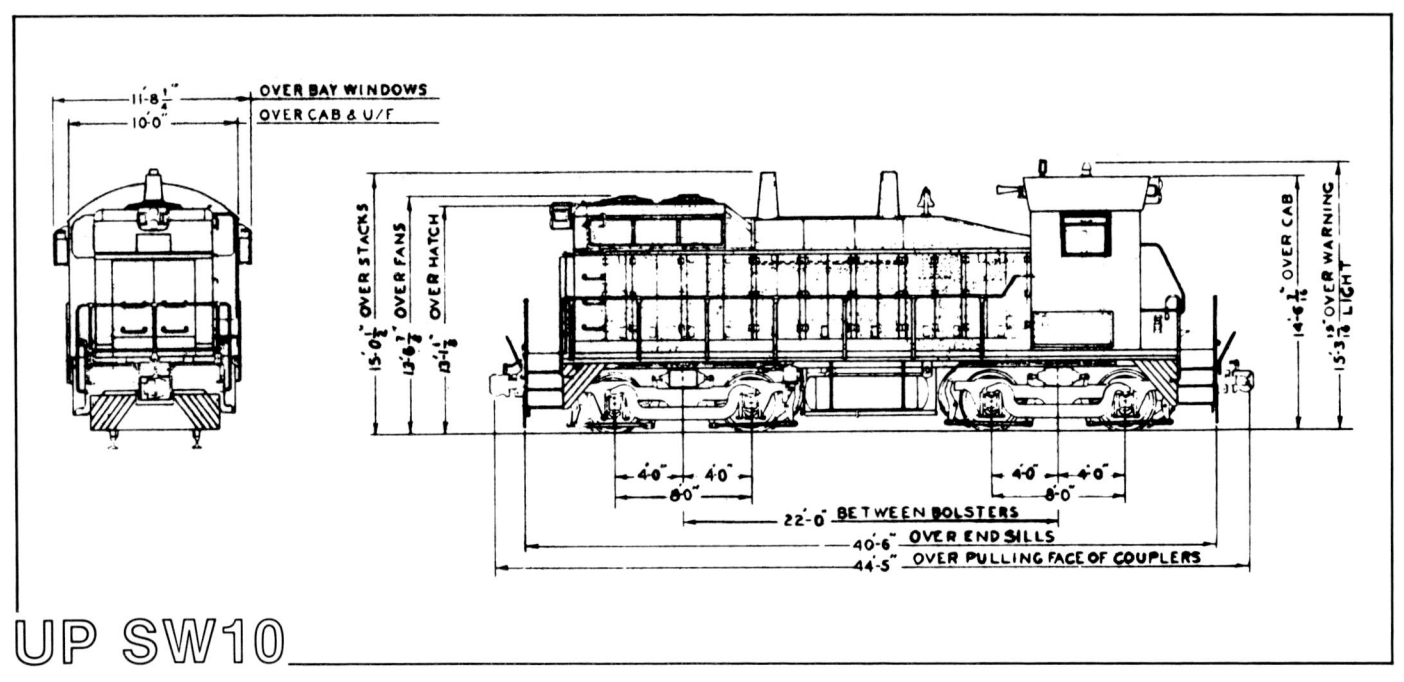

UP SW10

GENERAL DATA
A.A.R. DESIGNATION	B-B
GEAR RATIO	62/15
WEIGHT LOADED	251,200 LBS.
LIGHT WEIGHT	239,991 LBS.
MAXIMUM CURVATURE	WITH TRAIN
MAXIMUM CURVATURE	57° AS SINGLE UNIT
MAXIMUM SPEED	65 M.P.H.
MINIMUM CONT. SPEED	8 M.P.H.

SUPPLIES
FUEL	600 GALS.
LUBE OIL	165 GALS.
COOLING WATER	230 GALS.
SAND	41 CU. FT.

DIESEL ENGINE
MODEL	12-645-BC
TURBOCHARGER	NOT EQUIPPED
SPARK ARRESTER	EQUIPPED
AIR FILTER, BASIC:	
CARBODY	EQUIPPED
PRIMARY	AAF IMPINGEMENT TYPE (CARBODY)
ENGINE	AAF BAG TYPE
FUEL HEATER	NOT EQUIPPED

BRAKES
SCHEDULE	26 NL
AIR COMPRESSOR	WXO LOW MAINTENANCE
BRAKE SHOES	CAST IRON
SAFETY CONTROL	FOOT PEDAL

ELECTRICAL
MULTIPLE UNIT RECEPTACLES	NOT EQUIPPED
MAIN GENERATOR	D-12
ALTERNATOR	D-14
TRACTION MOTORS, TYPE	D-67
NUMBER OF TRACTION MOTORS	4
DYNAMIC BRAKES	NOT EQUIPPED
BATTERIES	64 V. 280 AMP. HRS.
HEADLIGHTS	TWIN SEALED BEAM 200W EA.
AUXILIARY GENERATOR	18 KW
COOLING FANS	(2) 36" 8-BLADE
CAB SIGNALS	NOT EQUIPPED
STROBE WARNING LIGHTS	EQUIPPED
R.C.S.	NOT EQUIPPED

RUNNING GEAR
DRAFT GEAR	NC-390
COUPLER	TYPE 'E'
JOURNALS	6½" x 12" ROLLER BEARING
WHEELS	40" DIA.
TRUCKS	4 WHEEL

MISCELLANEOUS
WHISTLE	LESLIE A-25
TOILET	NOT EQUIPPED
FIRE EXTINGUISHERS	(2) 30 LB. ANSUL
WATER COOLER	EQUIPPED
FUEL FILLER	BUCKEYE
SPEED RECORDER	NOT EQUIPPED

ELECTRO-MOTIVE'S SW10 ROSTER

UNIT	BUILDER DATE	REMARKS
1200:2	September 1979	Originally UP 1848 (bn 18836, 10/53) and rebuilt as SW10 with original number. Renumbered UP 1200 13 March 1980.
1201:2	November 1979	Originally UP 1839 (bn 17819, 4/53) and rebuilt as SW10 with original number. Renumbered UP 1201 1 April 1980.
1202:2	January 1980	Originally UP 1866 (bn 18854, 11/53) and rebuilt as SW10 with original number. Renumbered UP 1202 25 January 1980.
1203:2	March 1980	Originally UP 1864 (bn 18852, 11/53) and rebuilt as SW10. Renumbered UP 1203 9 March 1980.
1204:2	April 1980	Originally UP 1853 (bn 18841, 10/53) and rebuilt as SW10. Renumbered UP 1204 17 April 1980.
1205:2	May 1980	Originally UP 1865 (bn 18853, 11/53) and rebuilt as SW10. Renumbered UP 1205 21 May 1980.
1206:2	June 1980	Originally UP 1850 (bn 18838, 10/53) and rebuilt as SW10. Renumbered UP 1206 24 June 1980.
1207:2	July 1980	Originally UP 1859 (bn 18847, 11/53) and rebuilt as SW10. Renumbered UP 1207 14 July 1980.
1208:2	September 1980	Originally UP 1828 (bn 17808, 4/53) and rebuilt as SW10. Renumbered UP 1208 and released 4 September 1980.
1209:2	September 1980	Originally UP 1861 (bn 18849, 11/53) and rebuilt as SW10. To be renumbered UP 1209 and released in late September 1980.

NOTES:

A—The SW10 program calls for upgrading 15 SW7/9's by replacing the front-mounted mechanical radiator fan unit with two top-mounted electrically driven fans, installing "state-of-the-art" electrical circuitry, providing "clean cab" arrangement and adding modern crew comfort items.

B—The first 8 units have been assigned to Albina, Portland, OR.

C—UP 1208 and UP 1209 are shown in this roster; however, for accounting purposes, are considered as UP 1828 and UP 1861 in all other tallies of this book.

Taking a short break, newly painted SW10 1204 sits in front of the Omaha Shops on 19 April 1980. As each rebuilt switcher enters service, its breaks in by working Omaha's North Yard for about one month. After "qualifying," the units are assigned within the system . . . the first eight going to the Oregon Division.

Union Pacific began converting 15 SW9 switchers to "SW10's" in 1979. The pilot model was constructed from UP 1848 and released from the Omaha Shops in September 1979. After a thirty day qualification period in Omaha's North Yard, it was reassigned to the Oregon Division and shipped to Portland, OR for duty at the Albina Yard.

As the SW10 program continued, it was decided to create a new block of road numbers for these 1200-horsepower switchers. Instructions were issued to renumber UP 1848 to UP 1200, which was accomplished by Albina Shops on 13 March 1980.

Shown between assignments at Albina Yard, Portland OR on 12 July 1980.—*Photo by Ben Fredericks.*

The second SW10 was converted from UP 1839 in November 1979 and after its qualification at Omaha, was assigned to the Oregon Division for duty at Albina Yards. It was shipped as UP 1839.

In early 1980, the switcher was damaged sufficiently enough to have it returned to the Omaha Shops for repair. After being backshopped, it was released as UP 1201 on 1 April 1980. After requalification in Omaha's North Yard, it was shipped back to Portland, OR.

Shown during its Omaha North Yard stint, 13 April 1980.

Fresh from the paint shop, UP 1202 was converted from UP 1866. It was originally released as UP 1866 in early January 1980; however, due to painting problems it was returned to the paint shop. When released on 25 January 1980, it bore its new road number . . . 1202.

The first three conversions all had minor variations on the design changeover . . . primarily in engineering and electrical areas not identifiable from the exterior, since upgraded to standard. This unit represents the "standard" which has been incorporated in all follow-on rebuildings.

Shown in front of the Omaha Shops on 23 February 1980.

The distinctive SW10 roofline houses the two 36-inch 8-blade cooling fans in the raised radiator hatch. The engine cooling system is made up of six EMD 6-inch thick radiator cores in two banks of three cores each in a "V" configuration. They are cooled by the fans which are controlled by temperature switches. The cooling system capacity is 230 gallons of water.

Shutters are located on both sides of the radiator hatch, and are of the GP9 type which are operated by two air cylinders arranged to "fail safe" (open).

The cooling system accessories are mounted on a GP9 rack and consist of primarily GP9 components . . . the lubrication oil cooler, expansion water tank, two GP9-style venturi castings with associated plumbing.

Down on view of UP 1206 shows the standard EMD manifold exhaust stacks. Council Bluffs, IA, 29 August 1980.

The old and the new stand in front of the Omaha Shops on 21 June 1980. Just out of the shop is UP 1206, the ex-UP 1850 . . . and soon to be shipped west is UP 1205.

The removal of the front mounted radiator, shutters and fan allows the mounting of the large sand box. These modifications are more clearly seen in this during-construction view.

Completely qualified, UP 1206 awaits a westbound movement at Council Bluffs, IA on 30 August 1980. It is assigned to the Oregon Division and operates in the Albina Yard at Portland, OR. Its official conversion date to a SW10 is 24 June 1980.

It was during this time that the new marking standards were issued which eliminated the road numbers under the cab window. This unit went for a short time without these numbers; however, as no numbers are applied on the engine locker doors, an exception was made for these units.

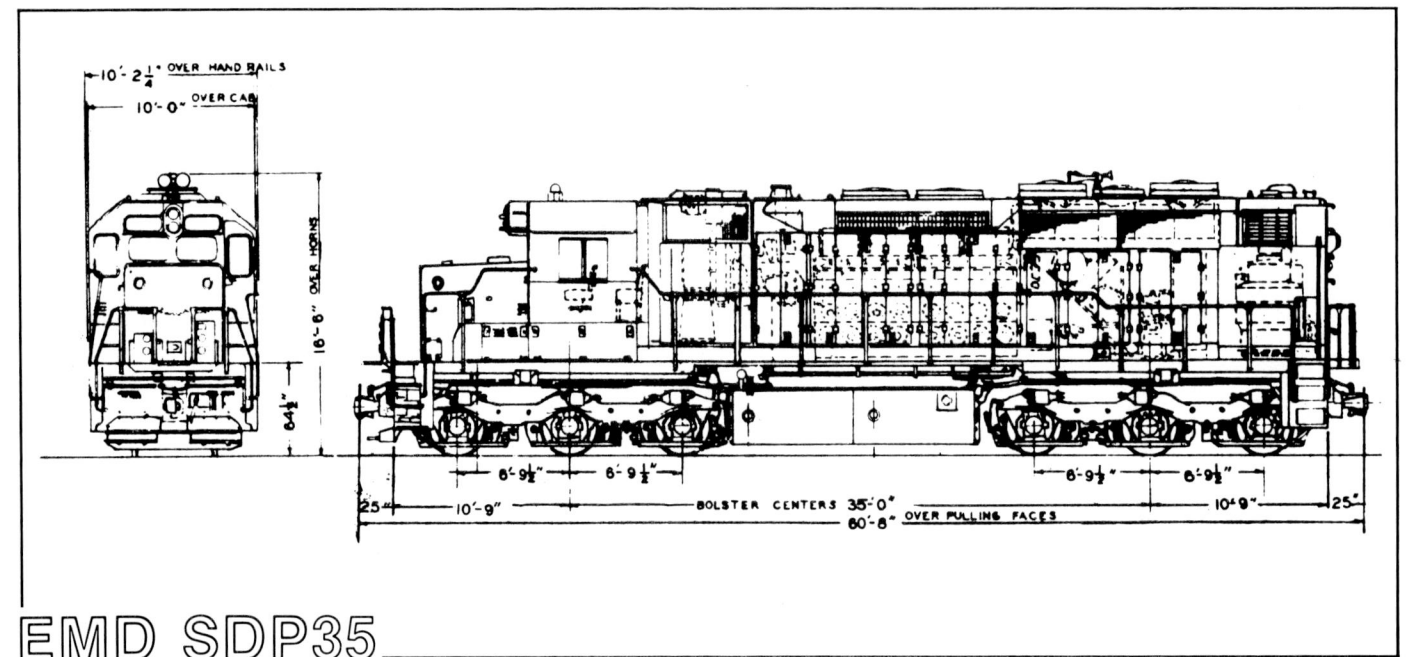

EMD SDP35

GENERAL DATA

A.A.R. DESIGNATION	C-C
GEAR RATIO	59/18
WEIGHT LOADED	379,560 LBS.*
LIGHT WEIGHT	345,447 LBS. APPROX.
MAXIMUM CURVATURE	WITH TRAIN
MAXIMUM CURVATURE	23° AS SINGLE UNIT
MAXIMUM SPEED	80 M.P.H.
MINIMUM CONT. SPEED	12 M.P.H.
CENTER OF GRAVITY	5.1" ABOVE RAIL (IN WORKING ORDER)

*FOR FREIGHT SERVICE W/O BOILER WATER

SUPPLIES

FUEL	2150 GALS.
LUBE OIL	374 GALS.
COOLING WATER	275 GALS.
SAND	40 CU. FT.
BOILER WATER	1150 GALS.

DIESEL ENGINE

MODEL	16-567-D3A
TURBOCHARGER	EQUIPPED
SPARK ARRESTER	NOT REQUIRED
AIR FILTER, BASIC:	
CARBODY	NOT EQUIPPED
PRIMARY	DYNAVANE
ENGINE	AAF BAG
FUEL HEATER	KELTY

BRAKES

SCHEDULE	26 L
AIR COMPRESSOR	WBO
BRAKE SHOES	HI PHOS. CAST IRON
SAFETY CONTROL	FOOT PEDAL

ELECTRICAL

MULTIPLE UNIT RECEPTACLES	12-21 & 27 PT
MAIN GENERATOR	D-32
ALTERNATOR	D-14
TRACTION MOTORS, TYPE	D-67B
NUMBER OF TRACTION MOTORS	6
DYNAMIC BRAKES*	POTENTIAL & FIELD LOOP
BATTERIES	32 CELL 64 V. 426 AMP. HRS.
HEADLIGHTS	TWIN SEALED BEAMS 200W EA.
AUXILIARY GENERATOR	18 KW A-8102-A3
COOLING FANS	(1) 36" & (2) 48" 6-BLADE
CAB SIGNALS	US&S TYPE 'E'
ROTATING WARNING LIGHTS	EQUIPPED
R.C.S.	NOT EQUIPPED

*EXTENDED RANGE

RUNNING GEAR

DRAFT GEAR	M-380A
COUPLER	TYPE 'F'
JOURNALS	6½" X 12" HYATT R.B.
WHEELS	40" DIA.
TRUCKS	6 WHL., FLEXICOIL, CLASP BRKS., HIGH CYL.

MISCELLANEOUS

WHISTLE	LESLIE S-3 LRF
TOILET	EQUIPPED
FIRE EXTINGUISHERS	30 LB. ANSUL
WATER COOLER	EQUIPPED
FUEL FILLER	BUCKEYE
SPEED RECORDER	CP
STEAM GENERATOR	(1) OK-4740

ELECTRO-MOTIVE'S SDP35 ROSTER

UNIT	BUILDER DATE	BUILDER NUMBER	UNIT	BUILDER DATE	BUILDER NUMBER	UNIT	BUILDER DATE	BUILDER NUMBER
1400:2	September 1965	30671	1404:2	September 1965	30675	1407:2	September 1965	30678
1401:2	September 1965	30672	1405:2	September 1965	30676	1408:2	September 1965	30679
1402:2	September 1965	30673	1406:2	September 1965	30677	1409:2	September 1965	30680
1403:2	September 1965	30674						

Extra 1409 East pulls across the Missouri River bridge on Mainline 2 as it approaches Council Bluffs, IA on 23 April 1977. Most of its 65-car consist is still in Nebraska. The horns are still rear-mounted; however, this unit had many different horn installations applied in the 1978-1979 period.

Not a particularly "hot seller"... some 35 units were produced in the mid-1960's. Union Pacific bought 10 to back-up its passenger locomotives. Steam generator equipped, they could perform standard freight service yet "protect" passenger service when needed.

As Union Pacific ran "fast varnish," the SDP35 quickly proved it was not capable of maintaining such demanding schedules. On occasions, these units have handled special company passenger operations, but never revenue passenger assignments.

These units have had different horn arrangements applied as part of Union Pacific's on-going audible alert testing, as evidenced by the pair of horns mounted on UP 1408.

Awaiting assignment at Council Bluffs, IA on 2 June 1978.

The extra radiator louver over the car body bulge is for the steam generator. The car body extension, housing the steam generator, can be quickly removed for ease in servicing. The bulge is on the left side only; however, the same radiator grill is on the opposite side. Otherwise, these units are just like the standard SD35. Council Bluffs, IA, 19 April 1978.

Heading out "light for Fremont" to pick-up a westbound C&NW freight, UP 1402 clears the Summit at Omaha on 17 August 1978. The air-raid siren was tested on this unit to measure its track-side warning effectiveness. It was later removed and applied to a DDA40X "Centennial" for further testing. The steam generator installation provides a major identifier.

Standing in the servicing area at Council Bluffs, IA on 19 June 1978 is UP 1403. The steam generator bulge at the left end of the car body, under the extra radiator louvers, is the major distinguishing feature between the standard SD35 and the SDP35 (Union Pacific owns no SD35's).

The turbocharger stack juts up aft of the clean air compartment, just forward of the fans . . . which boosts the 16-cylinder 567-D3A diesel engine to 2500 horsepower.

These ten units are currently stored serviceable at North Platte, NE, having been sidelined since late spring 1980.

Awaiting its crew at Council Bluffs, IA on 28 May 1979, it will soon run "light" to Fremont, NE to pick up a westbound C&NW train. Serving as a pilot-unit, it will head up the North Western's further movement to North Platte, NE.

The down-on view of UP 1405 shows off the short hood and cab details. The short hood has anti-glare, non-skid light green paint applied to the top.

The ground level view of the cab and front trucks of UP 1407 provides a good comparison to the overhead cab view above. Shown active at Council Bluffs, IA on 7 April 1980, just weeks before it was placed in storage at North Platte, NE. While built in the mid-1960's, the front shows a number of "first generation" mechanical details . . . the stacked MU-receptacles, the hose tray mounted on the flat pilot sheet and the modified auxiliary uncoupling lever converted from the older-style angle lever. Note the water manifold operating handle, located by the front step, which controls the flow of steam from the generator into the train line going forward.

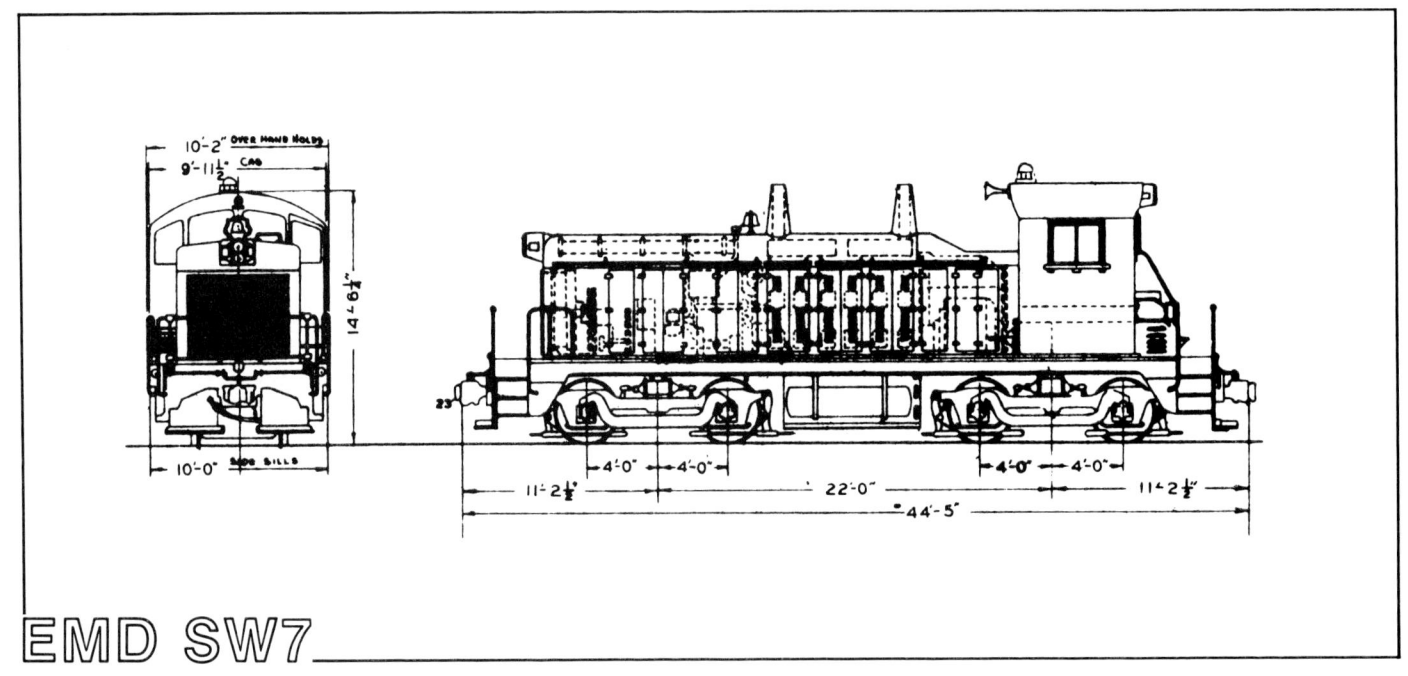

EMD SW7

GENERAL DATA
A.A.R. DESIGNATION	B-B
GEAR RATIO	62/15
WEIGHT LOADED	245,940 LBS.
LIGHT WEIGHT	235,732 LBS. APPROX.
MAXIMUM CURVATURE	WITH TRAIN
MAXIMUM CURVATURE	57° AS SINGLE UNIT
MAXIMUM SPEED	60 M.P.H.
MINIMUM CONT. SPEED	9.5 M.P.H.
CENTER OF GRAVITY	50.1" ABOVE RAIL (IN WORKING ORDER)

SUPPLIES
FUEL	600 GALS.
LUBE OIL	165 GALS.
COOLING WATER	223 GALS.
SAND	28 CU. FT.

DIESEL ENGINE
MODEL	12-567A
TURBOCHARGER	NOT EQUIPPED
SPARK ARRESTER	EQUIPPED
AIR FILTER, BASIC:	
CARBODY	NOT EQUIPPED
PRIMARY	NOT EQUIPPED
ENGINE	IMPINGEMENT (PANEL)
FUEL HEATER	KELTY

BRAKES
SCHEDULE	6-BL
AIR COMPRESSOR	WXE
BRAKE SHOES	CAST IRON
SAFETY CONTROL	FOOT PEDAL

ELECTRICAL
MULTIPLE UNIT RECEPTACLES	NOT EQUIPPED
MAIN GENERATOR	D-15-C
ALTERNATOR	NOT EQUIPPED
TRACTION MOTORS, TYPE	D-27-E
NUMBER OF TRACTION MOTORS	4
DYNAMIC BRAKES	NOT EQUIPPED
BATTERIES	32 CELL 64 V. 426 AH. AT 8 HRS.
HEADLIGHTS	TWIN SEALED BEAMS 200W EA.
AUXILIARY GENERATOR	A-7159
COOLING FANS	MECHANICAL
CAB SIGNALS	NOT EQUIPPED
ROTATING WARNING LIGHTS	EQUIPPED
R.C.S.	NOT EQUIPPED

RUNNING GEAR
DRAFT GEAR	MS-485-5A
COUPLER	TYPE 'E'
JOURNALS	6½" x 12" FRICTION BRGS.
WHEELS	40" DIA.
TRUCKS	4 WHL., EQUALIZER, CLASP BRKS.

MISCELLANEOUS
WHISTLE	LESLIE A-125
TOILET	NOT EQUIPPED
FIRE EXTINGUISHERS	(2) 30 LB. ANSUL
WATER COOLER	EQUIPPED
FUEL FILLER	BUCKEYE
SPEED RECORDER	NOT EQUIPPED

ELECTRO-MOTIVE'S SW7 ROSTER

UNIT	BUILDER DATE	BUILDER NUMBER	UNIT	BUILDER DATE	BUILDER NUMBER	UNIT	BUILDER DATE	BUILDER NUMBER
1800	September 1950	10752	1809[2]	September 1950	10761	1818	November 1950	10770
1801	August 1950	10753	1810	October 1950	10762	1819[3]	November 1950	10771
1802	August 1950	10754	1811	October 1950	10763	1820	November 1950	10772
1803[1]	August 1950	10755	1812	October 1950	10764	1821	November 1950	10773
1804	August 1950	10756	1813	October 1950	10765	1822	November 1950	10774
1805	September 1950	10757	1814	October 1950	10766	1823	November 1950	10775
1806	September 1950	10758	1815	November 1950	10767	1824	November 1950	10776
1807	September 1950	10759	1816	November 1950	10768			
1808	September 1950	10760	1817	November 1950	10769			

[1]Retired 12/78. Sold 12/79 to Chrome Crankshaft Company, Chicago, IL.
[2]Sold 2/77 to Chrome Crankshaft Company, Chicago, IL.
[3]Sold 10/78 to Precision National Corporation, Mt. Vernon, IL.

The "back porch" of the SW7 presents the "working-end" of the switcher, even though the other end is the front. The switching crew ride on the back . . . either on the "porch" or in the cab . . . when picking-up or setting-out cars according to their assignment sheets. Note the engineer's cold weather window extension. Awaiting duty at Council Bluffs, IA on 25 March 1979.

Almost 500 SW7's were constructed between October 1949 and January 1951. With a sizeable fleet of serviceable switchers, Union Pacific only purchased 25 of these 1200-horsepower units in late 1950. Easily distinguished from the twin-stacked earlier NW2's by the full-length front radiator grill, one must look closely at the engine locker door louvers to separate the SW7 from the SW9. The SW7 has the "letterboard" gap in the rows of louvering for the road name . . . the SW9 does not have the upper set of louvers. Council Bluffs, IA, 5 April 1977.

The two centered exhaust stacks on most units have the "cabbage-style" spark arrester installed. These venturi-concept spheres recirculate the exhaust to trap any hot carbon masses prior to venting . . . thus reducing the chance of trackside fires over the standard EMD manifold exhaust stack. Council Bluffs, IA, 30 November 1979.

The rounded roof of the SW7 is an EMD trade mark used in all of their basic switcher designs. It provides excellent 360° visibility for the engineer and weather protection for the switching crew. The back "porch" provides a large working space for switching crews during good weather. Council Bluffs, IA, 30 November 1979.

A pair of SW7's are lined up on parallel tracks at Council Bluffs, IA on 30 November 1979. The double row of car body louvers, providing a letterboard gap, is well displayed in this view . . . a spotting feature for this model. The bell on UP 1808 is attached by a double strap hangar . . . a "back shop" fabricated device replacing the original cast hangar assembly. Note the mid-section grab iron roof ladders and the sand box filler cover . . . both so placed due to the large overhead grill work, as shown on the opposite page.

These units weigh, fully loaded, 245,940 pounds and carry 600 gallons of diesel fuel, 165 gallons of lubrication oil, 223 gallons of water and 28 cubic feet of sand.

The double-equalized Type-A truck retains the original friction bearing journals, although Union Pacific has requalified some of these truck assemblies on other models with package roller bearings. Geared at 62:15 ratio, the unit's maximum speed is 60-mph.

Bearing the classic Union Pacific image, UP 1810 boasts *The Streamliners* at Ogden, UT on 18 September 1973. Equipped with number boards and classification lights, it certainly shows signs of being a "sports road model." While appearing in the Riverside Yard, several of these switchers acted as "coach yard goats" at Ogden during Union Pacific's passenger heydays.—*Photo by Brian Griebenow.*

Waiting out its new owner's shipping instructions, UP 1819 sits in the storage line at Council Bluffs, IA on 4 November 1978. Note the winterization window installed under the standard canvas awning. The wire VHF antenna points upward from its mount, the roof acting as its ground-plane. It was sold to Precision National Corporation in October 1978.

The roof line of UP 1800, showing the overhead grill work and exhaust stack arrangement, are typical construction features found both in the SW7 and the SW9 models. Council Bluffs, IA, 1 October 1979.

Just completing class repairs and sporting a new paint job, UP 1823 stands outside the North Platte Shops on 21 February 1979. This SW7 has been hustling locomotives around the heavy maintenance shops for the last several years... its "shop goat." The standard 12-cylinder 567A diesel engine can be seen.

While all conversions to SW10's have come from the SW9 fleet, the original plan was to consider the best units within the SW7/9 group for the conversion program. With the second-round for 15 additional conversions announced for 1981, it may include considering the SW7 fleet as possible candidates.

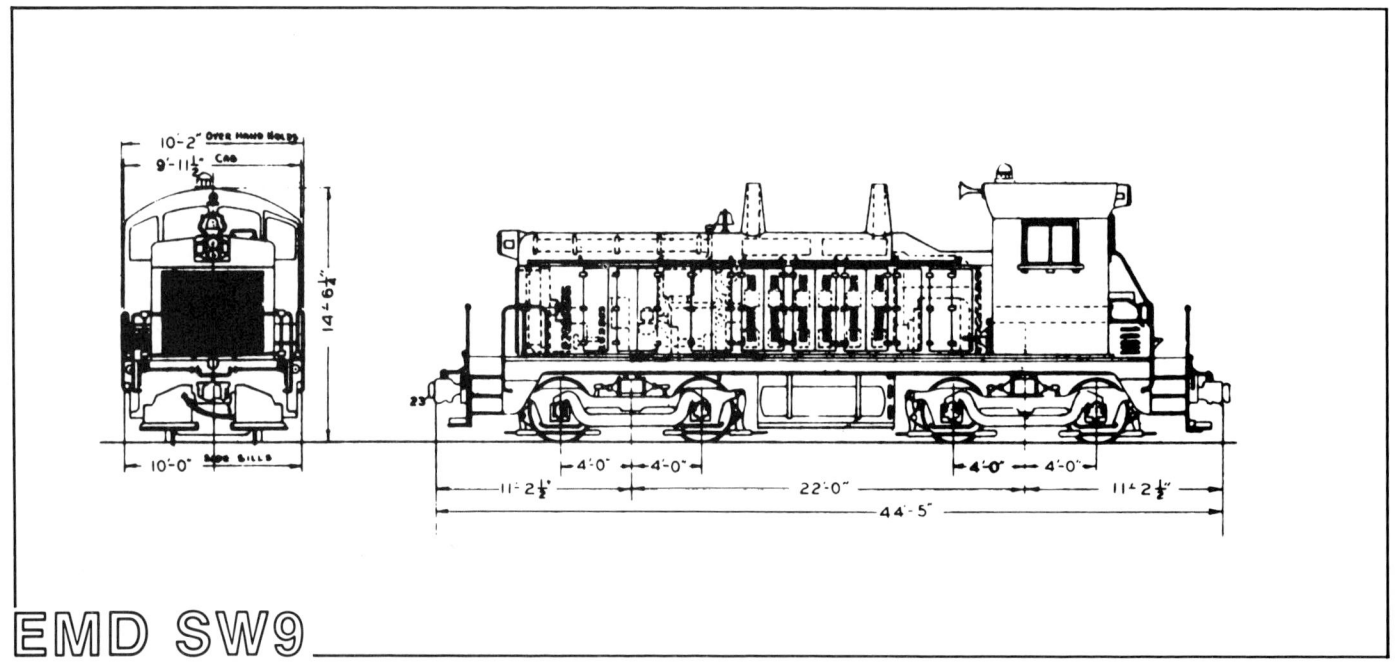

EMD SW9

GENERAL DATA

A.A.R. DESIGNATION	B-B
GEAR RATIO	62/15
WEIGHT LOADED	245,815 LBS.
LIGHT WEIGHT	235,606 LBS. APPROX.
MAXIMUM CURVATURE	WITH TRAIN
MAXIMUM CURVATURE	57° AS SINGLE UNIT
MAXIMUM SPEED	65 M.P.H.
MINIMUM CONT. SPEED	10.5 M.P.H.
CENTER OF GRAVITY	50.1" ABOVE RAIL (IN WORKING ORDER)

SUPPLIES

FUEL	600 GALS.
LUBE OIL	165 GALS.
COOLING WATER	223 GALS.
SAND	28 CU. FT.

DIESEL ENGINE

MODEL	12-567-BC
TURBOCHARGER	NOT EQUIPPED
SPARK ARRESTER	EQUIPPED
AIR FILTER, BASIC:	
CARBODY	NOT EQUIPPED
PRIMARY	NOT EQUIPPED
ENGINE	IMPINGEMENT (PANELS)
FUEL HEATER	KELTY

ELECTRICAL

MULTIPLE UNIT RECEPTACLES	NOT EQUIPPED
MAIN GENERATOR	D-15-C
ALTERNATOR	NOT EQUIPPED
TRACTION MOTORS, TYPE	D-27B
NUMBER OF TRACTION MOTORS	4
DYNAMIC BRAKES	NOT EQUIPPED
BATTERIES	64 V. 284 AMP. HRS.
HEADLIGHTS	TWIN SEALED BEAMS 200W EA.
AUXILIARY GENERATOR	A-7159
COOLING FANS	MECHANICAL
CAB SIGNALS	NOT EQUIPPED
ROTATING WARNING LIGHTS	EQUIPPED
R.C.S.	NOT EQUIPPED

RUNNING GEAR

DRAFT GEAR	MS-485-5A
COUPLER	TYPE 'E'
JOURNALS	6½" x 12" FRICTION BRGS.
WHEELS	40" DIA.
TRUCKS	4 WHL., EQUALIZER, CLASP BRKS.

BRAKES

SCHEDULE	6-BL
AIR COMPRESSOR	WXO
BRAKE SHOES	CAST IRON
SAFETY CONTROL	FOOT PEDAL

MISCELLANEOUS

WHISTLE	LESLIE A-125
TOILET	NOT EQUIPPED
FIRE EXTINGUISHERS	(2) 30 LB. ANSUL
WATER COOLER	EQUIPPED
FUEL FILLER	BUCKEYE
SPEED RECORDER	NOT EQUIPPED

ELECTRO-MOTIVE'S SW9 ROSTER

UNIT	BUILDER DATE	BUILDER NUMBER	UNIT	BUILDER DATE	BUILDER NUMBER	UNIT	BUILDER DATE	BUILDER NUMBER
1825	April 1953	17805	1840	April 1953	17820	1854	November 1953	18842
1826	April 1953	17806	1841	April 1953	17821	1855	November 1953	18843
1827[1]	April 1953	17807	1842[2]	April 1953	17822	1856	November 1953	18844
1828[13]	April 1953	17808	1843	April 1953	17823	1857	November 1953	18845
1829	April 1953	17809	1844	April 1953	17824	1858	November 1953	18846
1831	April 1953	17811	1845[3]	April 1953	17825	1859[12]	November 1953	18847
1832	April 1953	17812	1846	April 1953	17826	1860	November 1953	18848
1833	April 1953	17813	1847	October 1953	18835	1861[14]	November 1953	18849
1834	April 1953	17814	1848[5]	October 1953	18836	1862	November 1953	18850
1835	April 1953	17815	1849	October 1953	18837	1863[4]	November 1953	18851
1836	April 1953	17816	1850[11]	October 1953	18838	1864[8]	November 1953	18852
1837	April 1953	17817	1851	October 1953	18839	1865[10]	November 1953	18853
1838	April 1953	17818	1852	October 1953	18840	1866[7]	November 1953	18854
1839[6]	April 1953	17819	1853[9]	October 1953	18841			

[1] Sold 10/77 to Precision National Corporation, Mt. Vernon, IL.
[2] Sold 10/77 to Precision National Corporation, Mt. Vernon, IL.
[3] Sold 11/78 to Chrome Crankshaft Company, Chicago, IL.
[4] Sold 2/77 to Chrome Crankshaft Company, Chicago, IL.
[5] Rebuilt 9/79 as SW10. Renumbered UP 1200 13 March 1980.
[6] Rebuilt 11/79 as SW10. Renumbered UP 1201 1 April 1980.
[7] Rebuilt 1/80 as SW10. Renumbered UP 1202 25 January 1980.
[8] Rebuilt 3/80 as SW10 and renumbered UP 1203 9 March 1980.
[9] Rebuilt 4/80 as SW10 and renumbered UP 1204 17 April 1980.
[10] Rebuilt 5/80 as SW10 and renumbered UP 1205 21 May 1980.
[11] Rebuilt 6/80 as SW10 and renumbered UP 1206 24 June 1980.
[12] Rebuilt 7/80 as SW10 and renumbered UP 1207 14 July 1980.
[13] Rebuilt 9/80 as SW10. (Renumbered UP 1208 4 September 1980.)
[14] Rebuilt 9/80 as SW10. (To be renumbered UP 1209 and released in late September 1980.)

Trundling back to Omaha after an early morning delivery in Council Bluffs, IA on 10 May 1980, is 1953-built UP 1860. These Electro-Motive SW9's have proven their worth over the years . . . with ten converted into Union Pacific's SW10 version and more are selected as conversion candidates.—*Photo by Greg B. Davies.*

The SW9 model differs little from the SW7's, having the twin stacks and the full-sized front radiator. The subtle differences are the single blocks of engine locker-door vents running the length of the engine compartment.

Almost 800 of these switchers were built in the early 1950's. The 42 units bought in 1953 were the last "pure" switchers purchased by Union Pacific.

UP 1853 shown active at Council Bluffs, IA on 31 March 1979, will be converted in April 1980 to a SW10 and renumbered UP 1204.

Working the Omaha North Yard, it is seen from the Abbott Street bridge on 25 July 1979. The distinguishing features of the SW9 are clearly shown here . . . the two centered exhaust stacks, the large full-size front radiator and the locker-door louver arrangement.

This unit has not been earmarked for the SW10 conversion program. It serves as the "shop goat" and fills in on yard duties when needed.

Awaiting duties at Albina Yard in Portland, OR, UP 1833 is another unit that has not been selected as a candidate for the SW10 conversion program. A 1953 product of EMD, it does not show its 27 years of service. The SW9 fleet shows a very high daily availability on the mechanical records . . . 79 percent.

The "cabbage-style" exhaust stack spark arresters are credited with greatly reducing trackside fires during "high-index" summer and fall days.

Portland, OR, 3 August 1978.—*Photo by Vic F. Reyna.*

Being resupplied at the Provo, UT yard, UP 1848 idles in the shadows of the nearby hills which compartmentize the Salt Lake basin. Bearing "first generation" markings, it has served on the Utah Division for years. It has not been selected as a candidate for the SW10 conversion program; however, the second round of building will probably see it rebuilt to modern day standards. The Salt Lake area had a number of switchers assigned; however, many have been replaced with SD24's and GP30's.—
Photo by Kenneth M. Ardinger.

THE SW10 CONVERSION PROGRAM

The first conversion... UP 1848 sits in front of the Omaha Shops on 28 September 1980 fresh from the paint shop. Union Pacific is not interested in the currently available switchers, so it decided to upgrade its fleet of switchers. The SW9's were selected and engineering studies were started to convert these units with all of the 1980's "state-of-the-art" technology. A new cooling system was designed. The electrical cabinet was upgraded to include solid-state circuitry. A "clean cab" reconstruction included a modern control stand, electrical cab heat, modern human comfort items and changing the window arrangement somewhat.

UP 1848 and 1839 were assigned to Albina Yard in Portland, OR. In early 1980, they were renumbered to UP 1200 and 1201, respectively. Shown at Omaha, NE, 17 January 1980.

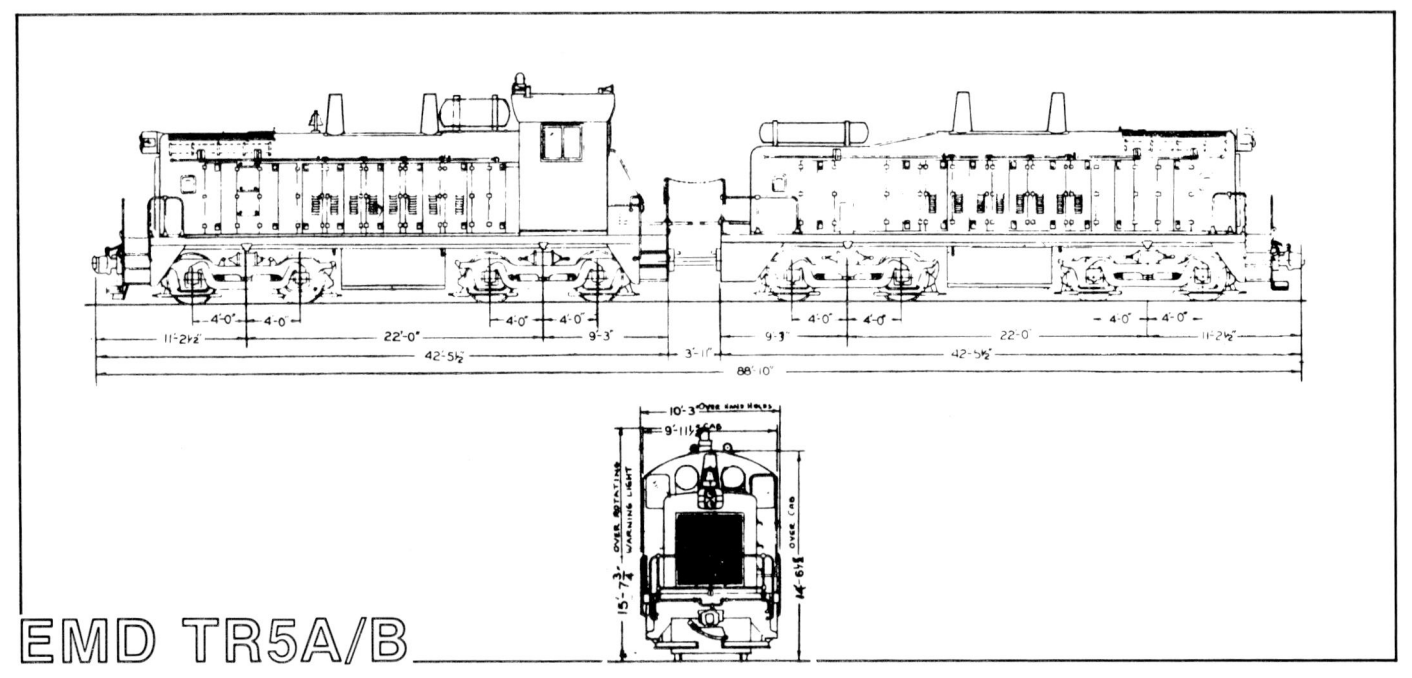

EMD TR5A/B

GENERAL DATA

A.A.R. DESIGNATION	B-B & B-B
GEAR RATIO	62/15
WEIGHT LOADED	521,600 LBS.
LIGHT WEIGHT	489,653 LBS. APPROX.
MAXIMUM CURVATURE	WITH TRAIN
MAXIMUM CURVATURE	57° AS SINGLE UNIT
MAXIMUM SPEED	65 M.P.H.
MINIMUM CONT. SPEED	10.5 M.P.H.

SUPPLIES

FUEL	(2) 1400 GALS.
LUBE OIL	(2) 165 GALS.
COOLING WATER	(2) 223 GALS.
SAND	(2) 28 CU. FT.

DIESEL ENGINE

MODEL	(2) 12-567-B
TURBOCHARGER	NOT EQUIPPED
SPARK ARRESTER	EQUIPPED
AIR FILTER, BASIC:	
CARBODY	NOT EQUIPPED
PRIMARY	NOT EQUIPPED
ENGINE	IMPINGEMENT PANELS
FUEL HEATER	KELTY

BRAKES

SCHEDULE	6 BL MOD. TO MU W/24 RL & 26 L EQUIPPED UNITS
AIR COMPRESSOR	WXO
BRAKE SHOES	CAST IRON
SAFETY CONTROL	FOOT PEDAL

ELECTRICAL

MULTIPLE UNIT RECEPTACLES	NOT EQUIPPED
MAIN GENERATOR	(2) D-15-C
ALTERNATOR	NOT EQUIPPED
TRACTION MOTORS, TYPE	D-27B
NUMBER OF TRACTION MOTORS	8
DYNAMIC BRAKES	NOT EQUIPPED
BATTERIES	64 V. 426 AMP. HRS.
HEADLIGHTS	TWIN SEALED BEAMS 200W EA.
AUXILIARY GENERATOR	A-7159
COOLING FANS	MECHANICAL
CAB SIGNALS	NOT EQUIPPED
ROTATING WARNING LIGHTS	EQUIPPED
R.C.S.	NOT EQUIPPED

RUNNING GEAR

DRAFT GEAR	MS-485-5A
COUPLER	TYPE 'E'
JOURNALS	6½" x 12" FRICT. BRGS.
WHEELS	40" DIA.
TRUCKS	4 WHL., EQUALIZER, CLSP. BRKS.

MISCELLANEOUS

WHISTLE	LESLIE A-125
TOILET	NOT EQUIPPED
FIRE EXTINGUISHERS	(3) 30 LB. ANSUL
WATER COOLER	EQUIPPED
FUEL FILLER	BUCKEYE
SPEED RECORDER	CP

ELECTRO-MOTIVE'S TR5A ROSTER

UNIT	BUILDER DATE	BUILDER NUMBER	REMARKS
1871	October 1951	15069	
1872	October 1951	15070	
1873	October 1951	15071	Dynamic brakes removed in 1972.
1874	October 1951	15072	Dynamic brakes removed in 1972.
1875	October 1951	15073	Dynamic brakes removed in 1972.
1876	October 1951	15074	Dynamic brakes removed in 1972.
1877	October 1951	15075	Dynamic brakes removed in 1972.

ELECTRO-MOTIVE'S TR5B ROSTER

UNIT	BUILDER DATE	BUILDER NUMBER	REMARKS
1870B	October 1951	15076	Mated to TR5A UP 1872.
1871B	October 1951	15077	
1873B	October 1951	15079	
1874B	October 1951	15080	
1875B	October 1951	15081	
1876B	October 1951	15082	
1877B	October 1951	15083	

Approaching Missouri Pacific's Neff Yard in Kansas City, MO is a heavy transfer drag from Union Pacific's Armstrong Yard in Kansas City, KS headed by a TR5 "cow and calf" set. This set was broken up in September 1976 when UP 1870 was sold. Later UP 1870B was mated to UP 1872 and is now assigned to Albina, OR. Kansas City, MO, 1 September 1975.

Awaiting yard assignments, "cow and calf set" 1876-1876B idle away at Pocatello, ID on 22 September 1973. The dynamic brakes, housed just forward of the cab, had been removed by a mechanical directive in 1972. The fuel capacity of the TR5's 1873-1873B through 1877-1877B is two 600 gallon capacity tanks per set. Note the first generation diesel paint scheme.—*Photo by Brian Griebenow*.

Having just delivered a transfer to Missouri Pacific's Neff Yard in Kansas City, MO, "cow and calf set" 1871-1871B will amble on back to Union Pacific's Armstrong Yard in Kansas City, KS. Having larger 1400 gallon fuel tanks, the air reservoir tanks are mounted atop the body . . . in front of the cab on the A-unit, and on the top front of the B-unit. 1 September 1975.

Preparing to pull a transfer drag back to Union Pacific's Albina Yard is "cow and calf set" 1874-1874B at Portland, OR on 12 April 1980. The location is the Portland Terminal Railroad's yard adjacent to the Portland Union Station. With the smaller 600 gallon fuel tanks, these sets weigh 494,720 pounds fully loaded. These units are not equipped with MU-receptacles.—*Photo by Charles W. Storz, Jr.*

Making set-outs and pick-ups just south of Provo, UT on 5 May 1976, "cow and calf set" 1874-1874B works its old Salt Lake haunts prior to being reassigned to the Oregon Division. These units are equipped with brake schedule 6BL which has been modified to MU with 24RL and 26L schedule units. Rated at 2400-horsepower, these 1951 transfer locomotives have done yeoman service across the system.

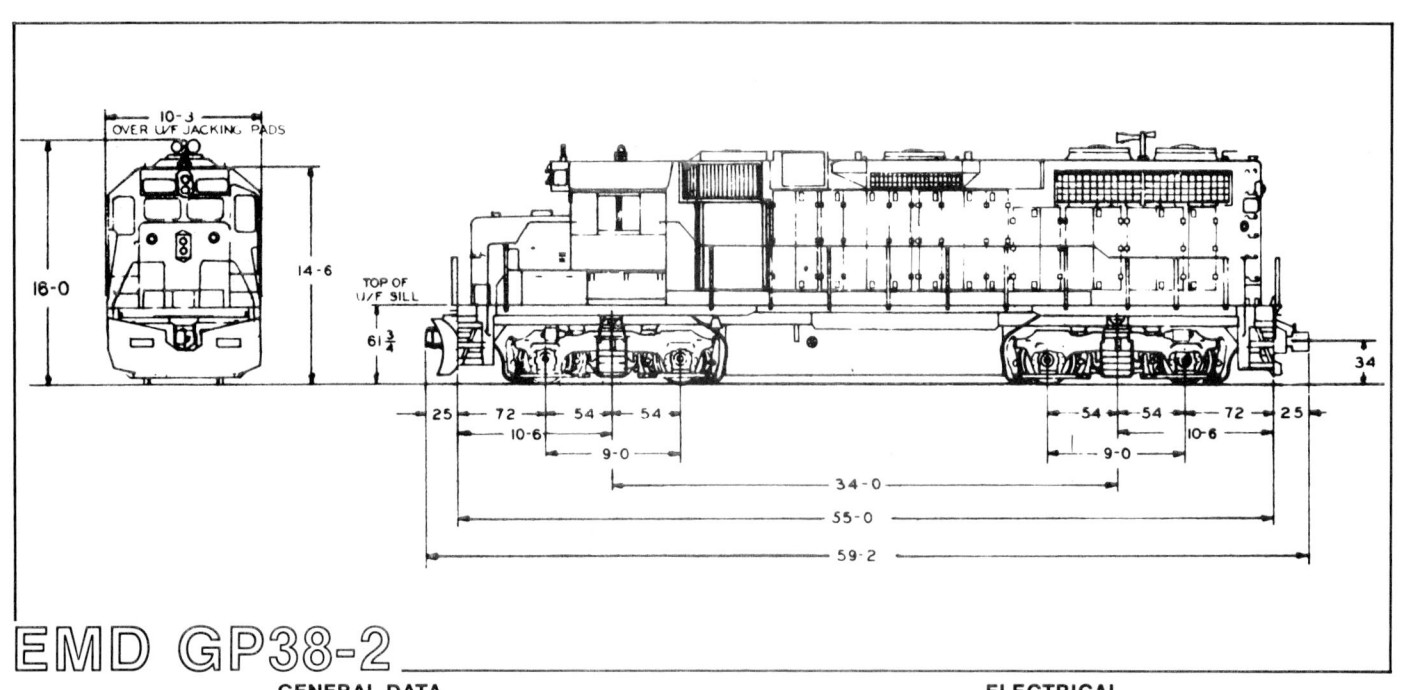

EMD GP38-2

GENERAL DATA
A.A.R. DESIGNATION	BB
GEAR RATIO	62/15
WEIGHT LOADED	269,460 LBS.*
LIGHT WEIGHT	232,880 LBS. APPROX.*
MAXIMUM CURVATURE	19° WITH TRAIN
MAXIMUM CURVATURE	42° AS SINGLE UNIT
MAXIMUM SPEED	65 M.P.H.
MINIMUM CONT. SPEED	12 M.P.H.
*2040-2059 LOADED WT.	272,367 LBS.
LIGHT WT.	235,787 LBS.

SUPPLIES
FUEL	3600 GALS.
LUBE OIL	243 GALS.
COOLING WATER	240 GALS.
SAND	72 CU. FT.

DIESEL ENGINE
MODEL	16-645-E
TURBOCHARGER	NOT EQUIPPED
SPARK ARRESTER	EQUIPPED
AIR FILTER, BASIC:	
CARBODY	NOT EQUIPPED
PRIMARY	DYNAVANE
ENGINE	AAF BAG
FUEL HEATER	KELTY 525-232

BRAKES
SCHEDULE	26L W/J1.6 (160%) RELAY VALVE
AIR COMPRESSOR	WBO
BRAKE SHOES	HI FRICT. COMP.
SAFETY CONTROL	FOOT PEDAL

ELECTRICAL
MULTIPLE UNIT RECEPTACLES	27 PT
MAIN GENERATOR	AR10E1
ALTERNATOR	D-14
TRACTION MOTORS, TYPE	D-77
NUMBER OF TRACTION MOTORS	4
DYNAMIC BRAKES	POTENTIAL CONTROL*
BATTERIES	32 CELL 64V. 420 AMP. HRS.
HEADLIGHTS	TWIN SEALED BEAMS 200W. EA.
AUXILIARY GENERATOR	18 KW. AC
COOLING FANS	(2) 48" FANS
CAB SIGNALS	US&S TYPE 'EL'
ROTATING WARNING LIGHTS	EQUIPPED
R.C.S.	NOT EQUIPPED
*EXTENDED RANGE	

RUNNING GEAR
DRAFT GEAR	NC-390
COUPLER	TYPE 'E'
JOURNALS	6⅞" x 12" HYATT-JEM
WHEELS	40" DIA.
TRUCKS	4 WHEEL

MISCELLANEOUS
WHISTLE	LESLIE 3-S LRF
TOILET	INCINOLET
FIRE EXTINGUISHERS	(2) 30 LB. ANSUL
WATER COOLER	STANRAY
FUEL FILLER	BUCKEYE
SPEED RECORDER	CP
SNOW PLOW	EQUIPPED
ELECT. CAB HEAT	EQUIPPED

ELECTRO-MOTIVE'S GP38-2 ROSTER

UNIT	BUILDER DATE	BUILDER NUMBER	UNIT	BUILDER DATE	BUILDER NUMBER	UNIT	BUILDER DATE	BUILDER NUMBER
2000	April 1974	73662-1	2020	April 1974	73662-21	2040	April 1975	74675-1
2001	February 1974	73662-2	2021	April 1974	73662-22	2041	April 1975	74675-2
2002	February 1974	73662-3	2022	April 1974	73662-23	2042	April 1975	74675-3
2003	February 1974	73662-4	2023	April 1974	73662-24	2043	April 1975	74675-4
2004	April 1974	73662-5	2024	April 1974	73662-25	2044	April 1975	74675-5
2005	April 1974	73662-6	2025	May 1974	73662-26	2045	April 1975	74675-6
2006	April 1974	73662-7	2026	May 1974	73662-27	2046	April 1975	74675-7
2007	April 1974	73662-8	2027	May 1974	73662-28	2047	April 1975	74675-8
2008	April 1974	73662-9	2028	May 1974	73662-29	2048	April 1975	74675-9
2009	April 1974	73662-10	2029	May 1974	73662-30	2049	April 1975	74675-10
2010[1]	April 1974	73662-11	2030	May 1974	73662-31	2050	April 1975	74675-11
2011	April 1974	73662-12	2031	May 1974	73662-32	2051	April 1975	74675-12
2012	April 1974	73662-13	2032	May 1974	73662-33	2052	April 1975	74675-13
2013	April 1974	73662-14	2033	May 1974	73662-34	2053	April 1975	74675-14
2014	April 1974	73662-15	2034	May 1974	73662-35	2054	April 1975	74675-15
2015	April 1974	73662-16	2035	May 1974	73662-36	2055	April 1975	74675-16
2016	April 1974	73662-17	2036	June 1974	73662-37	2056	April 1975	74675-17
2017	April 1974	73662-18	2037	May 1974	73662-38	2057	April 1975	74675-18
2018	April 1974	73662-19	2038	May 1974	73662-39	2058	April 1975	74675-19
2019	April 1974	73662-20	2039	June 1974	73662-40	2059	April 1975	74675-20

[1] UP 2010 leased 5 November 1979 to Federal Railroad Administration (FRA) Test Facilities, Pueblo, CO, and returned 7/80.

The "Clarnie Turn" rests at Meno, OR on 20 April 1979. GP38-2's have proved their suitability in the Pacific Northwest and seldom wander away from their primary area of assignment. Portland is some 58 miles west.—*Photo by Ben Fredericks.*

In 1972, Electro-Motive started producing the "dash 2" series of models already listed in their catalog. Most of the changes were either mechanical or electrical improvements reflecting the changing "state-of-the-art." It would be several years before Union Pacific would buy the GP38-2 when they started to retire the aging GP9's. Normally a "six-axle" railroad, they needed a light, but agile locomotive to work the branchlines in the Pacific Northwest. Thus the ordering of 40 units in 1974 and 20 more in 1975.

Representing the second order, UP 2050 sits at Council Bluffs, IA on 17 April 1975. This order arrived during a severe down-turn in traffic and the units were stored at Council Bluffs, IA for approximately nine months prior to being placed in service.

The face of UP 2035 shows all the safety appliances and pilot snow plow at Council Bluffs, IA on 22 April 1975. Note the auxiliary uncoupling lever arrangement . . . operated from either the ground level, step or platform.

A front and rear comparison view of Union Pacific's second order GP38-2's, as they sat stored new at Council Bluffs, IA on 21 April 1975. UP 2047 sports the "set-up" view, with antenna, arm rests and awnings installed. Once assigned to the Oregon Division, these units are seldom seen elsewhere. Note the bolted-on battery box plate, rather than a hinged door found on earlier EMD models. The paper filter box juts up, just behind the cab.

The Omaha Shop forces will set-up this unit with radios, window awnings and arm rests, rotating beacon, toilet and water cooler. The box-like arrangement just forward of the dynamic brake blister houses the paper filters for the clean air compartment. As Union Pacific purchased these units for branchline service in the Pacific Northwest, all GP38-2's have the front pilot snow plow as standard equipment. Omaha, NE, 2 May 1975.

The rear view of UP 2013 shows the EMD option of either a high or low position for the classification lights . . . Union Pacific elected the lower position for ease in reaching. The back is simply protected by a flat steel pilot sheet to which the uncoupling devices are attached. Council Bluffs, IA, 7 October 1975.

There are subtle differences between the left rear and the right rear . . . the sighting glass to quickly check the water level on the right side of UP 2048. The high-adhesion B-Type trucks give good traction to this unit. Note the oleo dampening strut mountings . . . they are diagonally opposite on each truck assembly. While delivered with the horns mounted over the radiator fans, many have been repositioned forward over the cab in compliance with new Mechanical Department standards. Council Bluffs, IA, 16 April 1975.

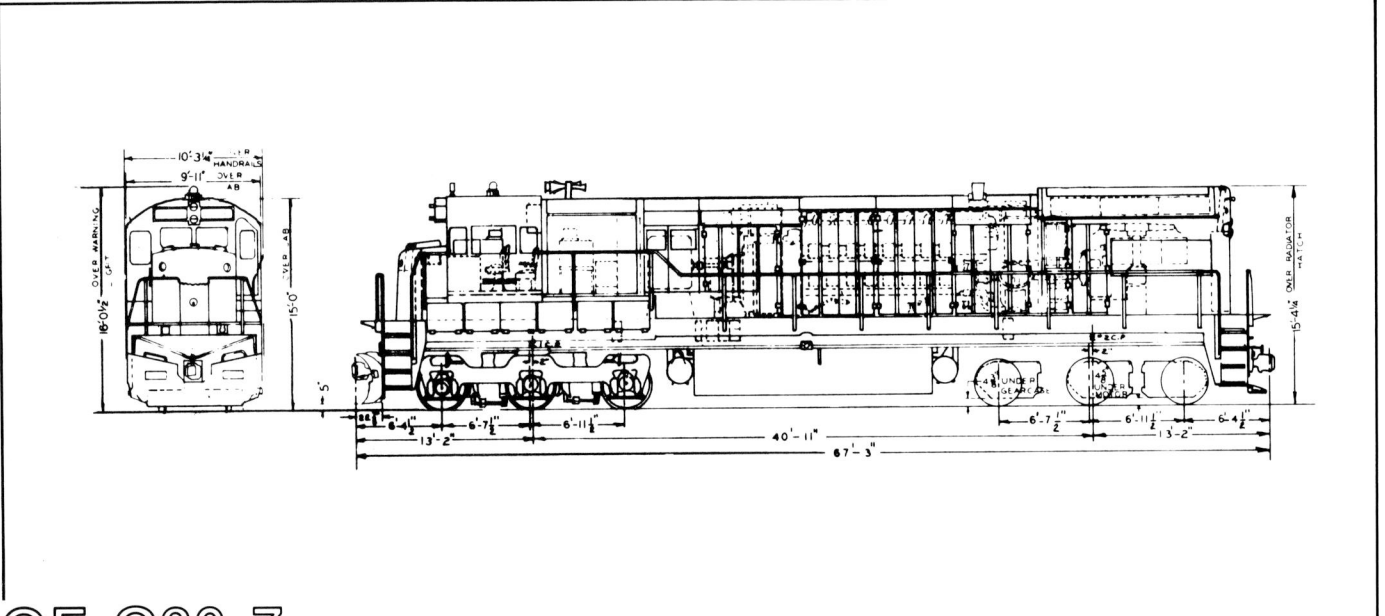

GE C30-7

GENERAL DATA
A.A.R. DESIGNATION	C-C
GEAR RATIO	74/18
WEIGHT LOADED	395,000 LBS.
LIGHT WEIGHT	357,626 LBS.
MAXIMUM CURVATURE	21° WITH TRAIN
MAXIMUM CURVATURE	21° AS SINGLE UNIT
MAXIMUM SPEED	65 M.P.H.
MINIMUM CONT. SPEED	10 M.P.H.
CENTER OF GRAVITY	62½" ABOVE RAIL (IN WORKING ORDER)

SUPPLIES
FUEL	4000 GALS.
LUBE OIL	380 GALS.
COOLING WATER	365 GALS.
SAND	60 CU. FT.

DIESEL ENGINE
MODEL	7-FDL-16E18
TURBOCHARGER	EQUIPPED
SPARK ARRESTER	NOT REQUIRED
AIR FILTER, BASIC:	
CARBODY	NOT EQUIPPED
PRIMARY	G. E. VORTOX TYPE
ENGINE	AAF BAG
FUEL HEATER	G. E. TYPE

BRAKES
SCHEDULE	26L W/J1.6-16
AIR COMPRESSOR	WABCO AIR COOLED
BRAKE SHOES	HI FRICT. COMP.
SAFETY CONTROL	FOOT PEDAL

ELECTRICAL
MULTIPLE UNIT RECEPTACLES	27 PT
MAIN GENERATOR	GTA-11
ALTERNATOR	NOT EQUIPPED
TRACTION MOTORS, TYPE	752-E8
NUMBER OF TRACTION MOTORS	6
DYNAMIC BRAKES	POTENTIAL CONTROL*
BATTERIES	64V. 426 AMP. HRS.
HEADLIGHTS	TWIN SEALED BEAMS 200W. EA.
AUXILIARY GENERATOR	GY-27
COOLING FANS	MECHANICAL
CAB SIGNALS	US&S TYPE 'EL'
WARNING LIGHTS	EQUIPPED
R.C.S.	NOT EQUIPPED

*EXTENDED RANGE

RUNNING GEAR
DRAFT GEAR	NC-390
COUPLER	TYPE 'E'
JOURNALS	6⅞" x 12" HYATT JMRA
WHEELS	40" DIA.
TRUCKS	6 WHL., SINGLE SHOE BRKS, HIGH CYL.

MISCELLANEOUS
WHISTLE	LESLIE RS-3 LRF
TOILET	INCINOLET MODEL S/A
FIRE EXTINGUISHERS	(3) 30 LB. ANSUL
WATER COOLER	EQUIPPED
FUEL FILLER	BUCKEYE
SPEED RECORDER	CP

NOTES:
CHEC EXCITATION SYSTEM
ALL ELECTRIC CAB HEATERS

A back and front design comparision can be made from these renumbered C30-7's. When initially delivered, this group . . . 2960-2974, thence 2400-2414 . . . were placed into unit coal train service. With Pacesetter Speed Control, these units can operate in the .1-1 mph range, which is suitable for tipple-style coal loading . . . yet retain full control over all speed regimes. Shown on the diesel service tracks at Kansas City, KS on 3 September 1978.

Easing over to Mainline 3 at Summit, Extra 2411 East will bring its train down the 1.25 percent grade into Omaha and over the bridge to Council Bluffs, IA. Mainline 1 and 2 are in the background. This is where the Old and New Mainlines split, and viewing action from the Vinton Street bridge is always rewarding.

Originally delivered as UP 2960 through 2974, the first 15 General Electric C30-7's were renumbered about 12 months later into the 2400-Class. This served to set them apart from the earlier C30-7 models, similar in general appearance; however, greatly different in many mechanical and electrical aspects.

A presentation of these units is made under their original number assignments and again here with the new numbers, heading up the follow-on orders for the C30-7's.

The distinct face of General Electric's C30-7 points west at Council Bluffs, IA on 15 August 1978. Originally numbered 2960, it was renumbered to 2400... the Class-unit. The low hood nose plate is an option offered by General Electric for either housing a *Mars* light or twin seal beam headlights... which Union Pacific did not choose. The MU-cable is plugged-in with its free end drapped over the pilot snow plow. The first order has canvas window awnings applied, while follow-on orders have the metal flap shade.

The engine locker box is starting to reveal the original road number on this unit... 2972. The 4000-gallon fuel tank appears monsterous, straddle the front and rear trucks. The horns are shown in their original rear position... later moved to the forward location now favored by the Union Pacific. Council Bluffs, IA on 21 August 1980.

A pair of brand new C30-7's rest on the diesel servicing tracks at Council Bluffs, IA on 10 July 1978. These will be sent over to the Omaha Shops for set-up and returned to fleet service promptly. These are the first "pure" C30-7's... as the first 15 units had been delivered in different road number assignments prior to renumbering into the 2400-Class. The extended radiator "wings" are primary spotting features for this model.

GENERAL ELECTRIC'S C30-7 ROSTER

UNIT	BUILDER DATE	BUILDER NUMBER	REMARKS
2400	July 1977	41558	Originally UP 2960, renumbered 5/78.
2401	July 1977	41559	Originally UP 2961, renumbered 5/78.
2402	August 1977	41560	Originally UP 2962, renumbered 7/78.
2403	August 1977	41561	Originally UP 2963, renumbered 7/78.
2404	August 1977	41562	Originally UP 2964, renumbered 6/78.
2405	August 1977	41563	Originally UP 2965, renumbered 6/78.
2406	September 1977	41564	Originally UP 2966, renumbered 6/78.
2407	September 1977	41565	Originally UP 2967, renumbered 6/78.
2408	September 1977	41566	Originally UP 2968, renumbered 6/78.
2409	September 1977	41567	Originally UP 2969, renumbered 6/78.
2410	September 1977	41568	Originally UP 2970, renumbered 6/78.
2411	September 1977	41569	Originally UP 2971, renumbered 6/78.
2412	September 1977	41570	Originally UP 2972, renumbered 6/78.
2413	September 1977	41571	Originally UP 2973, renumbered 5/78.
2414	September 1977	41572	Originally UP 2974, renumbered 6/78.

UNIT	BUILDER DATE	BUILDER NUMBER
2415	June 1978	41782
2416	June 1978	41783
2417	June 1978	41784
2418	June 1978	41785
2419	June 1978	41786
2420	June 1978	41787
2421	June 1978	41788
2422	July 1978	41789
2423	July 1978	41790
2424	July 1978	41791
2425	July 1978	41792
2426	July 1978	41793
2427	July 1978	41794
2428	July 1978	41795
2429	July 1978	41796
2430	December 1978	42093
2431	December 1978	42094
2432	December 1978	42095
2433	December 1978	42096
2434	December 1978	42097
2435	December 1978	42098
2436	December 1978	42099
2437	December 1978	42100
2438	December 1978	42101
2439	December 1978	42102
2440	January 1979	42103
2441	January 1979	42104
2442	January 1979	42105
2443	January 1979	42106
2444	January 1979	42107
2445	January 1979	42108
2446	January 1979	42109
2447	January 1979	42110
2448	January 1979	42111
2449	January 1979	42112
2450	January 1979	42113
2451	January 1979	42114
2452	January 1979	42115
2453	January 1979	42116
2454	January 1979	42117
2455	January 1979	42118
2456	January 1979	42119
2457	January 1979	42120
2458	January 1979	42121
2459	January 1979	42122
2460	January 1980	42700
2461	January 1980	42701
2462	January 1980	42702
2463	January 1980	42703
2464	January 1980	42704
2465	January 1980	42705
2466	January 1980	42706
2467	January 1980	42707
2468	January 1980	42708
2469	January 1980	42709
2470	January 1980	42710
2471	January 1980	42711
2472	January 1980	42712
2473	January 1980	42713
2474	January 1980	42714
2475	February 1980	42715
2476	February 1980	24716
2477	February 1980	24717
2478	February 1980	24718
2479	February 1980	24719
2480	February 1980	24720
2481	February 1980	24721
2482	February 1980	24722
2483	February 1980	24723
2484	February 1980	24724
2485	February 1980	24725
2486	February 1980	24726
2487	February 1980	24727
2488	February 1980	24728
2489	February 1980	24729
2490	February 1980	24730
2491	February 1980	24731
2492	February 1980	24732
2493	February 1980	24733
2494	February 1980	24734
2495	February 1980	24735
2496	February 1980	24736
2497	February 1980	24737
2498	February 1980	24738
2499	February 1980	24739
2500	August 1980	43067
2501	August 1980	43068
2502	August 1980	43069
2503	August 1980	43070
2504	August 1980	43071
2505	August 1980	43072
2506	August 1980	43073
2507	August 1980	43074
2508	August 1980	43075
2509	August 1980	43076
2510	August 1980	43077
2511	August 1980	43078
2512	August 1980	43079
2513	August 1980	43080
2514	August 1980	43081
2515	August 1980	43082
2516	August 1980	43083

Pulling the grade to Summit is a westbounder with a CN&W unit in trail. The roof details, or lack thereof . . . are obvious. The clean-line roof arrangement is typical of all General Electric designed diesel locomotives. These earlier production models do not have the larger stack of the later versions which house the exhaust silencer. The location of the horn is in accordance with Union Pacific's standards . . . part of an extensive horn testing program designed to maximize the sound pattern forward of the locomotive. Omaha, NE on 17 August 1978.

Freshly set-up at Omaha Shops, UP 2415 faces west at Council Bluffs, IA on 9 July 1978 on its first day of system service. This is the first "pure" C30-7 . . . delivered in proper road numbers. A total of fifteen units . . . UP 2415-2429, made up this second order for these highly sophisticated General Electric locomotives. The optional lower headlight installation is simply plated over . . . Union Pacific decided against such extras. All the major spotting features of this improved "U-boat" design can be seen . . . the extended radiator "wings," battery box "twist-knob" openers and the car body grill work.

Pulling in from the west, six-month-old UP 2433 arrives at Council Bluffs, IA on a very cold 6 January 1979. The brute design of these locomotives bespeaks its capabilities to perform work . . . all are equipped with the standard pilot snow plows enabling the units to handle all but the heaviest snows. The horns are mounted in the rear location; however, they have since been moved forward and mounted behind the cab . . . the older units have them behind the fireman's location, while the recent orders have them mounted behind the engineer's location.

The early 1980 order . . . UP 2460-2499, is represented by these two C30-7's idling at Council Bluffs, IA on 3 March 1980. Once again, these differ ever so slightly from their earlier counterparts . . . with most changes embodied in mechanical or electrical improvements based on reports from extended usage.

Due to severe winters, Union Pacific has caused the installation of "positive" (open) dump valves to release all liquids when the engine temperature reaches a "damaging point." Fuel tank heating units prevent diesel fuel separation, another major cold weather operation factor. Experimentation continues in using a 50-50 antifreeze and water mix over straight water in the cooling system. As the engine operates continuously, radiated heat offers passive protection to the unit; however, if the unit shuts down and becomes "cold soaked," there is a high risk that damage will be sustained to normally operating components.

Factory-fresh C30-7 has just arrived on property from General Electric's Erie, PA plant. Part of the forty-unit order scheduled for delivery in the 3rd quarter, 1980, UP 2505 was built in August 1980. First stop for this unit will be the Omaha Shops for "set-up." Council Bluffs, IA, 1 September 1980.

The first of 40 C30-7's ordered for delivery in late 1980 strikes a builder's pose for the General Electric's plant photographer at Erie, PA in mid-August 1980. This order was lettered in accordance with the new standards which omits the road number under the cab window. —*Photo by General Electric.*

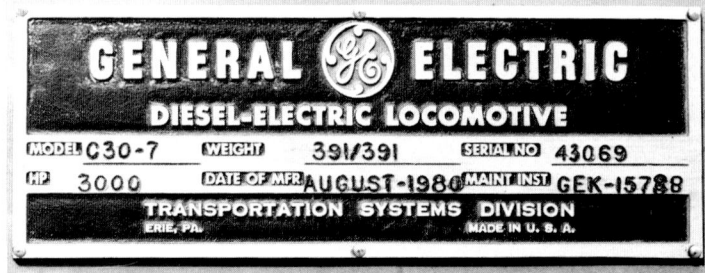

Just delivered at Council Bluffs, IA on 29 August 1980, it will be sent to Omaha Shops for set-up and placed into immediate revenue service. The builder's plate, attached near the left front under the battery box door, documents the primary data for UP 2502.

On its way to Omaha Shops, UP 2504 has just been delivered at Council Bluffs, IA on 27 August 1980. The shops forces immediately set-up the unit . . . installing the rotating beacon, awnings, arm-rests, radio and antenna and other standard company equipment . . . and released it to fleet service on 28 August 1980.

The extended "wings" of the larger radiator are prominent . . . one of the major spotting features of the C30-7 series. The horns are mounted just aft of the engineer's location.

A comparison view of the rear portion of the C30-7 . . . as shown by UP 2505 and 2503 at Council Bluffs, IA on 1 September 1980. Received earlier, both are on their way to Omaha Shops for set-up and will be released for system assignment the next day.

The first five units (UP 2500-2504) have an "Eddy current clutch" installed on the radiator fan. This permits the fan to operate "as needed," rather than continuously. In a fan no-load situation, the savings in horsepower (translates into a fuel economic factor) becomes an important consideration in these days of higher operating costs. If proven successful, this option will probably become standard on Union Pacific GE's.

The major spotting feature of General Electric's C30-7 model is the rear body construction of the radiator housing. The extended "wings" protrude dramatically away from the car body so as to permit a larger radiator cooling area. The car body also steps away two doors forward of the air-intake screening and in-line with the exhaust stack. The latest models have the enlarged, flat exhaust silencer installed.

The upper view shows the roof profile in the exhaust stack area. The jut in the car body is also clearly seen.

The overhead view offers another study of the exhaust stack and the forward portion of the extended radiator construction. The "clean line" General Electric roof is another distinguishing feature associated with the "U-boats."

Both views are of just delivered UP 2502, taken at Council Bluffs, IA on 29 August 1980.

Its pristine appearance indicates it has just arrived from the builder's Erie, PA plant. Idling at Council Bluffs, IA on 1 October 1980, it will be shipped over to Omaha Shops for immediate set-up and placed into system service. With more emphasis being placed on energy, the requirements for low-sulphur content Wyoming coal have placed heavy demands on the regional railroads. Union Pacific has found the 3000-horsepower GE's perfect for their head-end power, equipping all GE's with Pacesetter Speed control interface hardware.

The Pacesetter equipment allows operation in two speed regimes: .1-1 mph and 10-100 mph. The .1-1 mph is used during the loading of coal at the tipple.

NEWLY DELIVERED GE C30-7's • OCTOBER 1980

EDITOR'S NOTE:
The arrival of UP 2517-2539 has NOT been reflected in the locomotive summary and roster data presented . . . which had an editorial cut-off of 31 August 1980. In an effort to present the most complete overview of the Union Pacific right up to press time, pages were reserved to cover such contingencies.

The builder numbers for UP 2517-2529, built in September 1980, are 43084-43096. The builder numbers for UP 2530-2539, built in October 1980, are 43097-43106.

The standard pilot snow plow can be studied in this detail view . . . typical of the style used by General Electric over the last several years. This one is mounted on UP 2932, just delivered from General Electric, while at Council Bluffs, IA on 19 October 1980. The new-styled auxiliary uncoupling lever used to "pull-the-pin," mounts above the plow. The cut-outs in the face of the plow allow leading the operating hoses out for coupling to the adjacent unit, or remaining behind the closed door for protection when the unit is in the lead position.

Facing west on the diesel leads at Council Bluffs, IA on 19 October 1980, just-delivered UP 2529 awaits a hostler movement to Omaha Shops for set-up. The small windows on either side of the large side window became 1980 optional General Electric items . . . which Union Pacific did not purchase. In addition to the large, flat, reactive exhaust stack silencer, the missing small windows will help identify the mid-1980 production models from the earlier versions.

A trio of brand new General Electric C30-7's heads over to the Omaha Shops from Council Bluffs, IA on 19 October 1980. From front to rear are UP 2527, 2535 and 2536 . . . all built in October 1980. These units were immediately set-up at the shops and placed into fleet service. The big GE's are particularly well suited to loading and movement of coal from Wyoming . . . having Pacesetter equipment installed that permits "creep-control" at the coal loading tipples.

The hefty General Electric designed truck glistens with its new paint . . . almost factory fresh, under the cab of UP 2539 at Council Bluffs, IA on 1 November 1980. "U-boats" have been riding on this style side-frame casting that began its development in 1966. Castings are made by Adirondack, as evidenced by the AD initials on the frame.

The last C30-7 in the current order for 40 units idles at Council Bluffs, IA on 1 November 1980 . . . making 140 of these models now in service on the Union Pacific.

In its continuing effort to standardize its road power to several models, Union Pacific has settled on the C30-7 as one of its road units. Such action reduces the number of spare parts that must be maintained for a variety of models, insures a higher shop craft proficiency in dealing with just several standard units, and standardizes train-handling functions . . . all "pluses" on the "bottom line."

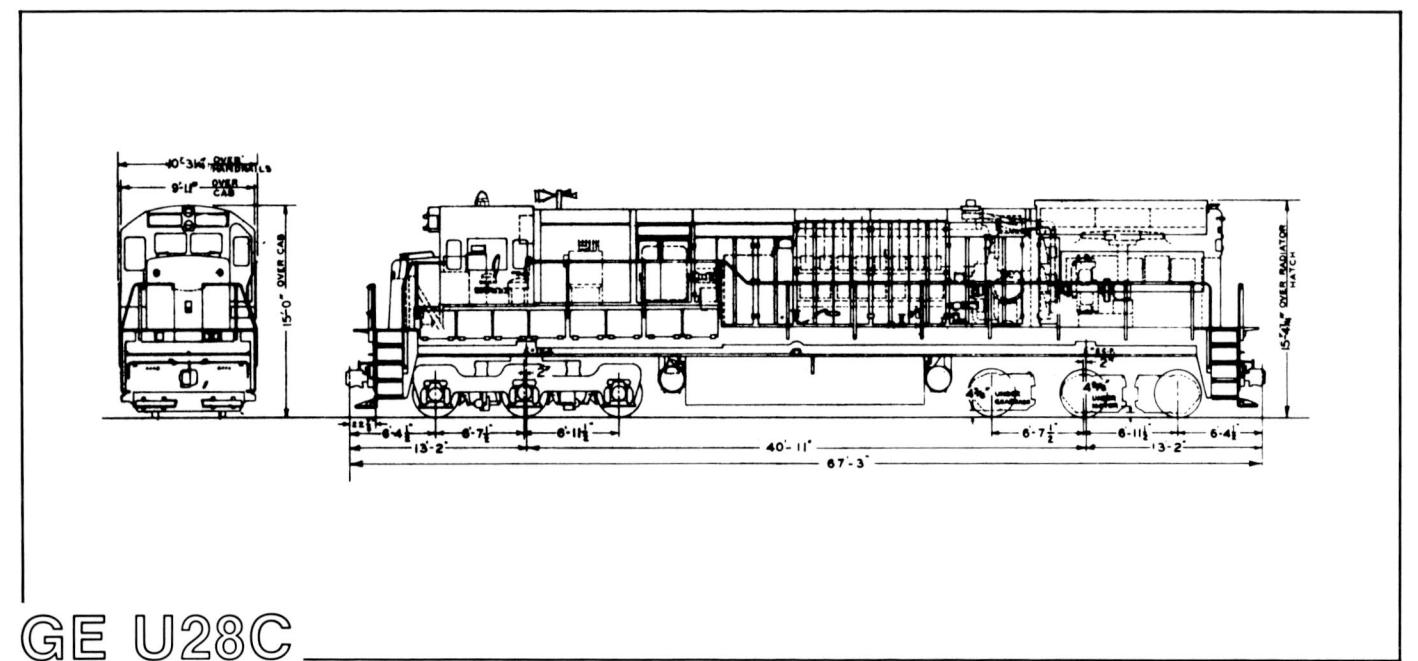

GE U28C

GENERAL DATA
A.A.R. DESIGNATION	C-C
GEAR RATIO	74/18
WEIGHT LOADED	373,600 LBS.
LIGHT WEIGHT	334,660 LBS. APPROX.
MAXIMUM CURVATURE	WITH TRAIN
MAXIMUM CURVATURE	21° AS SINGLE UNIT
MAXIMUM SPEED	65 M.P.H.
MINIMUM CONT. SPEED	11 M.P.H.
CENTER OF GRAVITY	62½" ABOVE RAIL (IN WORKING ORDER)

SUPPLIES
FUEL	4000 GALS.
LUBE OIL	380 GALS.
COOLING WATER	300 GALS.
SAND	48 CU. FT.

DIESEL ENGINE
MODEL	GE 7-FDL-16D1
TURBOCHARGER	EQUIPPED
SPARK ARRESTER	NOT REQUIRED
AIR FILTER, BASIC:	
CARBODY	NOT EQUIPPED
PRIMARY	DONALDSON CENTRIF.
ENGINE	OIL BATH (AIR MAZE)
FUEL HEATER	KELTY

BRAKES
SCHEDULE	26 L J1.6 (160%) RELAY VALVE
AIR COMPRESSOR	WESTINGHOUSE 3-CWDL.
BRAKE SHOES	HI FRICT. COMP.
SAFETY CONTROL	FOOT PEDAL

ELECTRICAL
MULTIPLE UNIT RECEPTACLES	12-21 & 27 PT
MAIN GENERATOR	GT-598
ALTERNATOR	NOT EQUIPPED
TRACTION MOTORS, TYPE	752-E-6
NUMBER OF TRACTION MOTORS	6
DYNAMIC BRAKES	POTENTIAL CONTROL
BATTERIES	64 V. 426 AMP. HRS.
HEADLIGHTS	TWIN SEALED BEAMS 200W EA.
AUXILIARY GENERATOR	10 KW
COOLING FANS	MECHANICAL
CAB SIGNALS	SEE NOTE
ROTATING WARNING LIGHTS	EQUIPPED
R.C.S.	NOT EQUIPPED
EXCITER	GY-50

NOTE:
C.C.S.
UNITS 2800-2806	US&S TYPE 'E'
2807-2809	US&S TYPE 'EL'

RUNNING GEAR
DRAFT GEAR	M-381 COUPLER — TYPE 'E'
JOURNALS	6½" x 12" TIMKEN SC CLASS GG
WHEELS	40" DIA.
TRUCKS	6 WHL., SINGLE SHOE BRK., LOW CYLS.

MISCELLANEOUS
WHISTLE	LESLIE S-3 LRF
TOILET	EQUIPPED
FIRE EXTINGUISHERS	(3) 30 LB. ANSUL
WATER COOLER	EQUIPPED
FUEL FILLER	BUCKEYE
SPEED RECORDER	CP

GENERAL ELECTRIC'S U28C ROSTER

UNIT	BUILDER DATE	BUILDER NUMBER	REMARKS
2800	July 1966	36014	Sold 7/80 to Bargains Galore, Portland, OR and shipped to J. Simon & Sons, Tacoma, WA.
2801	June 1966	36015	
2802	July 1966	36016	Retired 10/79. Sold 2/80 to Precision National Corporation, Mt. Vernon, IL.
2803	June 1966	36017	Retired 10/79. Sold 2/80 to Precision National Corporatin, Mt. Vernon, IL.
2804	July 1966	36018	
2805	September 1966	36063	Retired 12/79. Sold 7/80 to Railcar Corporation, Colorado Springs, CO.
2806	August 1966	36064	
2807	September 1966	36065	Retired 9/79. Sold 12/79 to Hyman-Michaels Company, Madison, IL.
2808	September 1966	36066	Retired 4/80. Sold 8/80 to Hyman-Michaels Company, Madison, IL.
2809	October 1966	36067	Sold 7/80 to Bargains Galore, Portland, OR and shipped to J. Simon & Sons, Tacoma, WA.

Rolling out of the super-elevated approach curve at Summit, an Iowa Power empty unit coal train heads west for another load of low-sulphur content Wyoming coal. The General Electric "clean roof" is a feature of their "U-boat" design... as presented here by one-of-ten U28C's on the roster. Viewed from Omaha's Vinton Street bridge on 25 August 1978.

Only ten U28C's were purchased during the summer of 1966. Not a popular model, General Electric produced a total of just over 70 of these units.

The Union Pacific units, having the radiator bulge and riding on the newly designed GE truck, were different in general appearance than the early production models that had the features of U25C's.

The class unit . . . UP 2800 . . . awaits a westbound assignment on the diesel lead at Council Bluffs, IA, 10 October 1978.

The U28C's did not receive pilot snow plows even though they were extensively operated in the eastern half of the system . . . noted for its severe winters.

The basic lines of the General Electric "U-boats" have changed little over the life span of their design . . . starting back with the original U25's demonstrators in 1960 through the U28's, U30's, U36's and into the current C30-7's.

Equipped with the proven 7-FDL engine, these units are now being retired from the system . . . their last assignments handling heavy yard transfer services at North Platte, NE.

Council Bluffs, IA, 7 June 1977.

The fireman's side of the front cab and short low hood offers a detailed study on the mechanical construction of a U28C. The "C" type trucks are the Adirondack version, having an extended ridge over the center pedestal.

The earlier slogan . . . "Dependable Transportation". . . applied to most first generation diesels, gave way to the "We Can Handle It" in the mid-1970's. The road numbers have been moved back two doors, a result of reinstalling the battery box doors in the wrong order.

Council Bluffs, IA, 18 June 1976.

UP 2806 has just been "cut-off" from an east-bound train and awaits movement to the Council Bluffs, IA servicing area on 19 October 1978. These units were relegated to heavy transfer service at North Platte during their last active years.

Another view of UP 2806, shows off the engineer's side of the front. The dropped inspection doors reveal the air brake equipment and its associated piping. Note the hand brake wheel mounted just forward of the engineer's window on the short hood.

The construction features of the U28C can be easily studied in this "elephant-style" lash-up. The radiator screens mask the large cooling fan mounted in the rear compartment of UP 2806. There is 300 gallons of cooling water on board. The cab of UP 2801 has the mid-1970 "We Can Handle It" slogan and is missing its road numbers usually applied on the battery box doors under the slogan or shield.

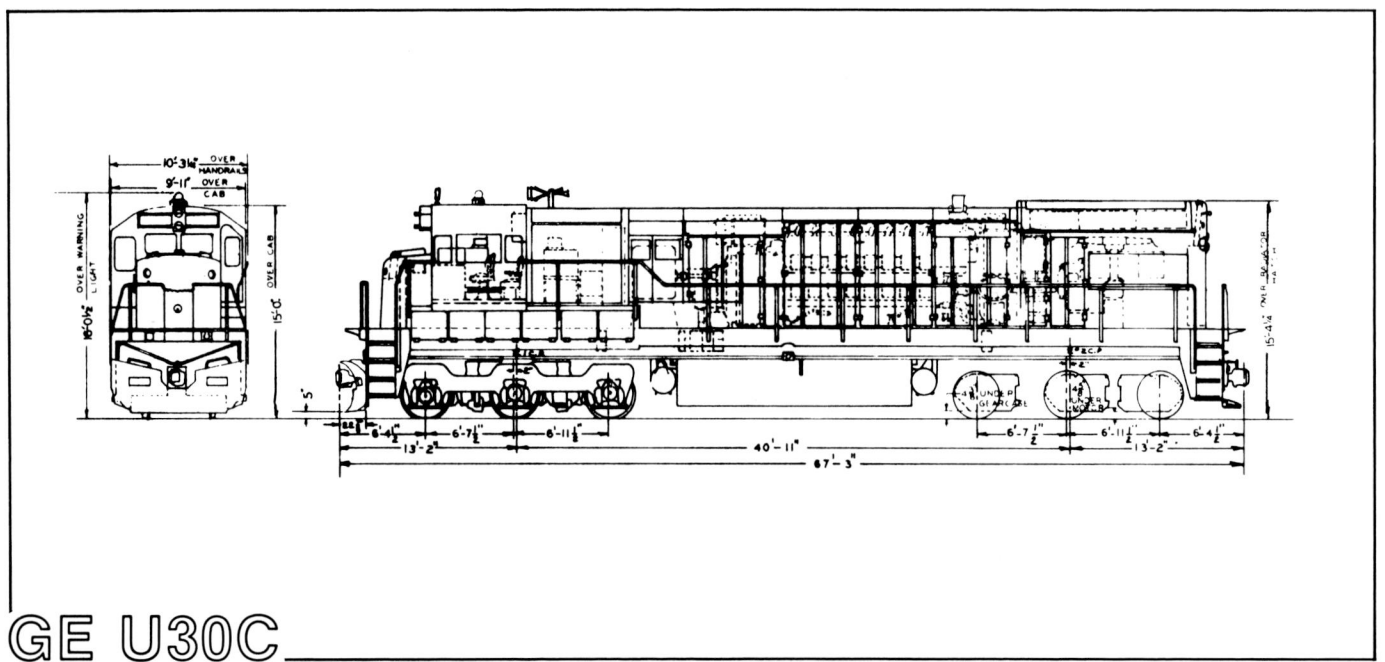

GE U30C

GENERAL DATA

A.A.R. DESIGNATION	C-C
GEAR RATIO	74/18
WEIGHT LOADED	392,951 LBS.
LIGHT WEIGHT	352,105 LBS. APPROX.*
MAXIMUM CURVATURE	21° WITH TRAIN
MAXIMUM CURVATURE	21° AS SINGLE UNIT
MAXIMUM SPEED	65 M.P.H.
MINIMUM CONT. SPEED	10 M.P.H.
ENTER OF GRAVITY	62½" ABOVE RAIL (IN WORKING ORDER)
*2870-2904 LOADED WEIGHT	389,980 LBS.
LIGHT WEIGHT	351,440 LBS. APPROX.

SUPPLIES

FUEL	4000 GALS.
LUBE OIL	380 GALS.
COOLING WATER	385 GALS.
SAND	60 CU. FT.

DIESEL ENGINE

MODEL (2915-2919 ONLY)	7-FCL-16A1
MODEL	7-FDL-16E18
TURBOCHARGER	EQUIPPED
SPARK ARRESTER	NOT REQUIRED
AIR FILTER, BASIC:	
CARBODY	NOT EQUIPPED
PRIMARY	G. E. VORTOX TYPE
ENGINE	G. E. PAPER*
FUEL HEATER	G. E. TYPE

*2870-2919 — A.A.F. BAG TYPE

RUNNING GEAR

DRAFT GEAR	NC-390
COUPLER	TYPE 'E'
JOURNALS	6½" x 12" HYATT JMRA

WHEELS	40" DIA.
TRUCKS	6 WHL., SINGLE SHOE BRKS., LOW CYL.

ELECTRICAL

MILTIPLE UNIT RECEPTACLES	27 PT
MAIN GENERATOR	GTA-11
ALTERNATOR	NOT EQUIPPED
TRACTION MOTORS, TYPE	752-E8
NUMBER OF TRACTION MOTORS	6
DYNAMIC BRAKES	POTENTIAL CONTROL*
BATTERIES	64V. 426 AMP. HRS.
HEADLIGHTS	TWIN SEALED BEAMS 200W. EA.
AUXILIARY GENERATOR	GY-27
COOLING FANS	MECHANICAL
CAB SIGNALS	US&S TYPE 'EL'
ROTATING WARNING LIGHTS	EQUIPPED
R.C.S.	NOT EQUIPPED

*EXTENDED RANGE

BRAKES

SCHEDULE	26L W/J1.6 RELAY W/PORTOPACK
AIR COMPRESSOR	WBO*
BRAKE SHOES	HI FRICT. COMP.
SAFETY CONTROL	FOOT PEDAL

*AIR COOLED WABCO 3-CDCL ON UNITS 2895-2915. AIR COMPRESSOR INTEGRAL WITH ENGINE ON UNITS 2916-2919.

MISCELLANEOUS

WHISTLE	LESLIE S-3 LRF
TOILET	INCINOLET MODEL S/A
FIRE EXTINGUISHERS	(3) 30 LB. ANSUL
WATER COOLER	EQUIPPED
FUEL FILLER	BUCKEYE
SPEED RECORDER	CP

Lined up across the servicing area at Council Bluffs, IA on 29 August 1978 are U30C UP 2902 built in 1974, SD40 UP 3094 built in 1971, and U30C UP 2831 built in 1973. This pretty well represents what the power looks like at any Union Pacific servicing area today. The wide variety of models of the past has given way to system standardization in the last several years. The road units boil down to General Electric's U30C/C30-7's and Electro-Motive's SD40/SD40-2's.

Pulling past Milepost 3/4 is a westbound unit grain train just departing Council Bluffs, IA on 8 August 1980. The consist stretches all the way back to the west departure tracks . . . some 70 cars behind the power. UP 2913 is a General Electric U30C built in May 1975.

Union Pacific initially ordered 20 General Electric U30C's in early 1972 and entered them on the roster after the earlier ten General Electric U28C's as UP 2810-2829. Going strong on 1 May 1979, UP 2810 leads a westbound freight out of Council Bluffs, IA.

A close inspection will reveal subtle differences between the U28C's and the early U30C's, but the biggest give away can be found in the cooling system area at the back. The U30C's have an arched roof construction for the radiator housing and smaller air intakes.

Experience with the first group of "U-boats" warranted a follow-on purchase in early 1973 for forty more units . . . numbered UP 2830-2869. While appearing similar to the first order, one unit was delivered with an experimental fiberglass short hood . . . UP 2851. This unit has the standard heavy crash posts built-in to the general superstructure, which the designers felt were sufficient to protect the crews. A fibre glass hood encloses the structural members and is marked on the outside with warnings not to use welding torches around it. Fortunately, the designer's theory has never been tested. While the experimental hood remains in service, Union Pacific has never opted for additional ones.

The clean roofline is a General Electric feature, as shown by Up 2832 as it tops the Summit at Omaha, NE on 23 August 1978.

Almost a year later, a third order was placed with General Electric for 35 more U30C's . . . UP 2870-2904. Again, these units were "kissin' cousins" of the previous order. With increased emphasis being placed on moving low-sulphur-content coal from Wyoming, Union Pacific found that the 3000-horsepower "U-boat" was a near perfect match for the job . . . capable of operating at coal mine head loading speeds of less than 1-mph and at handling 100-car unit trains at normal speeds on the mainline. Various devices were experimentally installed to increase overall performance such as "fuel savers" which could cut in or out units in the power consist when needed and *Pacesetter* two-speed control which allows a very low or normal speed regulation. UP 2900 represents this mid-1974 order . . . at Council Bluffs, IA on 17 August 1980.

GENERAL ELECTRIC'S U30C ROSTER

UNIT	BUILDER DATE	BUILDER NUMBER	UNIT	BUILDER DATE	BUILDER NUMBER	UNIT	BUILDER DATE	BUILDER NUMBER
2810	April 1972	38300	2860	June 1973	39200	2910	May 1975	40049
2811	April 1972	38301	2861	June 1973	39201	2911	May 1975	40050
2812	April 1972	38302	2862	June 1973	39202	2912	May 1975	40051
2813	April 1972	38303	2863	June 1973	39203	2913	May 1975	40052
2814	April 1972	38304	2864	June 1973	39204	2914	May 1975	40053
2815	April 1972	38305	2865	June 1973	39205	2915[4]	June 1975	40054
2816	April 1972	38306	2866	June 1973	39206	2916[4]	June 1975	40055
2817	April 1972	38307	2867	June 1973	39207	2917[4]	February 1976	40056
2818	May 1972	38308	2868	June 1973	39208	2918[4]	February 1976	40057
2819	May 1972	38309	2869	June 1973	39209	2919[4]	February 1976	40058
2820[1]	May 1972	38310	2870[3]	March 1974	39591	2920	July 1976	40925
2821	May 1972	38311	2871	March 1974	39592	2921	July 1976	40926
2822	May 1972	38312	2872	March 1974	39593	2922	July 1976	40927
2823	May 1972	38313	2873	March 1974	39594	2923	July 1976	40928
2824	May 1972	38314	2874	March 1974	39595	2924	July 1976	40929
2825	May 1972	38315	2875	March 1974	39596	2925	July 1976	40930
2826	May 1972	38316	2876	March 1974	39597	2926	July 1976	40931
2827	May 1972	38317	2877	April 1974	39598	2927	August 1976	40932
2828	June 1972	38318	2878	April 1974	39599	2928	August 1976	40933
2829	June 1972	38319	2879	April 1974	39600	2929	August 1976	40934
2830	February 1973	38795	2880	April 1974	39601	2930	August 1976	40935
2831	March 1973	38796	2881	April 1974	39602	2931	August 1976	40936
2832	February 1973	38797	2882	April 1974	39603	2932	August 1976	40937
2833	February 1973	38798	2883	April 1974	39604	2933	August 1976	40938
2834	March 1973	38799	2884	April 1974	39605	2934	August 1976	40939
2835	March 1973	38800	2885	June 1974	39606	2935	August 1976	40940
2836	March 1973	38801	2886	May 1974	39607	2936	August 1976	40941
2837	March 1973	38802	2887	June 1974	39608	2937	August 1976	40942
2838	March 1973	38803	2888	June 1974	39609	2938	September 1976	40943
2839	March 1973	38804	2889	June 1974	39610	2939	September 1976	40944
2840	March 1973	38805	2890	June 1974	39611	2940	September 1976	40945
2841	March 1973	38806	2891	June 1974	39612	2941	September 1976	40946
2842	March 1973	38807	2892	June 1974	39613	2942	September 1976	40947
2843	March 1973	38808	2893	June 1974	39614	2943	September 1976	40948
2844	April 1973	38809	2894	June 1974	39615	2944	September 1976	40949
2845	April 1973	38811	2895	June 1974	39616	2945	September 1976	40950
2846	April 1973	38812	2896	June 1974	39617	2946	September 1976	40951
2847	April 1973	38813	2897	June 1974	39618	2947	September 1976	40952
2848	April 1973	38814	2898	July 1974	39619	2948	September 1976	40953
2849	April 1973	38815	2899	July 1974	39620	2949	September 1976	40954
2850	April 1973	38810	2900:2	July 1974	39847	2950	October 1976	40955
2851[2]	April 1973	38816	2901:2	July 1974	39848	2951	October 1976	40956
2852	May 1973	38817	2902:2	July 1974	39849	2952	October 1976	40957
2853	May 1973	38818	2903:2	July 1974	39850	2953	October 1976	40958
2854	May 1973	38819	2904:2	July 1974	39851	2954	October 1976	40959
2855	May 1973	38820	2905:2	April 1975	40044	2955	October 1976	40960
2856	May 1973	38821	2906:2	April 1975	40045	2956	October 1976	40961
2857	May 1973	38822	2907:2	April 1975	40046	2957	October 1976	40962
2858	May 1973	38823	2908:2	April 1975	40047	2958	October 1976	40963
2859	May 1973	38824	2909:2	April 1975	40048	2959	October 1976	40964

[1] Accident Hayward, CA, 9 April 1980. To be retired, and charged to the Western Pacific Railroad.
[2] Delivered with experimental fibre glass short hood.
[3] Accident Hitchita, OK, 22 October 1979. Retired 24 January 1980, and charged to Missouri Pacific Railroad.
[4] Delivered with two of the 16 cylinders experimentally used as an integral air compressor with no decrease in available horsepower. Units reworked into standard configuration after performance proved less than satisfactory.

The experimentation with the "U-boats" continues . . . typical of the staff engineers at General Electric and Union Pacific. Five units were delivered, UP 2915-2919, which revised the rugged FDL-16 diesel engine to produce 3000-horsepower from 14 cylinders. The other two cylinders were used as integral air compressors, doing away with the separate air compressor. A number of small dynamic problems proved the revision less than satisfactory and these units were returned to standard 16-cylinder operations.

There is no outward appearance differences as shown by UP 2916 at Council Bluffs, IA, on 11 August 1975, shortly after delivery.

The balance of the 1976 order, which ended with UP 2959, remains similar in general appearance to the previous models.

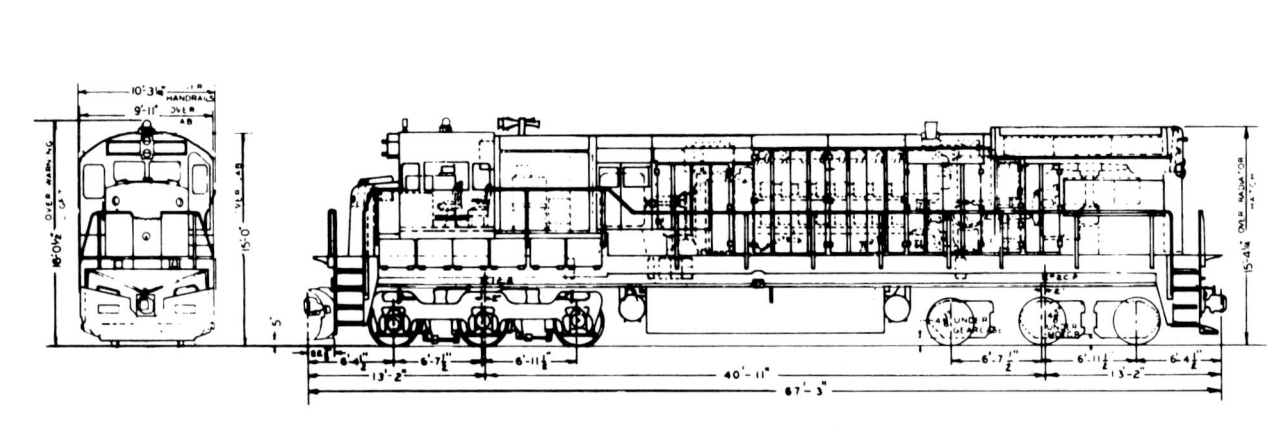

THE GENERAL DATA HAS BEEN OMITTED.

GE C30-7

GENERAL ELECTRIC C30-7 ROSTER

UNIT	BUILDER DATE	BUILDER NUMBER	REMARKS
2960	July 1977	41558	Renumbered 5-26-78 to UP 2400.
2961	July 1977	41559	Renumbered 5-30-78 to UP 2401.
2962	August 1977	41560	Renumbered 7-5-78 to UP 2402.
2963	August 1977	41561	Renumbered 7-5-78 to UP 2403.
2964	August 1977	41562	Renumbered 6-23-78 to UP 2404.
2965	August 1977	41563	Renumbered 6-8-78 to UP 2405.
2966	September 1977	41564	Renumbered 6-13-78 to UP 2406.
2967	September 1977	41565	Renumbered 6-1-78 to UP 2407.
2968	September 1977	41566	Renumbered 6-12-78 to UP 2408.
2969	September 1977	41567	Renumbered 6-2-78 to UP 2409.
2970	September 1977	41568	Renumbered 6-3-78 to UP 2410.
2971	September 1977	41569	Renumbered 6-2-78 to UP 2411.
2972	September 1977	41570	Renumbered 6-3-78 to UP 2412.
2973	September 1977	41571	Renumbered 5-28-78 to UP 2413.
2974	September 1977	41572	Renumbered 6-19-78 to UP 2414.

Newly-delivered General Electric C30-7's stand at the diesel servicing area at Council Bluffs, IA on 19 September 1977. These units were numbered in after the last U30C's . . . starting at UP 2960. Union Pacific directed that the units be delivered in the simple paint scheme—harbor-mist grey banding the Armour yellow with silvered running gear. As the units were set-up at Omaha Shops, they received the decorative trim and lettering before final release to fleet service. To avoid any possible confusion with the U30C's due to slightly differing mechanical and electrical arrangements, a new block of numbers were assigned to the C30-7's. These first fifteen units were renumbered into the 2400-Class and follow-on C30-7's have entered accordingly.

Basking in the bright sun in front of the Omaha Shops is a brand new General Electric C30-7. It has just been "set-up" with all the company equipment and is now ready for mainline action. This block of fifteen units (2960-2974) was renumbered to 2400-2414 in mid-1978. Omaha, NE, 22 September 1977.

Having just been "set-up" at Omaha Shops, Union Pacific's first C30-7 is ready for system assignment. This order for 15 units . . . 2960-2974 . . . were shipped from General Electric with no distinctive markings. Once on property, the locomotives were worked through the shops during which the Union Pacific lettering and stripping was applied.

The major spotting differences between the previous 219 U30C's on property and these new C30-7's is the larger top mounted radiator area extending away from the car body roof at the rear of engine and the front short low hood light assembly. The wingspan of the radiator also required the off-setting of the car body just forward of the air intake screens.

These units were renumbered UP 2400-2414 during the summer of 1973, so as to keep all C30-7's in numerical sequence.

Photographed on the Omaha Shop lead, 22 August 1977.

Two views of UP 2961 show the front end construction features. The front short low hood has an optional light assembly capable of housing a set of twin seal beams or a rotating Mars light . . . which Union Pacific did not opt for.

The approved FRA front mounting step and lift-pin lever are additional spotting features . . . along with the General Electric designed cast truck assembly.

Shown at Council Bluffs, IA, ready for assignment . . . 21 August 1977.

Without the distinctive red striping and Union Pacific markings, these undecorated yellow and grey units are less than attractive! Just delivered at Council Bluffs, IA on 19 September 1977, this unit will go directly to the Omaha Shops for "set-up" . . . receiving arm rests and window awnings, radio installation, water cooler, toilet, rotating beacon and application of all distinctive markings.

The fireman's side of just delivered UP 2965 . . . again showing the starkness of the undecorated grey over yellow paint scheme. Once the window awnings are applied, it will be difficult to study the original window arrangement . . . as seen here. The new FRA style mounting step is equally clear to study. Shown at Council Bluffs, IA on 7 September 1977 . . . just prior to going to the Omaha Shops for "set-up."

The rear view of fresh-out-of-Omaha Shops UP 2970 shows the unit fully decorated in Union Pacific's scheme and ready for system assignment. The extended radiator area is housed in the top rear "wing" assembly . . . a spotting item of the C30-7's. This unit is prepared as a westbound lead unit as evidenced by the draped MU-cable on the rear pilot . . . and will soon be backed on to the balance of the power consist. Shown at the diesel servicing area at Council Bluffs, IA, 22 September 1977.

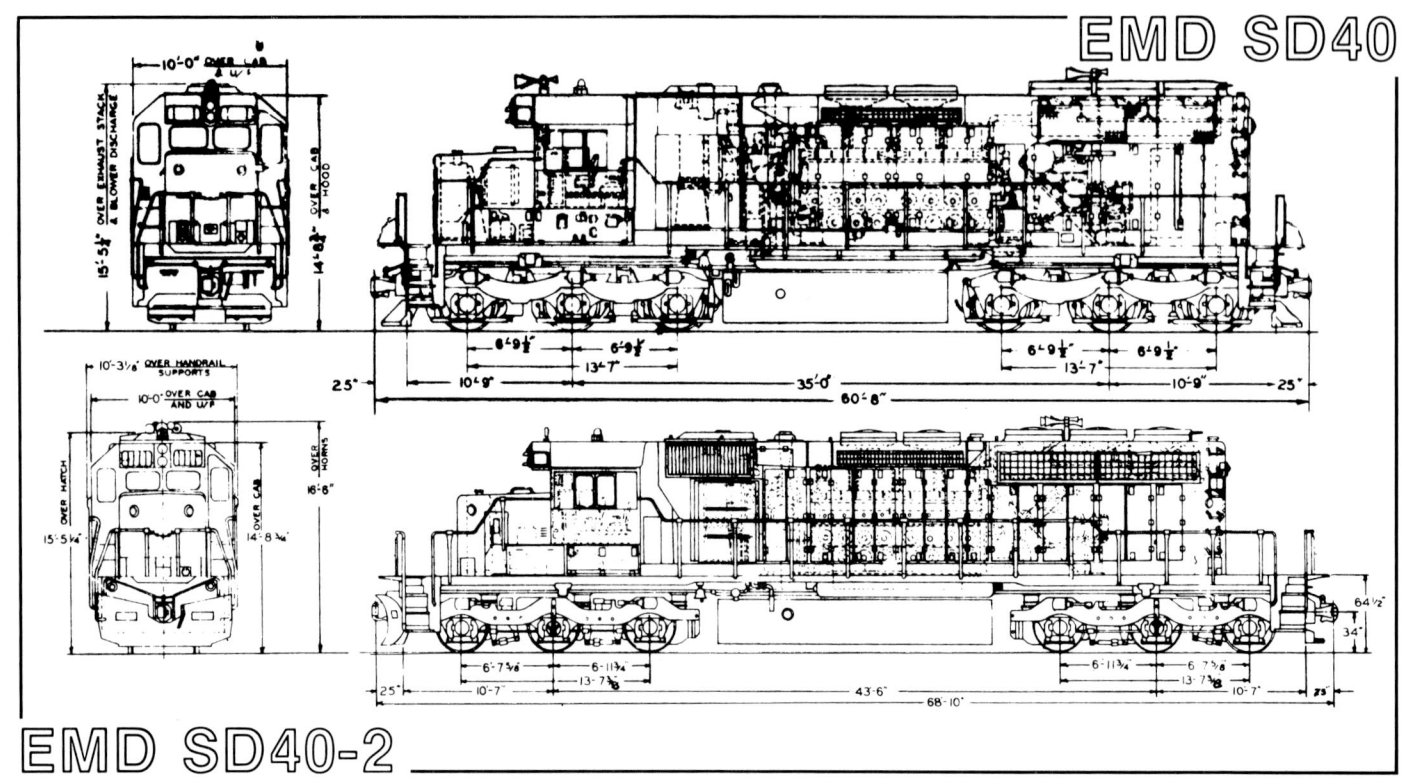

EMD SD40
EMD SD40-2

SD40			SD40-2		
	GENERAL DATA			**GENERAL DATA**	
A.A.R. DESIGNATION		C-C	A.A.R. DESIGNATION		C-C
GEAR RATIO		62/15	GEAR RATIO		62/15
WEIGHT LOADED		391,822 LBS.	WEIGHT LOADED		392,000 LBS.
LIGHT WEIGHT		360,810 LBS. APPROX.	LIGHT WEIGHT		351,065 LBS. APPROX.
MAXIMUM CURVATURE		WITH TRAIN	MAXIMUM CURVATURE		16° WITH TRAIN
MAXIMUM CURVATURE		21° AS SINGLE UNIT	MAXIMUM CURVATURE		30° AS SINGLE UNIT
MAXIMUM SPEED		65 M.P.H.	MAXIMUM SPEED		65 M.P.H.
MINIMUM CONT. SPEED		11 M.P.H.	MINIMUM CONT. SPEED		11 M.P.H.
CENTER OF GRAVITY		59.6" ABOVE RAIL (IN WORKING ORDER)	CENTER OF GRAVITY		60.9" ABOVE RAIL (IN WORKING ORDER)
	SUPPLIES			**SUPPLIES**	
FUEL		3000 GALS.	FUEL		4000 GALS.
LUBE OIL		395 GALS.	LUBE OIL		395 GALS.
COOLING WATER		295 GALS.	COOLING WATER		254 GALS.
SAND		40 CU. FT.	SAND		72 CU. FT.
	DIESEL ENGINE			**DIESEL ENGINE**	
MODEL		16-645-E3	MODEL		16-645-E3
TURBOCHARGER		EQUIPPED	TURBOCHARGER		EQUIPPED
SPARK ARRESTER		NOT REQUIRED	SPARK ARRESTER		NOT REQUIRED
AIR FILTER, BASIC:			AIR FILTER, BASIC:		
CARBODY		NOT EQUIPPED	CARBODY		NOT EQUIPPED
PRIMARY		DYNAVANE	PRIMARY		DYNAVANE
ENGINE		AAF BAG	ENGINE		AAF BAG
FUEL HEATER		*KELTY	FUEL HEATER		KELTY NO. 525-232
*SOME MODIFIED WITH FARR					
	ELECTRICAL			**ELECTRICAL**	
MULTIPLE UNIT RECEPTACLES		12-21 & 27 PT	MULTIPLE UNIT RECEPTACLES		27 PT
MAIN GENERATOR		AR-10	MAIN GENERATOR		AR-10
ALTERNATOR		D-14	ALTERNATOR		D-14
TRACTION MOTORS, TYPE		D-77	TRACTION MOTORS, TYPE		D-77
NUMBER OF TRACTION MOTORS		6	NUMBER OF TRACTION MOTORS		6
DYNAMIC BRAKES		POTENTIAL CONTROL**	DYNAMIC BRAKES		POTENTIAL CONTROL*
BATTERIES		64V. 426 AMP. HRS.	BATTERIES		64V. 426 AMP. HRS.
HEADLIGHTS		TWIN SEALED BEAMS 200W. EA.	HEADLIGHTS		TWIN SEALED BEAMS 200W. EA.
AUXILIARY GENERATOR		10 KW.	AUXILIARY GENERATOR		18 KW.
COOLING FANS		(3) 48" 8-BLADE	COOLING FANS		(3) 48" 8-BLADE
CAB SIGNALS		US&S TYPE 'E'	CAB SIGNALS		US&S TYPE 'EL'
ROTATING WARNING LIGHTS		EQUIPPED	ROTATING WARNING LIGHTS		EQUIPPED
R.C.S.		NOT EQUIPPED	R.C.S.		NOT EQUIPPED
**EXTENDED RANGE			*EXTENDED RANGE		
	RUNNING GEAR			**RUNNING GEAR**	
DRAFT GEAR		M-381	DRAFT GEAR		NC-390
COUPLER		TYPE 'E'	COUPLER		TYPE 'E'
JOURNALS		6½" x 12" HYATT R.B.	JOURNALS		6⅞" x 12" HYATT R.B.
WHEELS		40" DIA.	WHEELS		40" DIA.
TRUCKS		6-WHL., FLEXICOIL, CLSP. BRKS., HIGH CYL.	TRUCKS		6 WHL., HTC SINGLE SHOE BRKS., HIGH BRK. CYL.

ELECTRO-MOTIVE'S SD40 ROSTER

UNIT	BUILDER DATE	BUILDER NUMBER	UNIT	BUILDER DATE	BUILDER NUMBER	UNIT	BUILDER DATE	BUILDER NUMBER
3000	April 1966	31414	3014	April 1966	31428	3028	April 1966	31578
3001	April 1966	31415	3015	April 1966	31429	3029	April 1966	31579
3002	April 1966	31416	3016	April 1966	31430	3030	April 1966	31580
3003	April 1966	31417	3017	April 1966	31431	3031	April 1966	31581
3004	April 1966	31418	3018	April 1966	31432	3032	April 1966	31582
3005	April 1966	31419	3019	April 1966	31433	3033	April 1966	31583
3006	April 1966	31420	3020	April 1966	31434	3034	April 1966	31584
3007	April 1966	31421	3021	April 1966	31435	3035	April 1966	31585
3008	April 1966	31422	3022	April 1966	31436	3036	April 1966	31586
3009	April 1966	31423	3023	April 1966	31437	3037	April 1966	31587
3010	April 1966	31424	3024	April 1966	31438	3038	April 1966	31588
3011	April 1966	31425	3025	April 1966	31575	3039	April 1966	31589
3012	April 1966	31426	3026	April 1966	31576			
3013	April 1966	31427	3027	April 1966	31577			

Starting to show signs of the many miles rolled up, UP 3004 idles at Council Bluffs, IA on 23 April 1977. The 1966 order received the double rotating beacon installation; however, some have been converted to a single top-centered mounted beacon.

The SD40X's, shown below, were on property two months before the first production models (UP 3000-3039) were delivered.

The SD40 shares the same basic frame with the SD38 and SD45, which results in the large front and rear platforms.

Union Pacific purchased the eight EMD SD40X demonstrators (434A-434H) and numbered them UP 3040-3047. The first six have the flared radiator, while the remaining two have the standard flush-body radiator. UP 3044 faces west at Kansas City, KS on 23 April 1977, and shows off its flared radiators at Omaha, NE on 7 October 1980. All are in heavy transfer yard service.

ELECTRO-MOTIVE'S SD40 ROSTER

UNIT	BUILDER DATE	BUILDER NUMBER	REMARKS	UNIT	BUILDER DATE	BUILDER NUMBER	REMARKS
3040	April 1965	29873	Originally EMD demonstrator #434A. Purchased second-hand 2/66.	3044	May 1965	30499	Originally EMD demonstrator #434E. Purchased second-hand 2/66.
3041	April 1965	29874	Originally EMD demonstrator #434B. Purchased second-hand 2/66.	3045	June 1965	30500	Originally EMD demonstrator #434F. Purchased second-hand 2/66.
3042	May 1965	29875	Originally EMD demonstrator #434C. Purchased second-hand 4/66.	3046	July 1965	30501	Originally EMD demonstrator #434G. Purchased second-hand 2/66.
3043	April 1965	29876	Originally EMD demonstrator #434D. Purchased second-hand 4/66.	3047	July 1965	30502	Originally EMD demonstrator #434H. Purchased second-hand 2/66.

ELECTRO-MOTIVE'S SD40 ROSTER

UNIT	BUILDER DATE	BUILDER NUMBER	UNIT	BUILDER DATE	BUILDER NUMBER	UNIT	BUILDER DATE	BUILDER NUMBER
3048	October 1966	32400	3060	October 1966	32412	3072	December 1966	32424
3049	October 1966	32401	3061	October 1966	32413	3073	December 1966	32425
3050	October 1966	32402	3063	October 1966	32415	3074	December 1966	32426
3051	October 1966	32403	3064	October 1966	32416	3075	December 1966	32427
3052	October 1966	32404	3065	December 1966	32417	3076	December 1966	32428
3053	October 1966	32405	3066	November 1966	32418	3077	December 1966	32429
3054	October 1966	32406	3067	November 1966	32419	3078	December 1966	32430
3055	October 1966	32407	3068	November 1966	32420	3079	December 1966	32431
3056	October 1966	32408	3069	December 1966	32421	3080	December 1966	32432
3057	October 1966	32409	3070	December 1966	32422	3081	December 1966	32433
3058	October 1966	32410	3071¹	December 1966	32423	3082	December 1966	32434
3059	October 1966	32411						

¹Accident Lake Point, UT 8/77. Scrapped at scene.

Heading up a string of brand-new SD40-2's, UP 3054 offers a fourteen-year comparison to the near classic Electro-Motive 6-axle, 3000-horsepower design. Pilot snow plows were first installed on 1972 production models. A proven performer, this model will probably end-up as EMD's all-time, forever, most-built unit.

ELECTRO-MOTIVE'S SD40-2 ROSTER

UNIT	BUILDER DATE	BUILDER NUMBER	UNIT	BUILDER DATE	BUILDER NUMBER	UNIT	BUILDER DATE	BUILDER NUMBER
3083	August 1971	37639	3097	September 1971	37653	3111	October 1971	37917
3084	August 1971	37640	3098	September 1971	37904	3112	October 1971	37918
3085	August 1971	37641	3099	September 1971	37905	3113	October 1971	37919
3086	August 1971	37642	3100:²	September 1971	37906	3114	October 1971	37920
3087	August 1971	37643	3101	September 1971	37907	3115	October 1971	37921
3088	August 1971	37644	3102	September 1971	37908	3116	October 1971	37922
3089	August 1971	37645	3103	September 1971	37909	3117	October 1971	37923
3090	August 1971	37646	3104	September 1971	37910	3118	October 1971	37924
3091	August 1971	37647	3105	September 1971	37911	3119	October 1971	37925
3092	August 1971	37648	3106	September 1971	37912	3120	October 1971	37926
3093	September 1971	37649	3107	September 1971	37913	3121	October 1971	37927
3094	September 1971	37650	3108	September 1971	37914	3122	October 1971	37928
3095	September 1971	37651	3109	September 1971	37915			
3096	September 1971	37652	3110	September 1971	37916			

Striking a typical builder's pose, UP 3107 awaits the signal "bug" on the throat to the mainline at Council Bluffs, IA on 5 February 1978. These units built in 1971 have the brake wheel mounted on a vertical stand at the very back of the car body . . . under the rear twin sealed-beam light. This location protected the assembly from being packed with ice and snow during cold weather operations; however, it proved to be poorly located to the head-end crew. This order was the last to have an individual builder number assigned to each unit.

ELECTRO-MOTIVE'S SD40-2 ROSTER

UNIT	BUILDER DATE	BUILDER NUMBER	UNIT	BUILDER DATE	BUILDER NUMBER	UNIT	BUILDER DATE	BUILDER NUMBER
3123	January 1972	7334-1	3150	February 1972	7334-28	3177	June 1972	5819-5
3124	January 1972	7334-2	3151	February 1972	7334-29	3178	June 1972	5819-6
3125	January 1972	7334-3	3152	February 1972	7334-30	3179	June 1972	5819-7
3126	January 1972	7334-4	3153	February 1972	7334-31	3180	June 1972	5819-8
3127	January 1972	7334-5	3154	February 1972	7334-32	3181	June 1972	5819-9
3128	January 1972	7334-6	3155	February 1972	7334-33	3182	June 1972	5819-10
3129	January 1972	7334-7	3156	February 1972	7334-34	3183	July 1972	5819-11
3130	January 1972	7334-8	3157	February 1972	7334-35	3184	July 1972	5819-12
3131	January 1972	7334-9	3158	February 1972	7334-36	3185	July 1972	5819-13
3132	January 1972	7334-10	3159	February 1972	7334-37	3186	July 1972	5819-14
3133	January 1972	7334-11	3160	February 1972	7334-38	3187	July 1972	5819-15
3134	January 1972	7334-12	3161	February 1972	7334-39	3188	July 1972	5819-16
3135	January 1972	7334-13	3162	February 1972	7334-40	3189	July 1972	5819-17
3136	January 1972	7334-14	3163	February 1972	7334-41	3190	July 1972	5819-18
3137	January 1972	7334-15	3164	February 1972	7334-42	3191	July 1972	5819-19
3138	January 1972	7334-16	3165	February 1972	7334-43	3192	July 1972	5819-20
3139	January 1972	7334-17	3166	February 1972	7334-44	3193	August 1972	5819-21
3140	January 1972	7334-18	3167	February 1972	7334-45	3194	August 1972	5819-22
3141	January 1972	7334-19	3168	February 1972	7334-46	3195	August 1972	5819-23
3142	January 1972	7334-20	3169	February 1972	7334-47	3196	August 1972	5819-24
3143	January 1972	7334-21	3170	February 1972	7334-48	3197	August 1972	5819-25
3144	January 1972	7334-22	3171	February 1972	7334-49	3198	August 1972	5819-26
3145	January 1972	7334-23	3172	February 1972	7334-50	3199	August 1972	5819-27
3146[1]	January 1972	7334-24	3173	June 1972	5819-1	3200:2	August 1972	5819-28
3147	January 1972	7334-25	3174	June 1972	5819-2	3201	August 1972	5819-29
3148	February 1972	7334-26	3175	June 1972	5819-3	3202	August 1972	5819-30
3149	February 1972	7334-27	3176	June 1972	5819-4			

[1] Accident Lake Point, UT 8/77. Scrapped at scene.

The first unit of the 1973 order... UP 3203 was delivered in April. These units have the ratchet-style hand brake mounted on the fireman's side of the short hood. Cold weather operation found these assemblies getting packed with ice and snow and very difficult to clear and operate with gloved hands. Follow-on units have the brake wheel installed. The last three units of this order were converted to "fast forties" in February 1976 and renumbered UP 8000-8002... the only high-speed units with short front noses (the other 97 units have the extended short hood). UP 8000 reverted back to a standard 65-mph SD40-2 and regained its original road number... UP 3240 in June 1980.

ELECTRO-MOTIVE'S SD40-2 ROSTER

UNIT	BUILDER DATE	BUILDER NUMBER	UNIT	BUILDER DATE	BUILDER NUMBER	UNIT	BUILDER DATE	BUILDER NUMBER
3203	April 1973	72684-1	3216	April 1973	72684-14	3229	May 1973	72684-27
3204	April 1973	72684-2	3217	April 1973	72684-15	3230	May 1973	72684-28
3205	April 1973	72684-3	3218	April 1973	72684-16	3231	May 1973	72684-29
3206	April 1973	72684-4	3219	April 1973	72684-17	3232	May 1973	72684-30
3207	April 1973	72684-5	3220	April 1973	72684-18	3233	May 1973	72684-31
3208	April 1973	72684-6	3221	April 1973	72684-19	3234	May 1973	72684-32
3209	April 1973	72684-7	3222	May 1973	72684-20	3235	May 1973	72684-33
3210	April 1973	72684-8	3223	May 1973	72684-21	3236	May 1973	72684-34
3211	April 1973	72684-9	3224	May 1973	72684-22	3237	May 1973	72684-35
3212	April 1973	72684-10	3225	May 1973	72684-23	3238	May 1973	72684-36
3213	April 1973	72684-11	3226	May 1973	72684-24	3239	May 1973	72684-37
3214	April 1973	72684-12	3227	May 1973	72684-25			
3215	April 1973	72684-13	3228	May 1973	72684-26			

The following units were converted to SD40-2H High Speed Units:

UNIT	BUILDER DATE	BUILDER NUMBER	REMARKS	UNIT	BUILDER DATE	BUILDER NUMBER	REMARKS
3240	May 1973	72684-38	Converted and renumbered UP 8000 2/76. Reverted to standard SD40-2 and renumbered UP 3240 6/80.	3261	June 1974	73661-19	Converted and renumbered UP 8021 4/76. Reverted to standard SD40-2 and renumbered UP 3261 6/80.
3257	June 1974	73661-15	Converted and renumbered UP 8017 4/76. Reverted to standard SD40-2 and renumbered UP 3257 7/80.				

ELECTRO-MOTIVE'S SD40-2 ROSTER

UNIT	BUILDER DATE	BUILDER NUMBER	UNIT	BUILDER DATE	BUILDER NUMBER	UNIT	BUILDER DATE	BUILDER NUMBER
3275	July 1974	73661-33	3285	July 1974	73661-43	3295	July 1974	74676-8
3276	July 1974	73661-34	3286	July 1974	73661-44	3296	July 1974	74676-9
3277	July 1974	73661-35	3287	July 1974	73661-45	3297	July 1974	74676-10
3278	July 1974	73661-36	3288	July 1974	74676-1	3298	July 1974	74676-11
3279	July 1974	73661-37	3289	July 1974	74676-2	3299	July 1974	74676-12
3280	July 1974	73661-38	3290	July 1974	74676-3	3300	April 1975	74676-13
3281	July 1974	73661-39	3291	July 1974	74676-4	3301	April 1975	74676-14
3282	July 1974	73661-40	3292	July 1974	74676-5	3302	April 1975	74676-15
3283	July 1974	73661-41	3293	July 1974	74676-6	3303	April 1975	74676-16
3284	July 1974	73661-42	3294	July 1974	74676-7	3304	April 1975	74676-17

Extra 3289 West pulls through the Armstrong Yards at Kansas City, KS on 28 May 1978. This is a typical power lash-up . . . 12,000-horsepower. The longer short hood on the SD40-2 units has been dubbed by some wag as "snoot-noses." These extra-length short hoods were designed to house additional radio gear suitable for RCS operations; however, these plans never materialized. The compartment is walled off from the crew toilet and serves as storage space for extra tools and coupler knuckles. Electro-Motive shortened the short hood length in follow-on models . . . however, Union Pacific has these long hoods on UP 8003-8074; UP 3288-3304; UP 3335; UP 3337-3399; UP 3410-3488.

Representing one of the SD40-2's that returned to its reserved road number slot, UP 3317 shows off its originally-assigned number on the battery box door. Admittedly, "8047" has been removed; however, it is still clearly visible. The roster below shows the renumbered units delivered as high-speed units numbered in the 8000-Class. Holes in the sequential roster were reserved for just this purpose . . . so if and when any "fast forties" would revert to standard 65-mph road units they would be in proper year/model order. Council Bluffs, IA, 12 October 1980.

ELECTRO-MOTIVE'S SD40-2 ROSTER

UNIT	BUILDER DATE	BUILDER NUMBER	REMARKS	UNIT	BUILDER DATE	BUILDER NUMBER	REMARKS
3305	July 1976	767021-1	Originally UP 8035 delivered as SD40-2M. Converted to standard SD40-2 and renumbered UP 3305 6/80.	3317	August 1976	767021-13	Originally UP 8047 delivered as SD40-2M. Converted to standard SD40-2 and renumbered UP 3317 8/80.
3306	July 1976	767021-2	Originally UP 8036 delivered as SD40-2M. Converted to standard SD40-2 and renumbered UP 3306 6/80.	3319	August 1976	767021-15	Originally UP 8049 delivered as SD40-2M. Converted to standard SD40-2 and renumbered UP 3319 7/80.
3312	July 1976	767021-8	Originally UP 8042 delivered as SD40-2M. Converted to standard SD40-2 and renumbered UP 3312 7/80.	3329	September 1976	767021-25	Originally UP 8059 delivered as SD40-2M. Converted to standard SD40-2 and renumbered UP 3329 8/80.
3313	July 1976	767021-9	Originally UP 8043 delivered as SD40-2M. Converted to standard SD40-2 and renumbered UP 3313 6/80.	3330	September 1976	767021-26	Originally UP 8060 delivered as SD40-2M. Converted to standard SD40-2 and renumbered UP 3330 6/80.

NOTES:

A—Original instructions were issued 6/80 to change the gear ratio from 59/18 to 62/15 on units 8000-8099 and apply a PF17 module in place of the PF18 module. These instructions were later modified to include only units 8000-8074 in the conversion to standard SD40-2's. On 21 August 1980 the program was suspended.

ELECTRO-MOTIVE'S SD40-2 ROSTER

UNIT	BUILDER DATE	BUILDER NUMBER	UNIT	BUILDER DATE	BUILDER NUMBER	UNIT	BUILDER DATE	BUILDER NUMBER
3335	February 1977	766056-1	3357	March 1977	766056-23	3379	April 1977	766056-45
3336[1]	February 1977	766056-2	3358	March 1977	766056-24	3380	April 1977	766056-46
3337	February 1977	766056-3	3359	March 1977	766056-25	3381	April 1977	766056-47
3338	February 1977	766056-4	3360	March 1977	766056-26	3382	April 1977	766056-48
3339	February 1977	766056-5	3361	March 1977	766056-27	3383	April 1977	766056-49
3340	February 1977	766056-6	3362	March 1977	766056-28	3384	April 1977	766056-50
3341	February 1977	766056-7	3363	March 1977	766056-29	3385	April 1977	766056-51
3342	February 1977	766056-8	3364	March 1977	766056-30	3386	April 1977	766056-52
3343	February 1977	766056-9	3365	March 1977	766056-31	3387	April 1977	766056-53
3344	February 1977	766056-10	3366	March 1977	766056-32	3388	April 1977	766056-54
3345	March 1977	766056-11	3367	March 1977	766056-33	3389	April 1977	766056-55
3346	March 1977	766056-12	3368	March 1977	766056-34	3390	April 1977	766056-56
3347	March 1977	766056-13	3369	March 1977	766056-35	3391	April 1977	766056-57
3348	March 1977	766056-14	3370	March 1977	766056-36	3392	April 1977	766056-58
3349	March 1977	766056-15	3371	March 1977	766056-37	3393	April 1977	766056-59
3350	March 1977	766056-16	3372	March 1977	766056-38	3394	April 1977	766056-60
3351	March 1977	766056-17	3373	March 1977	766056-39	3395	April 1977	766056-61
3352	March 1977	766056-18	3374	April 1977	766056-40	3396	April 1977	766056-62
3353	March 1977	766056-19	3375	April 1977	766056-41	3397	April 1977	766056-63
3354	March 1977	766056-20	3376	April 1977	766056-42	3398	April 1977	766056-64
3355	March 1977	766056-21	3377	April 1977	766056-43	3399:2	May 1977	766056-65
3356	March 1977	766056-22	3378	April 1977	766056-44			

[1]*Accident Lake Point, UT 8/77. Scrapped at scene.*

Newly delivered UP 3399 sits at the diesel servicing area at Council Bluffs, IA on 13 May 1977. It sports the Union Pacific shield on the cab and the larger road name and numbers on the car body. This unit received the "Canadian ditch lights and stop box" the following year, so that it could be assigned to "run-through operations" into Canada.

Another mid-1977 delivery, UP 3380 shows the rear construction features which include the new styled double auxiliary uncoupling lever which can be functioned from either the ground, step or from the platform. Note the double classification light arrangement . . . Union Pacific opted for the lower set of lights. Council Bluffs, IA, 14 April 1977.

The cab and truck view of UP 3363 shows the extended hood SD40-2 . . . dubbed by some wag as "snoot."

ELECTRO-MOTIVE'S SD40-2 ROSTER

UNIT	BUILDER DATE	BUILDER NUMBER	UNIT	BUILDER DATE	BUILDER NUMBER	UNIT	BUILDER DATE	BUILDER NUMBER
3410	March 1978	776088-1	3437	April 1978	776088-28	3464	April 1978	776088-55
3411	March 1978	776088-2	3438	April 1978	776088-29	3465	April 1978	776088-56
3412	March 1978	776088-3	3439	April 1978	776088-30	3466	April 1978	776088-57
3413	March 1978	776088-4	3440	April 1978	776088-31	3467	April 1978	776088-58
3414	March 1978	776088-5	3441	April 1978	776088-32	3468	April 1978	776088-59
3415	March 1978	776088-6	3442	April 1978	776088-33	3469	April 1978	776088-60
3416	March 1978	776088-7	3443	April 1978	776088-34	3470	April 1978	776088-61
3417	March 1978	776088-8	3444	April 1978	776088-35	3471	April 1978	776088-62
3418	March 1978	776088-9	3445	April 1978	776088-36	3472	April 1978	776088-63
3419	March 1978	776088-10	3446	April 1978	776088-37	3473	April 1978	776088-64
3420	March 1978	776088-11	3447	April 1978	776088-38	3474	May 1978	776088-65
3421	March 1978	776088-12	3448	April 1978	776088-39	3475	May 1978	776088-66
3422	March 1978	776088-13	3449	April 1978	776088-40	3476	May 1978	776088-67
3423	March 1978	776088-14	3450	April 1978	776088-41	3477	May 1978	776088-68
3424	March 1978	776088-15	3451	April 1978	776088-42	3478	May 1978	776088-69
3425	March 1978	776088-16	3452	April 1978	776088-43	3479	May 1978	776088-70
3426	March 1978	776088-17	3453	April 1978	776088-44	3480	May 1978	776088-71
3427	March 1978	776088-18	3454	April 1978	776088-45	3481	May 1978	776088-72
3428	March 1978	776088-19	3455	April 1978	776088-46	3482	May 1978	776088-73
3429	March 1978	776088-20	3456	April 1978	776088-47	3483	May 1978	776088-74
3430	April 1978	776088-21	3457	April 1978	776088-48	3484	May 1978	776088-75
3431	April 1978	776088-22	3458	April 1978	776088-49	3485	May 1978	776088-76
3432	April 1978	776088-23	3459	April 1978	776088-50	3486	May 1978	776088-77
3433	April 1978	776088-24	3460	April 1978	776088-51	3487	May 1978	776088-78
3434	April 1978	776088-25	3461	April 1978	776088-52	3488	May 1978	776088-79
3435	April 1978	776088-26	3462	April 1978	776088-53			
3436	April 1978	776088-27	3463	April 1978	776088-54			

Just delivered to Council Bluffs, IA on 27 March 1978 are three brand new Electro-Motive SD40-2's built in March 1978. They will be scheduled into the Omaha Shops for set-up . . . receiving the window awnings and arm rests, the radio antenna, rotating beacon, refrigerator and toilet. These were part of a 79-unit order (UP 3410-3488) delivered between March and May 1978. Note that the horns are mounted in the aft position, over the radiator fans . . . the last order received in this configuration. The system's servicing areas are starting to look like EMD's shipping yard . . . what with all the SD40-2's around.

The middle unit of a ten-unit December 1978 order . . . UP 3493 heads up another new unit from the next order which started arriving in January 1979.

These are near duplicates to the orders before and after . . . and extend out the SD40/SD40-2 fleet that Union Pacific started building in 1966 when they purchased the eight SD40X Electro-Motive demonstrators 434A-434H. Almost 800 of these styled units are on the current locomotive roster, with more on order in 1981.

Shown active at Council Bluffs, IA on 6 May 1979.

ELECTRO-MOTIVE'S SD40-2 ROSTER

UNIT	BUILDER DATE	BUILDER NUMBER	UNIT	BUILDER DATE	BUILDER NUMBER	UNIT	BUILDER DATE	BUILDER NUMBER
3489	December 1978	786163-1	3493	December 1978	786163-5	3497	December 1978	786163-9
3490	December 1978	786163-2	3494	December 1978	786163-6	3498	December 1978	786163-10
3491	December 1978	786163-3	3495	December 1978	786163-7			
3492	December 1978	786163-4	3496	December 1978	786163-8			

ELECTRO-MOTIVE'S SD40-2 ROSTER

UNIT	BUILDER DATE	BUILDER NUMBER	UNIT	BUILDER DATE	BUILDER NUMBER	UNIT	BUILDER DATE	BUILDER NUMBER
3499	January 1979	786170-1	3528	February 1979	786170-30	3556	March 1979	786170-58
3500	January 1979	786170-2	3529	February 1979	786170-31	3557	March 1979	786170-59
3501	January 1979	786170-3	3530	February 1979	786170-32	3558	March 1979	786170-60
3502	January 1979	786170-4	3531	February 1979	786170-33	3559	March 1979	786170-61
3503	January 1979	786170-5	3532	February 1979	786170-34	3560	March 1979	786170-62
3504	January 1979	786170-6	3533	February 1979	786170-35	3561	March 1979	786170-63
3505	January 1979	786170-7	3534	February 1979	786170-36	3562	March 1979	786170-64
3506	January 1979	786170-8	3535	February 1979	786170-37	3563	March 1979	786170-65
3507	January 1979	786170-9	3536	February 1979	786170-38	3564	March 1979	786170-66
3508	January 1979	786170-10	3537	February 1979	786170-39	3565	March 1979	786170-67
3509	January 1979	786170-11	3538	February 1979	786170-40	3566	March 1979	786170-68
3510	January 1979	786170-12	3539	March 1979	786170-41	3567	March 1979	786170-69
3511	January 1979	786170-13	3540	March 1979	786170-42	3568	March 1979	786170-70
3512	January 1979	786170-14	3541	March 1979	786170-43	3569	March 1979	786170-71
3513	January 1979	786170-15	3542	March 1979	786170-44	3570	March 1979	786170-72
3514	January 1979	786170-16	3543	March 1979	786170-45	3571	March 1979	786170-73
3515	January 1979	786170-17	3544	March 1979	786170-46	3572	March 1979	786170-74
3516	January 1979	786170-18	3545	March 1979	786170-47	3573	March 1979	786170-75
3517	January 1979	786170-19	3546	March 1979	786170-48	3574	July 1979	786218-1
3518	January 1979	786170-20	3547	March 1979	786170-49	3575	July 1979	786218-2
3519	January 1979	786170-21	3548	March 1979	786170-50	3576	July 1979	786218-3
3520	January 1979	786170-22	3549	March 1979	786170-51	3577	July 1979	786218-4
3521	January 1979	786170-23	3550	March 1979	786170-52	3578	July 1979	786218-5
3522	January 1979	786170-24	3551	March 1979	786170-53	3579	July 1979	786218-6
3523	January 1979	786170-25	3552	March 1979	786170-54	3580	July 1979	786218-7
3524	February 1974	786170-26	3553	March 1979	786170-55	3581	July 1979	786218-8
3525	February 1979	786170-27	3554	March 1979	786170-56	3582	July 1979	786218-9
3526	February 1979	786170-28	3555	March 1979	786170-57	3583	July 1979	786218-10
3527	February 1979	786170-29						

Repair of damages complete, UP 3574 sits in front of Omaha Shops on 24 August 1980. Brand new and only five days on property, this unit was heavily damaged in a soda ash train (GRX) derailment on 31 July 1979 just east of Granite, WY where Interstate 80 crosses mainline 1 and 2. Initially thought to be a total loss, it was evacuated to Omaha Shops for evaluation and possible repair. Once again, the Omaha back shop skills have prevailed.

Having been serviced at Council Bluffs, IA on 20 September 1980, UP 3506 has been placed on the assignment board as "ready." The brake wheel mounted on the short hood serves the head-end crew much better than the ratchet-styled handle found on earlier SD40's. Ever try to dig a handle out of packed ice and snow and then jack it in sub-zero temperatures in gloved hands?... Not easy! The large wheel is much easier to grip in gloved hands and can be cleared of most ice and snow... so as to at least turn the wheel.

This was #8 in a seventy-five unit order delivered in early 1979.

ELECTRO-MOTIVE'S SD40-2 ROSTER

UNIT	BUILDER DATE	BUILDER NUMBER	UNIT	BUILDER DATE	BUILDER NUMBER	UNIT	BUILDER DATE	BUILDER NUMBER
3609:2	September 1979	786263-1	3626:2	November 1979	786263-18	3643:2	December 1979	786263-35
3610:2	September 1979	786263-2	3627:2	November 1979	786263-19	3644:2	December 1979	786263-36
3611:2	September 1979	786263-3	3628:2	November 1979	786263-20	3645:2	December 1979	786263-37
3612:2	September 1979	786263-4	3629:2	November 1979	786263-21	3646:2	December 1979	786263-38
3613:2	September 1979	786263-5	3630:2	November 1979	786263-22	3647:2	December 1979	786263-39
3614:2	September 1979	786263-6	3631:2	November 1979	786263-23	3648:2	December 1979	786263-40
3615:2	September 1979	786263-7	3632:2	November 1979	786263-24	3649:2	December 1979	786263-41
3616:2	September 1979	786263-8	3633:2	November 1979	786263-25	3650	December 1979	786263-42
3617:2	October 1979	786263-9	3634:2	November 1979	786263-26	3651	December 1979	786263-43
3618:2	October 1979	786263-10	3635:2	November 1979	786263-27	3652	December 1979	786263-44
3619:2	October 1979	786263-11	3636:2	November 1979	786263-28	3653	December 1979	786263-45
3620:2	October 1979	786263-12	3637:2	November 1979	786263-29	3654	December 1979	786263-46
3621:2	October 1979	786263-13	3638:2	November 1979	786263-30	3655	December 1979	786263-47
3622:2	October 1979	786263-14	3639:2	November 1979	786263-31	3656	December 1979	786263-48
3623:2	November 1979	786263-15	3640:2	November 1979	786263-32	3657	December 1979	786263-49
3624:2	November 1979	786263-16	3641:2	November 1979	786263-33	3658	December 1979	786263-50
3625:2	November 1979	786263-17	3642:2	November 1979	786263-34			

Pulling in California sunshine near Walnut, CA, UP 3700 leads a brace of power which includes two trailing Western Pacific units. It's unusual to spot a General Electric U30C on the California Division; however, UP 2821 runs in third position. UP 3700 has factory-installed front mounted horns, while UP 3162 sports "flying" horns relocated from the rear.—*Photo by Martin Bosynak.*

ELECTRO-MOTIVE'S SD40-2 ROSTER

UNIT	BUILDER DATE	BUILDER NUMBER	UNIT	BUILDER DATE	BUILDER NUMBER	UNIT	BUILDER DATE	BUILDER NUMBER
3659	January 1980	796297-1	3696	January 1980	796297-38	3733	February 1980	796297-75
3660	January 1980	796297-2	3697	January 1980	796297-39	3734	February 1980	796297-76
3661	January 1980	796297-3	3698	January 1980	796297-40	3735	February 1980	796297-77
3662	January 1980	796297-4	3699	January 1980	796297-41	3736	February 1980	796297-78
3663	January 1980	796297-5	3700	January 1980	796297-42	3737	February 1980	796297-79
3664	January 1980	796297-6	3701	January 1980	796297-43	3738	February 1980	796297-80
3665	January 1980	796297-7	3702	January 1980	796297-44	3739	February 1980	796297-81
3666	January 1980	796297-8	3703	January 1980	796297-45	3740	February 1980	796297-82
3667	January 1980	796297-9	3704	January 1980	796297-46	3741	February 1980	796297-83
3668	January 1980	796297-10	3705	January 1980	796297-47	3742	February 1980	796297-84
3669	January 1980	796297-11	3706	January 1980	796297-48	3743	February 1980	796297-85
3670	January 1980	796297-12	3707	January 1980	796297-49	3744	February 1980	796297-86
3671	January 1980	796297-13	3708	January 1980	796297-50	3745	February 1980	796297-87
3672	January 1980	796297-14	3709	January 1980	796297-51	3746	February 1980	796297-88
3673	January 1980	796297-15	3710	January 1980	796297-52	3747	February 1980	796297-89
3674	January 1980	796297-16	3711	January 1980	796297-53	3748	February 1980	796297-90
3675	January 1980	796297-17	3712	January 1980	796297-54	3749	February 1980	796297-91
3676	January 1980	796297-18	3713	January 1980	796297-55	3750	March 1980	796297-92
3677	January 1980	796297-19	3714	January 1980	796297-56	3751	March 1980	796297-93
3678	January 1980	796297-20	3715	January 1980	796297-57	3752	March 1980	796297-94
3679	January 1980	796297-21	3716	February 1980	796297-58	3753	March 1980	796297-95
3680	January 1980	796297-22	3717	February 1980	796297-59	3754	March 1980	796297-96
3681	January 1980	796297-23	3718	February 1980	796297-60	3755	March 1980	796297-97
3682	January 1980	796297-24	3719	February 1980	796297-61	3756	March 1980	796297-98
3683	January 1980	796297-25	3720	February 1980	796297-62	3757	March 1980	796297-99
3684	January 1980	796297-26	3721	February 1980	796297-63	3758	March 1980	796297-100
3685	January 1980	796297-27	3722	February 1980	796297-64	3759	March 1980	796297-101
3686	January 1980	796297-28	3723	February 1980	796297-65	3760	March 1980	796297-102
3687	January 1980	796297-29	3724	February 1980	796297-66	3761	March 1980	796297-103
3688	January 1980	796297-30	3725	February 1980	796297-67	3762	March 1980	796297-104
3689	January 1980	796297-31	3726	February 1980	796297-68	3763	March 1980	796297-105
3690	January 1980	796297-32	3727	February 1980	796297-69	3764	March 1980	796297-106
3691	January 1980	796297-33	3728	February 1980	796297-70	3765	March 1980	796297-107
3692	January 1980	796297-34	3729	February 1980	796297-71	3766	March 1980	796297-108
3693	January 1980	796297-35	3730	February 1980	796297-72	3767	March 1980	796297-109
3694	January 1980	796297-36	3731	February 1980	796297-73	3768	March 1980	796297-110
3695	January 1980	796297-37	3732	February 1980	796297-74			

Running eastward on Santa Fe rails is the first of a three section LABN (Los Angeles—Yermo) train on 26 May 1980. Exiting the tunnel at Alray, CA, the nine-thousand horsepower is fully employed in pulling the grade to Cajon Summit. The nearly new lead unit was delivered in February 1980.—*Photo by James R. Doughty.*

The most recent order for EMD's SD40-2's started arriving in October 1980 carrying master builder number 796345. The first of the 40-unit order is UP 3769, being -1 with a builder's date of October 1980. These units arrived in basic yellow and grey with silvered trucks . . . lacking all red stripings and other Union Pacifc markings. Union Pacific will apply the scotchlite decorative materials during the shop set-ups at Omaha. Council Bluffs, IA, 25 October 1980.

NEWLY DELIVERED EMD SD40-2's • OCTOBER 1980

The sharp nosey-angle shows off the starkness of this undecorated SD40-2 just delivered at Council Bluffs, IA on 22 October 1980. The only construction change noted on this new order is the fabrication of the access door by the step-up box to the cab. The door is made with an overlap sheet having a fluted edge that ends at nearly mid-point on the door.—Photo by Gerald J. Bosanek.

During set-up at Omaha Shops, UP 3771 was run through a fuel consumption testing project. Results will be compared with similar tests run on the newly arrived General Electric C30-7's and actual operating figures from the field. With the soaring costs of diesel fuels, Union Pacific is making every effort to maximize efficiency and minimize expenditures.

It is shown, just delivered, at Council Bluffs, IA on 22 October 1980.

A trio of newly arrived SD40's idles at Council Bluffs, IA on 25 October 1980. This view allows a comparison of the rear construction features for both sides. Not visible are the new quiet 8-blade "Q-fans" used on all current SD40-2 EMD deliveries . . . expected to meet Environmental Protection Agency's newest noise level standards.

In addition to applying all decorative markings, the Omaha Shops will stencil on other mechanical data during set-up, e.g., gear ratio markings on trucks, operating procedures on engine locker doors, and location of critical items.

EDITOR'S NOTE:
The arrival of UP 3769-3808 has NOT been reflected in the locomotive summary and roster data presented . . . which had an editorial cut-off of 31 August 1980. In an effort to present the most complete overview of the Union Pacific right up to press time, pages were reserved to cover such contingencies.

The master builder number for these 40 units is 796345. UP 3769-3789 carries -1 to -21, all built during October 1980; the highest number on property at this time is UP 3790 which carries -22, built in November 1980.

While appearing non-standard due to no decorations, the front construction features of the newly delivered SD40-2 order are the same as with the last order. Just delivered UP 3776 awaits movement at Council Bluffs, IA on 25 October 1980 to the Omaha Shops for set-up and application of all decals and stencilling.

Design 80's locomotive painting and lettering appears on the last of the current SD40-2 order . . . as on UP 3779 at Council Bluffs, IA on 19 November 1980. The 20-inch road numbers on the car body are moved forward to under the cab window. The 24-inch Union Pacific shield, which was under the cab window, is moved forward and centered on the front of the short hood.

The large numbers will be more easily "read" by video camera installations in the system's yard. Further testing with decal materials and black edging combinations will solidify the program which, once settled, will become standard markings.

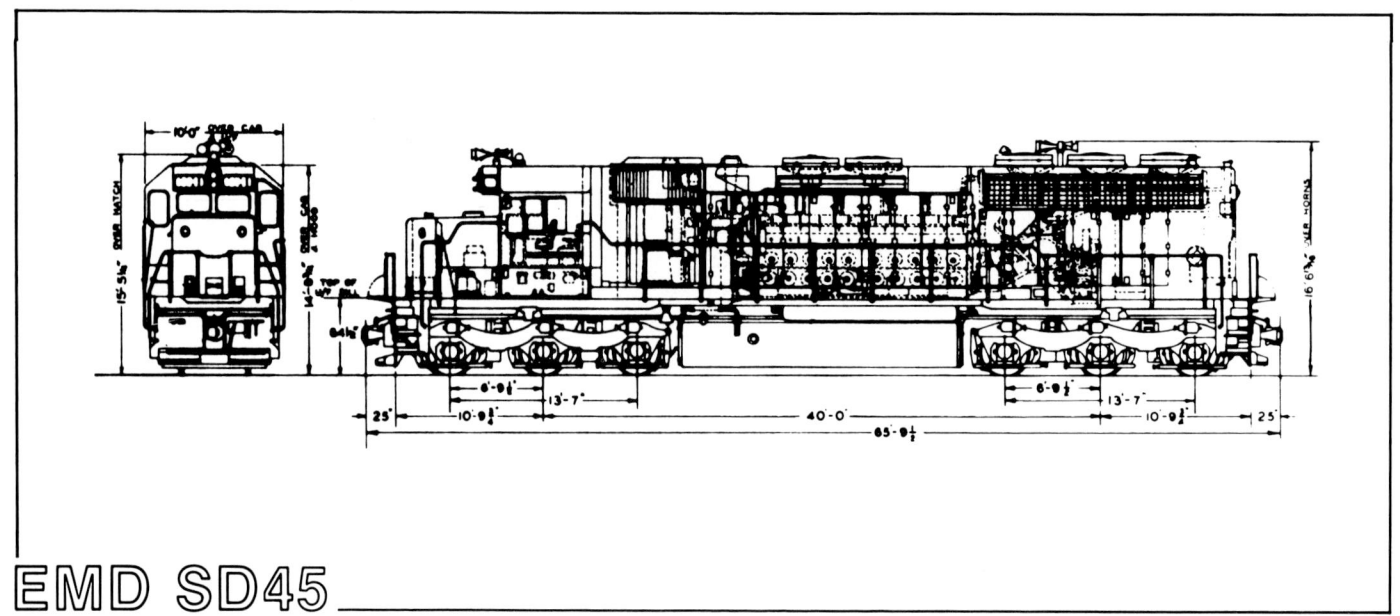

EMD SD45

GENERAL DATA

A.A.R. DESIGNATION	C-C
GEAR RATIO	62/15
WEIGHT LOADED	393,300 LBS.
LIGHT WEIGHT	353,015 LBS. APPROX.
MAXIMUM CURVATURE	17° WITH TRAIN
MAXIMUM CURVATURE	22° AS SINGLE UNIT
MAXIMUM SPEED	65 M.P.H.
MINIMUM CONT. SPEED	11 M.P.H.

DIESEL ENGINE

MODEL	20-645-E3
TURBOCHARGER	EQUIPPED
SPARK ARRESTER	NOT REQUIRED
AIR FILTER, BASIC:	
CARBODY	NOT EQUIPPED
PRIMARY	DYNAVANE
ENGINE	AAF BAG
FUEL HEATER	KELTY

ELECTRICAL

MULTIPLE UNIT RECEPTACLES	12-21 & 27 PT
MAIN GENERATOR	AR-10
ALTERNATOR	D-14
TRACTION MOTORS, TYPE	D-17
NUMBER OF TRACTION MOTORS	6
DYNAMIC BRAKES	POTENTIAL CONTROL
BATTERIES	64 V. 426 AMP. HRS.
HEADLIGHTS	TWIN SEALED BEAMS 200W EA.
AUXILIARY GENERATOR	10 KW
COOLING FANS	(3) 48" 9-BLADE
CAB SIGNALS	US&S TYPE 'EL'
ROTATING WARNING LIGHTS	EQUIPPED

*EXTENDED RANGE

SUPPLIES

FUEL	4000 GALS.
LUBE OIL	466 GALS.
COOLING WATER	288 GALS.
SAND	56 CU. FT.

ELECTRO-MOTIVE'S SD45 ROSTER

UNIT	BUILDER DATE	BUILDER NUMBER	REMARKS	UNIT	BUILDER DATE	BUILDER NUMBER	REMARKS
3600	March 1968	33409	Renumbered UP 50, 22 September 1978.	3624	March 1968	33433	Renumbered UP 24, 10 October 1978.
3601	March 1968	33410	Renumbered UP 1, 14 November 1978.	3625	March 1968	33434	Renumbered UP 25, 16 November 1978.
3602	March 1968	33411	Renumbered UP 2, 11 October 1978.	3626	April 1968	33435	Renumbered UP 26, 7 October 1978.
3603	March 1978	33412	Renumbered UP 3, 20 October 1978.	3627	March 1968	33436	Renumbered UP 27, 7 November 1978.
3604	March 1978	33413	Renumbered UP 4, 18 October 1978.	3628	March 1968	33437	Renumbered UP 28, 31 December 1978.
3605	April 1968	33414	Renumbered UP 5, 24 October 1978.	3629	March 1968	33438	Renumbered UP 29, 17 October 1978.
3606	April 1968	33415	Renumbered UP 6, 6 November 1978.	3630	March 1968	33439	Renumbered UP 30, 2 December 1978.
3607	April 1968	33416	Renumbered UP 7, 5 October 1978.	3631	March 1968	33440	Renumbered UP 31, 17 November 1978.
3608	April 1968	33417	Renumbered UP 8, 22 October 1978.	3632	March 1968	33441	Renumbered UP 32, 30 October 1978.
3609	April 1968	33418	Renumbered UP 9, 23 September 1978.	3633	March 1968	33442	Renumbered UP 33, 4 October 1978.
3610	April 1968	33419	Renumbered UP 10, 6 October 1978.	3634	March 1968	33443	Renumbered UP 34, 17 November 1978.
3611	April 1968	33420	Renumbered UP 11, 3 November 1978.	3635	March 1968	33444	Renumbered UP 35, 26 November 1978.
3612	April 1968	33421	Renumbered UP 12, 4 November 1978.	3636	March 1968	33445	Renumbered UP 36, 28 November 1978.
3613	April 1968	33422	Renumbered UP 13, 2 October 1978.	3637	March 1968	33446	Renumbered UP 37, 9 October 1978.
3614	April 1968	33423	Renumbered UP 14, 4 December 1978.	3638	March 1968	33447	Renumbered UP 38, 24 March 1979.
3615	April 1968	33424	Renumbered UP 15, 28 October 1978.	3639	March 1968	33448	Renumbered UP 39, 17 April 1979.
3616	April 1968	33425	Renumbered UP 16, 30 November 1978.	3640	March 1968	34016	Renumbered UP 40, 16 April 1979.
3617	April 1968	33426	Renumbered UP 17, 23 October 1978.	3641	March 1969	34017	Renumbered UP 41, 13 December 1978.
3618	April 1968	33427	Renumbered UP 18, 19 December 1978.	3642	March 1968	34018	Renumbered UP 42, 13 April 1979.
3619	April 1968	33428	Renumbered UP 19, 12 December 1978.	3643	March 1968	34019	Renumbered UP 43, 17 April 1979.
3620	April 1968	33429	Renumbered UP 20, 15 November 1978.	3644	March 1968	34020	Renumbered UP 44, 15 March 1979.
3621	April 1968	33430	Renumbered UP 21, 21 September 1978.	3645	March 1968	34021	Renumbered UP 45, 17 March 1979.
3622	April 1968	33431	Renumbered UP 22, 14 December 1978.	3646	March 1968	34022	Renumbered UP 46, 12 March 1979.
3623	April 1968	33432	Renumbered UP 23, 16 December 1978.	3647	March 1968	34023	Renumbered UP 47, 19 March 1979.
				3648	April 1968	34024	Renumbered UP 48, 15 March 1979.
				3649	April 1968	34025	Renumbered UP 49, 18 March 1979.

NOTES:
[1] Renumbered UP 1, 2 and 50 were the third locomotive assignments to these numbers.
[2] Renumbered UP 3 through 49 were the second locomotive assignment to these numbers.

Once a stomping grounds for SD45's, the Provo, UT yard hosts two sets of SD45's on 5 May 1976. The even-numbered units (3600-3636) are equipped as control RCS units, while the odd-numbered (3601-3635) are equipped as remote RCS units; UP 3638-3649 are not so equipped. These units have been renumbered into the "spot-series" . . . 1 through 50, in late 1978 through early 1979.

Air test complete and crew on board . . . UP 3604 awaits the clearing signal "bug" to pull out on the mainline and head westward at Council Bluffs, IA on 28 December 1977. The flared radiators serve as the major spotting feature for this model; however, closer inspection will disclose a longer engine hood with three large fans mounted atop.

Even numbered SD45's (3600-3636) were set-up as control RCS units, accounting for the "ping-pong" table over the cab . . . the antenna system mounted on a ground plane plate.

Awaiting call at Green River, WY, 30 August 1977, UP 3617 shows off its C-Type truck assembly.

Extra 3606 East pulls into Green River, WY on 31 August 1977. The large fuel tank holds 4000 gallons.

Pointing west, UP 3601 puts in a rare appearance on the eastern end of the system. These units are almost "captive" to the west, operating out of the Salt Lake City area. Equipped with RCS, the odd-numbered units (3601-3635) operate as the remote RCS units in mid-train location. The heavy ore movements from Wyoming are frequently handled by SD45 control units on the head end and remote units spliced into the middle.

These units were renumbered in the Fall of 1978, so as to clear the way for sequential numbering of the swelling SD40-2 ranks. UP 3601 became UP 1. The first three digits were dropped and the unit picked up the last number as it entered the "Spot"-Class. In the case of UP 3600, it went from the front of the SD45 roster to the back . . . becoming UP 50 (the exception to the rule).

More complete SD45 coverage is presented in the renumbered "Spot"-Class section.

Under menacing winter skies, UP 3642 awaits signal clearance to back on to its train at Council Bluffs, IA on 6 March 1977. It will pick-up a C&NW unit coal train just delivered to the Union Pacific and head it out westward . . . probably cutting off at North Platte, NE.

It still carries the "first generation" slogan declaring "Dependable Transportation" under the cab windows. When renumbered, most received a new paint job and the larger lettering and number scheme using the shield under the window.

Sporting the intermediate lettering and painting scheme of the mid-1970's identified by the slogan "We Can Handle It," UP 3644 shows off the engineer's side of the cab at Provo, UT on 5 May 1976.

UP 3638 through 3649 were not equipped with RCS equipment, thus the clean top of the cab . . . with only the "firecracker" VHF antenna and rotating beacon breaking the outline. On the RCS-equipped units, the radio antenna is mounted at the very rear of the roof, just aft of the sand box filler lid.

The big 6-wheel, flexicoil trucks are equipped with clasp brakes actuated by the high-mounted cylinders. The brake system uses the 26L schedule with automatic retainer control.

Moving east through Yermo, CA on 17 February 1979 with the *BNSL,* UP 3647 begins to accelerate on the California First Subdivision as it clears the yard limits. While Daggett is the west gateway to using Santa Fe trackage into the Los Angeles area . . . some 5 miles west of Yermo, clearances to operate on the AT&SF are given at Yermo.

This is one of the non-RCS control equipped units. The most recent standard lettering and numbering scheme is applied using the road numbers under the cab (this scheme was modified to eliminate the cab road numbers in 1980).

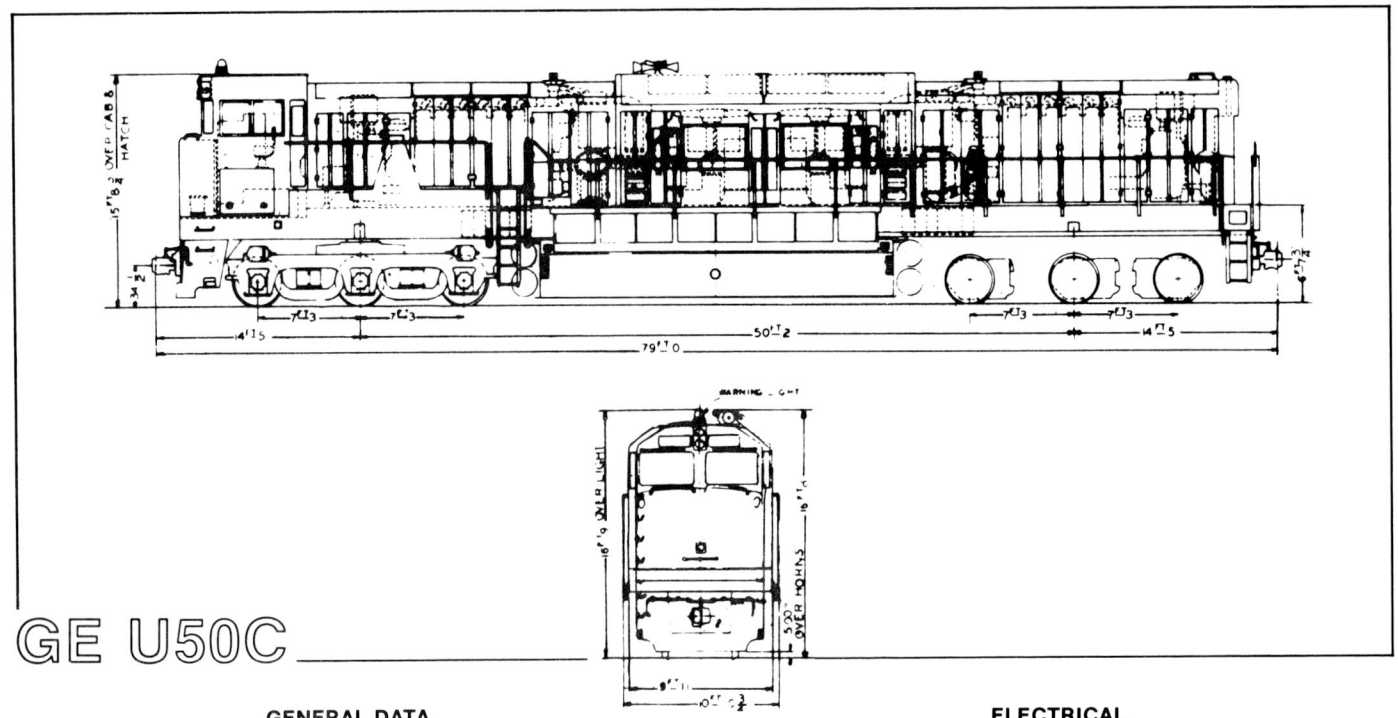

GE U50C

GENERAL DATA
A.A.R. DESIGNATION	C-C
GEAR RATIO	79/24
WEIGHT LOADED	442,660 LBS.
LIGHT WEIGHT	388,605 LBS. APPROX.
MAXIMUM CURVATURE	16° WITH TRAIN
MAXIMUM CURVATURE	19.1° AS SINGLE UNIT
MAXIMUM SPEED	85 M.P.H.
MINIMUM CONT. SPEED	14.7 M.P.H.

SUPPLIES
FUEL	6000 GALS.
LUBE OIL	300 GALS.
COOLING WATER	350 GALS.
SAND	57 CU. FT.

DIESEL ENGINE
MODEL	7FDL12
TURBOCHARGER	EQUIPPED
SPARK ARRESTER	NOT REQUIRED
AIR FILTER, BASIC:	
CARBODY	NOT EQUIPPED
PRIMARY	G.E. VORTEX
ENGINE	DYNACELL
FUEL HEATER	KELTY

BRAKES
SCHEDULE	26L W/PORTOPACK
AIR COMPRESSOR	SEE NOTE
BRAKE SHOES	CAST IRON
SAFETY CONTROL	FOOT PEDAL

NOTES:
AIR COMPRESSOR:
5000-5019	(2) 3CWDL
5020-5033	(2) WBO
5034-5039	(1) WBO + (1) WXO

ELECTRICAL
MULTIPLE UNIT RECEPTACLES	27 PT
MAIN GENERATOR	5-GTA11-A2
ALTERNATOR	NOT EQUIPPED
TRACTION MOTORS, TYPE	752-E8
NUMBER OF TRACTION MOTORS	6
DYNAMIC BRAKES	POTENTIAL CONTROL*
BATTERIES	64V. 426 AMP. HRS.
HEADLIGHTS	TWIN SEALED BEAMS 200W. EA.
AUXILIARY GENERATOR	5GY27HIR
COOLING FANS	MECHANICAL
CAB SIGNALS	US&S TYPE 'EL'
ROTATING WARNING LIGHTS	EQUIPPED
R.C.S.	NOT EQUIPPED

*EXTENDED RANGE

RUNNING GEAR
DRAFT GEAR	M-380A
COUPLER	TYPE 'E'
JOURNALS	7" TIMKEN OR SKF BRGS.
WHEELS	40" DIA.
TRUCKS	6 WHL., EQUALIZER, CLASP BRKS., HIGH CYLS.

MISCELLANEOUS
WHISTLE	LESLIE S-5 TRF
TOILET	EQUIPPED
FIRE EXTINGUISHERS	(5) 30 LB. ANSUL
WATER COOLER	EQUIPPED
FUEL FILLER	BUCKEYE
SPEED RECORDER	CP

GENERAL ELECTRIC'S U50C ROSTER

UNIT	BUILDER DATE	BUILDER NUMBER	UNIT	BUILDER DATE	BUILDER NUMBER	UNIT	BUILDER DATE	BUILDER NUMBER
5000[2]	November 1969	37139	5014[2]	December 1970	37153	5028[3]	July 1971	37281
5001[2]	October 1969	37140	5015[2]	December 1970	37154	5029[3]	July 1971	37282
5002[1]	March 1970	37141	5016[1]	December 1970	37155	5030[3]	August 1971	37283
5003[2]	March 1970	37142	5017[3]	January 1971	37156	5031[3]	August 1971	37284
5004[2]	March 1970	37143	5018[3]	January 1971	37157	5032[3]	August 1971	37285
5005[4]	April 1970	37144	5019[3]	February 1971	37158	5033[3]	September 1971	37286
5006[1]	April 1970	37145	5020[3]	May 1971	37273	5034[3]	September 1971	37287
5007[2]	May 1970	37146	5021[3]	May 1971	37274	5035[3]	September 1971	37288
5008[2]	May 1970	37147	5022[3]	May 1971	37275	5036[3]	October 1971	37289
5009[1]	May 1970	37148	5023[3]	June 1971	37276	5037[3]	October 1971	37290
5010[1]	May 1970	37149	5024[3]	June 1971	37277	5038[3]	November 1971	37291
5011[1]	May 1970	37150	5025[3]	June 1971	37278	5039[3]	November 1971	37292
5012[1]	November 1970	37151	5026[3]	June 1971	37279			
5013[1]	December 1970	37152	5027[3]	July 1971	37280			

[1] Sold 5/77 to Erman Corporation, Turner, KS.
[2] Sold 8/77 to Erman Corporation, Turner, KS.
[3] Sold 6/78 to Erman Corporation, Turner, KS.
[4] Scrapped 8/77 at Omaha Shops.

A pair of giant-sized General Electric U50C's angles through the turnouts as they gain mainline 4 and proceeds towards the Council Bluffs yards on 31 May 1976. Shortly after, all the U50's were sidelined, although several saw service as stand-by power plants during the 1977-78 eastern coal strikes.

Sporting a brand-new paint job, UP 5006 idles in front of the old diesel house at Council Bluffs, IA on 28 April 1975. The front door on the face of the cab was a safety modification applied by Union Pacific after the first units were delivered.

The unit embodied the basic engineering established with the earlier U50 model but faced the two engines so that a common radiator area could be built-in at mid-center. Equipped with two FDL-12 diesel engines, the unit turns out 5000 horsepower.

Riding on C-Type truck assemblies traded in from Union Pacific's Gas Electric Turbine Locomotives (GETL's), the 5000-Class U50C's are quickly identifiable over the sister U50D's which ride on pairs of 4-wheel trucks connected by a span bolster (B+B–B+B wheel arrangement).

The high, pug-nosed cab also serves to identify both U50 versions, as does the giant-sized fuel tank holding 5000 gallons. In fact, everything about these General Electric units is BIG!

UP 5013 awaits its westbound crew at Council Bluffs, IA on 12 August 1975. In their last years of service, they remained close to heavy support shops in the Kansas City, KS-North Platte, NE-Council Bluffs, IA triangle. Electric problems plagued both versions, which was a major contributor to their being sidelined about seven years after manufacture.

Ready for action, UP 5018 glistens in the bright sun at Council Bluffs, IA on 5 June 1975. Many westbound freights were handled by single units; however, in the later years a protection unit was added, in case of engine failure. This proved to be a serious problem too... having the equivalent of two units mounted on a single chassis, if one engine failed one basically lost two locomotives—not a good trade-off! A number of engineering changes were tried over the course of seven years to remedy the electrical and mechanical problems... with little success.

The engineer's side of the unit is almost a flip-flop of the opposite side, except for the mounting grab-irons used by the hostlers to service the unit. The large sanding boxes are located over each truck assembly. The unit, being so big, presents no easy way to mount/dismount from the unit except via the ladders located aft of the truck assemblies. There is the emergency exit door let into the face of the unit. It appears this unit has had some turbocharger problems, evidenced by the scorched locker box wall. Council Bluffs, IA, 5 June 1975.

The short, pug-nosed face of the U50 models places the front-end crew high above the rails . . . a super vantage location for train handling. The front emergency door provides an escape route from the crew deck through the toilet/radio compartment to the front. Exit doors are located on the back of the cab on either side for the fireman and engineer to use. Only two U50C's were involved in serious front-end accidents, both proving the high cab design as a major safety item.

EDITOR'S NOTE: For a more detailed presentation on the two U50 versions, refer to *ROARING U50's . . . Union Pacific's Twin Diesels* by Reverend Harold Keekley, available from George R. Cockle & Associates, Box 1224-DTS, Omaha, NE 68101.

Retired after seven years of fleet service, the U50C's led one of the shortest lives of any mainline road units. Plagued with mechanical and electrical problems, the units presented design challenges to both General Electric and Union Pacific mechanical engineers. After attempting several major changes in rerouting primary wiring, replacing aluminum wiring with copper wiring, using heat sensors to react to high wire temperatures . . . the units were sidelined. All U50C's were sold, in several purchases, to Erman Corporation, Turner, KS. Long lines of units edge their scrap yards, as seen in this 1 July 1978 view.

173

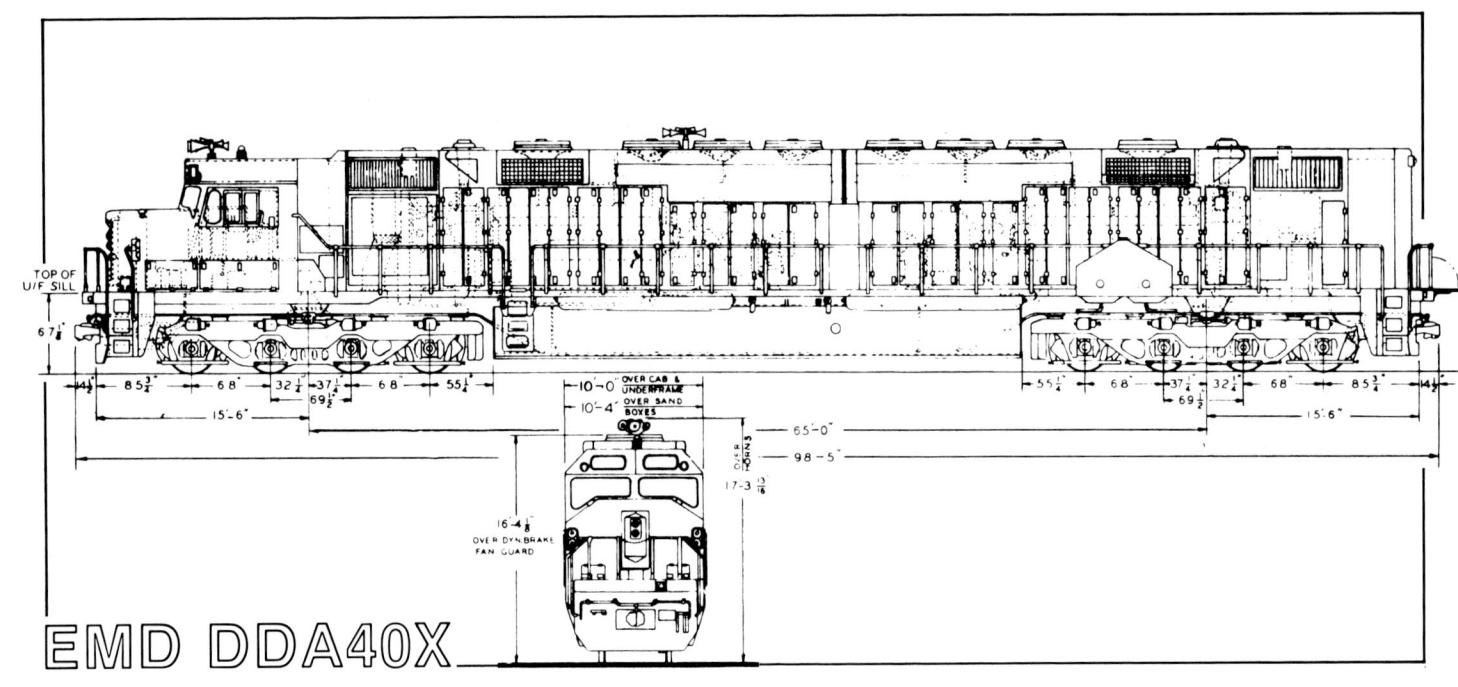

EMD DDA40X

GENERAL DATA

A.A.R. DESIGNATION	D-D
GEAR RATIO	59/18
WEIGHT LOADED (AVERAGE)	545,432 LBS.
LIGHT WEIGHT	475,630 LBS. APPROX.
MAXIMUM CURVATURE	16° WITH TRAIN
MAXIMUM CURVATURE	19.4° AS SINGLE UNIT
MAXIMUM SPEED	80 M.P.H.
MINIMUM CONT. SPEED	11 M.P.H.
CENTER OF GRAVITY	66½" ABOVE RAIL (IN WORKING ORDER)

SUPPLIES

FUEL	8200 GALS.
LUBE OIL	395 GALS.
COOLING WATER	300 GALS.
SAND	53 CU. FT.

DIESEL ENGINE

MODEL	(2) 16-645 E3A
TURBOCHARGER	EQUIPPED
SPARK ARRESTER	NOT REQUIRED
AIR FILTER, BASIC:	
CARBODY	NOT EQUIPPED
PRIMARY	DYNAVANE
ENGINE	AAF BAG
FUEL HEATER	FARR FILTER-HEATER

BRAKES

SCHEDULE	26 L WITH PORTOPACK J-1 RELAY (100%)
AIR COMPRESSOR	(2) WBO
BRAKE SHOES	HI PHOS. CAST IRON
SAFETY CONTROL	FOOT PEDAL

ELECTRICAL

MULTIPLE UNIT RECEPTACLES	27 PT
MAIN GENERATOR	(2) AR12
ALTERNATOR	(2) D14
TRACTION MOTORS, TYPE	D-77X
NUMBER OF TRACTION MOTORS	8
DYNAMIC BRAKES	POTENTIAL CONTROL*
BATTERIES	64 VOLTS 426 AMP. HRS.
HEADLIGHTS	TWIN SEALED BEAM 200W EA.
AUXILIARY GENERATOR	18 KW. 74 V.
COOLING FANS	(3) 48" 9-BLADE
CAB SIGNALS	US&S TYPE 'EL'
ROTATING WARNING LIGHT	EQUIPPED
R.C.S.	NOT EQUIPPED

*EXTENDED RANGE

RUNNING GEAR

DRAFT GEAR	NC-391
COUPLER	TYPE 'E'
JOURNALS	6⅞" x 12" HYATT R.B.
WHEELS	40" DIA.
TRUCKS	8 WHL., FLEXICOIL, CLASP BRKS.

MISCELLANEOUS

WHISTLE	LESLIE S-5 TRF
TOILET	INCINOLET TOILET
FIRE EXTINGUISHERS	(5) 30 LB. ANSUL
WATER COOLER	PORTACOOL AIR REFRIG.
FUEL FILLER	BUCKEYE
SPEED RECORDER	C.P.

ELECTROMOTIVE'S DDA40X ROSTER

UNIT	BUILDER DATE	BUILDER NUMBER	UNIT	BUILDER DATE	BUILDER NUMBER	UNIT	BUILDER DATE	BUILDER NUMBER
6900	April 1969	34526	6917	November 1969	34543	6933	December 1970	35507
6901	August 1969	34527	6918	November 1969	34544	6934	December 1970	35508
6902	July 1969	34528	6919	November 1969	34545	6935	January 1971	35509
6904	August 1969	34530	6920	December 1969	34546	6936	January 1971	35510
6905	August 1969	34531	6921[1]	December 1969	34547	6937	January 1971	35511
6906	August 1969	34532	6922	December 1969	34548	6938	June 1971	35512
6907	August 1969	34533	6923	December 1969	34549	6939	June 1971	35513
6908	August 1969	34534	6924	December 1969	34550	6940	June 1971	35514
6909	September 1969	34535	6925	June 1970	34599	6941	July 1971	35515
6910	September 1969	34536	6926	June 1970	35500	6942	July 1971	35516
6911	September 1969	34537	6927	June 1970	35501	6943	August 1971	35517
6912	October 1969	34538	6928	July 1970	35502	6944	August 1971	35518
6913	October 1969	34539	6929	August 1970	35503	6945	August 1971	35519
6914	October 1969	34540	6930	August 1970	35504	6946	September 1971	35520
6915	October 1969	34541	6931	September 1970	35505			
6916	November 1969	34542	6932	December 1970	35506			

[1] Retired. Accident 28 August 1978, Point of Rocks, WY. Scrapped 28 December 1978 Salt Lake City, UT. Sold 12/78 to Durbano Metal Company, Ogden, UT.

Getting its face washed at North Platte diesel facilities is "Centennial" UP 6907. Part of the standard summer servicing at this large Nebraska rail center is running the units through the wash racks. The harsh winter weather precludes much of this type servicing, due to potential "freeze-ups."—*Photo by James W. Watson.*

The DDA40X "Centennial" shows off its many faces at Council Bluffs, IA. The painting and lettering standards have never been changed for this unit, except for the dropping of *railroad* from the shield in 1970. The class unit, UP 6900, shows off its 98' 5" length.

The front sanding fillers are top mounted on either side of the short hood, while the rear sand supplies are held in boxes mounted on the walkway above the rear trucks on both sides... totalling 53 cubic feet.

The large "D" or 6-axle truck measures 272-inches or 22.6 feet! The 40-inch wheels and clasp brake arrangement are clearly visible on UP 6911's freshly painted front truck assembly.

Rear truck detail study of the 4-axle "D" truck on 6920. The large sanding box is mounted on the walkway above the truck assembly. Council Bluffs, IA, 9 March 1979.

Front view of 6930 shows the forwarded mounted horn installation. Council Bluffs, IA, 1 July 1980.

Two "Centennials" sport air raid sirens . . . 6918 and this installation atop 6924. Council Bluffs, IA, 15 May 1980.

Rear details of 6922. Council Bluffs, IA, 10 May 1978.

Standing in the servicing area at Portland, OR in August 1979 is 6941. The "Centennial" roams the system handling whatever assignment given with ease. This class locomotive is as synonymous with Union Pacific as the shield!—*Photo by Vic Reyna.*

For a more detailed presentation on the DDA40X "Centennial," an 88 page book . . . CENTENNIALS IN ACTION . . . is available, published by Overland Models, Inc.—*Editor.*

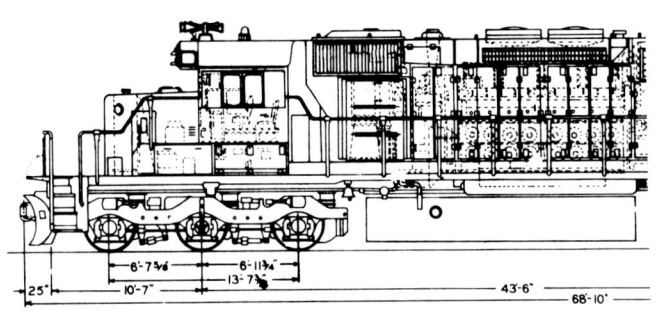
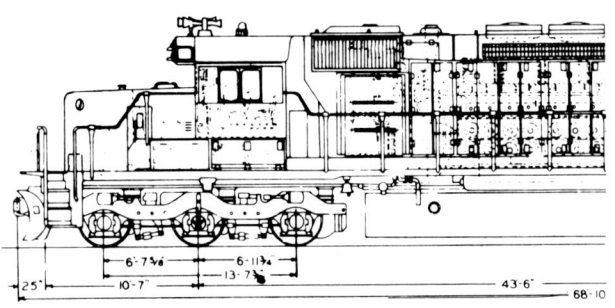

THE GENERAL DATA HAS BEEN OMITTED.

EMD SD40-2H / EMD SD40-2M

ELECTRO-MOTIVE'S SD40-2 ROSTER

UNIT	BUILDER DATE	BUILDER NUMBER	REMARKS	UNIT	BUILDER DATE	BUILDER NUMBER	REMARKS
8000	May 1973	72684-38	Originally UP 3240, renumbered 2/76. Renumbered UP 3240, 6/80.	8018	June 1974	73661-16	Originally UP 3258, renumbered 4/76.
8001	May 1973	72684-39	Originally UP 3241, renumbered 3/76.	8019	June 1974	73661-17	Originally UP 3259, renumbered 6/76.
8002	May 1973	72674-40	Originally UP 3242, renumbered 4/76.	8020	June 1974	73661-18	Originally UP 3260, renumbered 6/76.
8003	June 1974	73661-1	Originally UP 3243, renumbered 5/76.	8021	June 1974	73661-19	Originally UP 3261, renumbered 4/76. Renumbered UP 3261, 6/80.
8004	June 1974	73661-2	Originally UP 3244, renumbered 5/76.	8022	June 1974	73661-20	Originally UP 3262, renumbered 5/76.
8005	June 1974	73661-3	Originally UP 3245, renumbered 7/76.	8023	June 1974	73661-21	Originally UP 3263, renumbered 6/76.
8006	June 1974	73661-4	Originally UP 3246, renumbered 6/76.	8024	June 1974	73661-22	Originally UP 3264, renumbered 4/76.
8007	June 1974	73661-5	Originally UP 3247, renumbered 3/76.	8025	June 1974	73661-23	Originally UP 3265, renumbered 5/76.
8008	June 1974	73661-6	Originally UP 3248, renumbered 6/76.	8026	June 1974	73661-24	Originally UP 3266, renumbered 4/76.
8009	June 1974	73661-7	Originally UP 3249, renumbered 5/76.	8027	June 1974	73661-25	Originally UP 3267, renumbered 6/76.
8010	June 1974	73661-8	Originally UP 3250, renumbered 5/76.	8028	June 1974	73661-26	Originally UP 3268, renumbered 3/76.
8011	June 1974	73661-9	Originally UP 3251, renumbered 6/76.	8029	June 1974	73661-27	Originally UP 3269, renumbered 5/76.
8012	June 1974	73661-10	Originally UP 3252, renumbered 4/76.	8030	June 1974	73661-28	Originally UP 3270, renumbered 7/76.
8013	June 1974	73661-11	Originally UP 3253, renumbered 7/76.	8031	July 1974	73661-29	Originally UP 3271, renumbered 6/76.
8014	June 1974	73661-12	Originally UP 3254, renumbered 7/76.	8032	July 1974	73661-30	Originally UP 3272, renumbered 6/76.
8015	June 1974	73661-13	Originally UP 3255, renumbered 5/76.	8033	July 1974	73661-31	Originally UP 3273, renumbered 6/76.
8016	June 1974	73661-14	Originally UP 3256, renumbered 5/76.	8034	July 1974	73661-32	Originally UP 3274, renumbered 7/76.
8017	June 1974	73661-15	Originally UP 3257, renumbered 4/76. Renumbered UP 3257, 7/80.				

UNIT	BUILDER DATE	BUILDER NUMBER	UNIT	BUILDER DATE	BUILDER NUMBER	UNIT	BUILDER DATE	BUILDER NUMBER
8035[1]	July 1976	767021-1	8057	September 1976	767021-23	8079	July 1979	786218-15
8036[2]	July 1976	767021-2	8058	September 1976	767021-24	8080:2	July 1979	786218-16
8037	July 1976	767021-3	8059[6]	September 1976	767021-25	8081	August 1979	786218-17
8038	July 1976	767021-4	8060[7]	September 1976	767021-26	8082	August 1979	786218-18
8039	July 1976	767021-5	8061	September 1976	767021-27	8083	August 1979	786218-19
8040	July 1976	767021-6	8062	September 1976	767021-28	8084	August 1979	786218-20
8041	July 1976	767021-7	8063	September 1976	767021-29	8085	August 1979	786218-21
8042[3]	July 1976	767021-8	8064	September 1976	767021-30	8086	August 1979	786218-22
8043[4]	July 1976	767021-9	8065	May 1977	776013-1	8087	August 1979	786218-23
8044	July 1976	767021-10	8066	May 1977	776013-2	8088	August 1979	786218-24
8045	August 1976	767021-11	8067	May 1977	776012-3	8089	August 1979	786218-25
8046	August 1976	767021-12	8068	May 1977	776012-4	8090	August 1979	786218-26
8047	August 1976	767021-13	8069	May 1977	776013-5	8091	August 1979	786218-27
8048	August 1976	767021-14	8070	May 1977	776013-6	8092	August 1979	786218-28
8049[5]	August 1976	767021-15	8071	May 1977	776013-7	8093	August 1979	786218-29
8050	August 1976	767021-16	8072	May 1977	776013-8	8094	August 1979	786218-30
8051	August 1976	767021-17	8073	May 1977	776013-9	8095	August 1979	786218-31
8052	August 1976	767021-18	8074	May 1977	776013-10	8096	August 1979	786218-32
8053	August 1976	767021-19	8075	July 1979	786218-11	8097	August 1979	786218-33
8054	August 1976	767021-20	8076	July 1979	786218-12	8098	August 1979	786218-34
8055	September 1976	767021-21	8077	July 1979	786218-13	8099	August 1979	786218-35
8056	September 1976	767021-22	8078	July 1979	786218-14			

[1]Renumbered UP 3305, 6/80.
[2]Renumbered UP 3306, 6/80.
[3]Renumbered UP 3312, 7/80.
[4]Renumbered UP 3313, 6/80.
[5]Renumbered UP 3319, 7/80.
[6]Renumbered UP 3329, 6/80.
[7]Renumbered UP 3330, 6/80.

NOTES:

A—Instructions were issued 6/80 to change the gear ratio from 59/18 to 62/15 and exchange the PF18 module for a PF17 module on units 8000-8074. As modifications are accomplished, the unit will be renumbered back into its original block of road numbers, as follows: 8000-8034 to 3240-3274; 8035-8064 to 3305-3334; 8065-8074 to 3400-3409. This program was suspended 21 Aug. 1980.
B—UP 8000-8034 were modified by Union Pacific shops for high-speed operations and are identified as SD40-2H's by Union Pacific.
C—UP 8035-3099 were constructed by EMD for high-speed operations and are identified as SD40-2M's by Union Pacific.
D—UP 8000-8002 are the standard short low nose unit; UP 8003-8099 have the extended low nose.

The *LAD* rolls east through Afton Canyon, some 25 miles east of Barstow, CA in May 1977. A rain storm has just past through the usually dry Mojave desert. The piggyback train's power includes three "fast-forties," a C&NW SD40-2 and a DDA40X "Centennial."—*Photo by Jim Nelson.*

"FAST FORTIES"

When Union Pacific decided to regear a group of SD40-2's to high speed performance standards, it programmed the newest thirty-five units for the conversion. Three standard short hood units from the last of the 1973 order and thirty-two of the extended short hood units from the 1974 order . . . all running in numerical sequence from 3240 through 3274 . . . were selected. The changing-out of regeared wheel-sets along with associated speed performance control modules were accomplished by the company shops. Once accomplished, these units were identified as SD40-2H's and renumbered into the 8000-Class as 8000-8034 . . . so as to differentiate between the standard 65-mph SD40-2 and this new 80-mph classification.

The first three regeared "fast forties" have standard short hoods and were renumbered from 3240-3242 to 8000-8002 in early 1976. While originally operating in sets handling "hot trains," they ended split up spending lots of time spliced between a pair of DDA40X "Centennials" hauling premium freight. A few were used to protect Amtrak's *San Francisco Zephyr* in 1980. These company converted SD40-2's . . . identified as "H-models" . . . were changed over between January and July 1976. UP 8000 has already been changed back to a standard SD40-2 and renumbered 3240, its original road number, June 1980. Shown on the west departure tracks at Council Bluffs, IA, 28 December 1977.

EMD SD40-2H

Awaiting assignment at Council Bluffs, IA, the weather is bitter cold on New Years Day, 1978. This overhead view shows the long "snoot" nose off to best advantage. Green anti-glare, non-skid paint is applied to the top of the low hood . . . access is via the step-irons on the engineer's side of the hood.

This cab and front truck study shows the last of the ratchet-type hand brake installations on Union Pacific SD40-2's. Due to severe winter weather that produces bone-chilling cold temperatures and snow-packed front-ends, the brake wheel provides for easier handling with gloves and can be cleared of snow and ice more readily. The "firecracker-styled" antenna has since been moved to the right which allows remounting the horns forward above the headlights. These units have the "Touchstone" fuel-saver device installed which permits the unit's operation to be controlled by the engineer when in multiple-consist lash-ups . . . to "pull" or reduction to "idle." Council Bluffs, IA, 18 June 1977.

The rear truck and platform area length can be studied in this view taken at Council Bluffs, IA, 9 January 1978. The horns have been moved forward to a top-center position on the cab in accordance with current operating practices. The gear ratio of these high-speed units is 59:18 with a maximum speed of 80-mph.

A fast running east-bound merchandiser pulls through the Omaha "Union Station" area . . . now converted in a TOFC/COFC "Pig Yard" . . . as it heads toward the Missouri River bridge and its destination—Council Bluffs, IA on a cold 10 December 1977. The "snoot" nose houses the crew toilet and has a large forward compartment for radios and other special electronic equipment.

EMD SD40-2M

UP 8035 was the first "pure" SD40-2M, delivered as a "fast-forty" in July 1976. Equipped with the long "snoot" short hood, these units handle all the "hot-shot" fast freight... frequently spliced between two DDA40X "Centennials." This unit has been renumbered back to its reserved sequential 3000-Class position as UP 3305 in June 1980. Shown at Council Bluffs, IA, 1 January 1978.

UP 8047 is another SD40-2M that has since been returned to the 3000-Class as UP 3317. The "snoot" nose is quite obvious. At the diesel servicing docks at Council Bluffs, IA, 28 December 1977.

The rear view shows the construction features of later built SD40-2's... noted for the long "back porch." This unit has since been renumbered back to UP 3319 on 10 July 1980. Council Bluffs, IA, 1 January 1978.

Next to the last unit ordered under builder number block 767021 of 1976, it shows off the engineer's side of the cab. These were designated SD40-2M locomotives, indicating that EMD had delivered them as high-speed units. Council Bluffs, IA, 8 May 1977.

The 1977 order for SD40-2M's called for 10 units . . . UP 8065-8074. These were delivered in May. Yet to be "set-up" is newly delivered UP 8067 at Council Bluffs, IA, 28 May 1977.

The cab and front truck view shows sister UP 8068 as a "set-up" unit at Council Bluffs, IA, 1 January 1978.

Another newly delivered 1977 unit, UP 8071 points its long "snoot" forward. The pilot plow is standard on all Union Pacific road units. Council Bluffs, IA, 26 May 1977.

The large "back porch" is one of the major spotting features of the EMD SD40-2 series locomotives. The safety appliance and grab-iron installations are clearly evident in this rear view. Council Bluffs, IA, 1 June 1977.

183

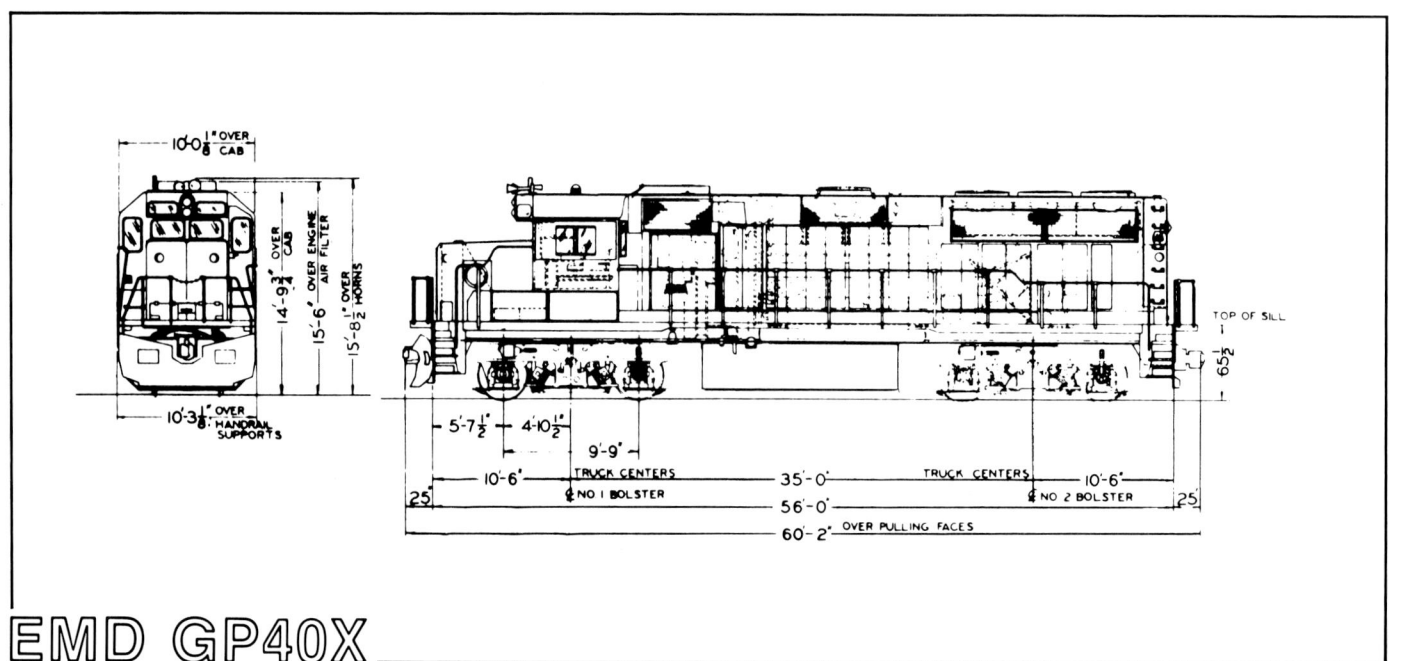

EMD GP40X

GENERAL DATA

A.A.R. DESIGNATION	B-B
GEAR RATIO	SEE NOTE
WEIGHT LOADED	274,000 LBS.
LIGHT WEIGHT	237,579 LBS. APPROX.
MAXIMUM CURVATURE	21° WITH TRAIN
MAXIMUM CURVATURE	42° AS SINGLE UNIT
MAXIMUM SPEED	80 M.P.H.
MINIMUM CONT. SPEED	11 M.P.H.
CENTER OF GRAVITY	63.4" ABOVE RAIL (IN WORKING ORDER)

NOTES:
UNITS 9000-9002 . . . . GEAR RATIO 66/20 WITH TRACTION MOTOR TYPE D-87X
UNITS 9003-9005 . . . . GEAR RATIO 59/18 WITH TRACTION MOTOR TYPE D-87Y

SUPPLIES

FUEL	3600 GALS.
LUBE OIL	396 GALS.
COOLING WATER	276 GALS.
SAND	56 CU. FT.

DIESEL ENGINE

MODEL	16-645-F3
TURBOCHARGER	EQUIPPED
SPARK ARRESTER	NOT REQUIRED
AIR FILTER, BASIC:	
CARBODY	NOT EQUIPPED
PRIMARY	DYNAVANE
ENGINE	AAF BAG
FUEL HEATER	KELTY NO. 525-232

BRAKES

SCHEDULE	26 L W/PORTOPACK W/J-16 (160%) RELAY VALVE
AIR COMPRESSOR	WBO
BRAKE SHOES	HI FRICT. COMP.
SAFETY CONTROL	FOOT PEDAL

ELECTRICAL

MULTIPLE UNIT RECEPTACLES	27 PT
MAIN GENERATOR	AR10X2
ALTERNATOR	D-14
TRACTION MOTORS, TYPE	SEE NOTE
NUMBER OF TRACTION MOTORS	4
DYNAMIC BRAKES	POTENTIAL CONTROL*
BATTERIES	64 V. 426 AMP. HRS.
HEADLIGHTS	TWIN SEALED BEAMS 200W EA.
AUXILIARY GENERATOR	18 KW
COOLING FANS	(3) 48" 9-BLADE
CAB SIGNALS	US&S TYPE 'EL'
ROTATING WARNING LIGHTS	EQUIPPED
R.C.S.	NOT EQUIPPED

*EXTENDED RANGE

RUNNING GEAR

DRAFT GEAR	NC-390
COUPLER	TYPE 'E'
JOURNALS	6⅞" x 12" HYATT R.B.
WHEELS	42" DIA.
TRUCKS	4 WHL. HTB SINGLE SHOE BRKS., HIGH BRK. CYL.

MISCELLANEOUS

WHISTLE	S-3 LRF
TOILET	INCINOLET MODEL S/A
FIRE EXTINGUISHERS	(3) 30 LB. ANSUL
WATER COOLER	EQUIPPED
FUEL FILLER	BUCKEYE
SPEED RECORDER	C.P. MODEL 'E'

ELECTRO-MOTIVE'S GP40X ROSTER

UNIT	BUILDER DATE	BUILDER NUMBER	UNIT	BUILDER DATE	BUILDER NUMBER	UNIT	BUILDER DATE	BUILDER NUMBER
9000	December 1977	766068-1	9002	February 1978	766068-3	9004	March 1978	766068-5
9001	March 1978	766068-2	9003	March 1978	766068-4	9005	March 1978	766068-6

[1]EMD Demonstrator 9000 used for testing prior to delivery 7/78 to UP.

Heading out west on mainline 2 is a North Platte-bound manifest. Initial entry of the GP40X's on the system saw high utilization on all types of consists and terrain. The high mileages and heavy schedules of the six units were evaluated to rate the dependability of this new model. Union Pacific has not indicated any further interest in the production "follow-on" GP50's. Council Bluffs, IA, 31 March 1978.

Released from Electro-Motive's LaGrange, IL facility in December 1977, EMD 9000 demonstrated on a number of railroads prior to being delivered to Union Pacific in July 1978. Painted Armour yellow and topped with Harbourmist grey, all that is lacking to be "UP" is the scotchlite stripes and lettering. The new-styled 2-axle HT-B truck, an option item installed on Union Pacific's six locomotives, has a lowered center of gravity intended to improve adhesion by reducing weight transfer. Wheel slip detection is monitored by a low-powered radar system.—*Both photos by James Claflin.*

The GP40X represents the most changed EMD locomotive since the introduction of the GP30 back in 1961. The powerful 16-645F-3 diesel engine produces 3500-horsepower at 950 rpm. The HT-B truck has a longer wheel base, and a lower center of gravity. EMD's "Super Series" system of wheel control is installed on all GP40X's as part of General Motor's "SS" field testing program. Shown in service, but not "set-up" as yet, at Council Bluffs, IA, 28 March 1978.

The engineer's side of the cab houses the air brake equipment and associated piping. The drop doors allow easy access to any component in the compartment. The unit is being sent to the Omaha Shops for "set-up," having just been received at Council Bluffs, IA on 8 March 1978. The HT-B has two rubber-metal "sandwiches" per side which result in a stiffer suspension system. The D87X traction motor, first introduced on the SD45X, produces an 11% current rating increase over the standard D77B traction motor.

Most noticeable on the GP40X is the large flared radiator area. While delivered with the horns mounted near the rear, new mechanical directives have called for the relocation of all horns to the front-top-center of the cab. A new main generator has been installed in these units . . . AR10X2-D14's. The HT-B truck, with its longer wheelbase, allows using 42-inch wheels. Nearly every circuit uses integrated circuits (IC), reflecting "state-of-the-art" electronic technology. Council Bluffs, IA, 26 April 1978.

Just released from Omaha Shops after being "set-up," it awaits delivery to Council Bluffs, IA for system assignments. Company property installed during "set-up" includes radio equipment, arm-rests and overhead awnings, water coolers, toilets, seats, rotating beacon and safety equipment. A complete mechanical inspection is performed and any additional stencilling is applied prior to the shop's release. Omaha, NE, 31 March 1978.

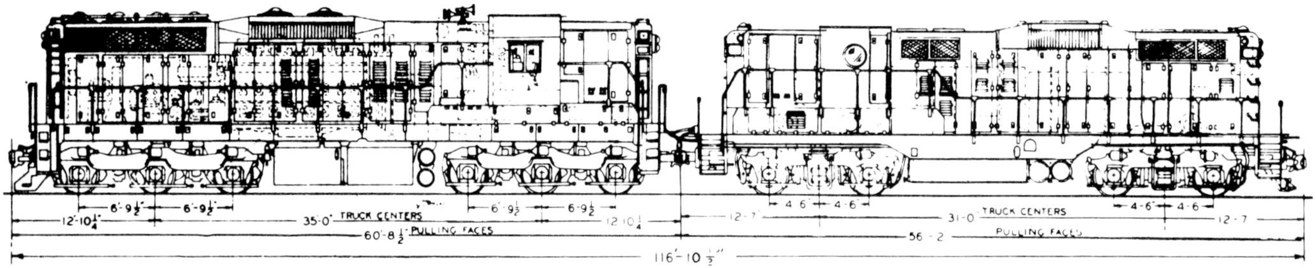

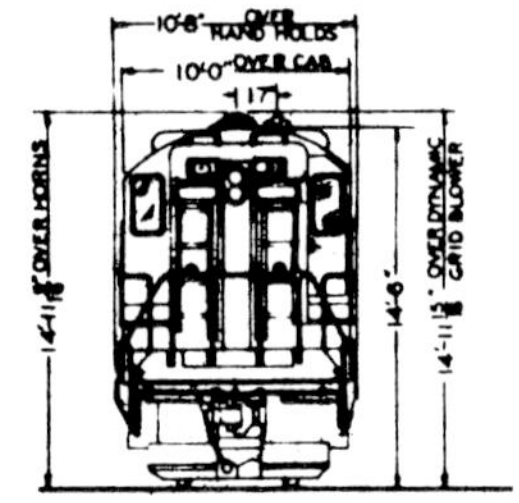

SD7 WITH 4-AXLE SLUG — 10 MOTOR UNIT

MODIFIED GP9 TO SLUG UNIT

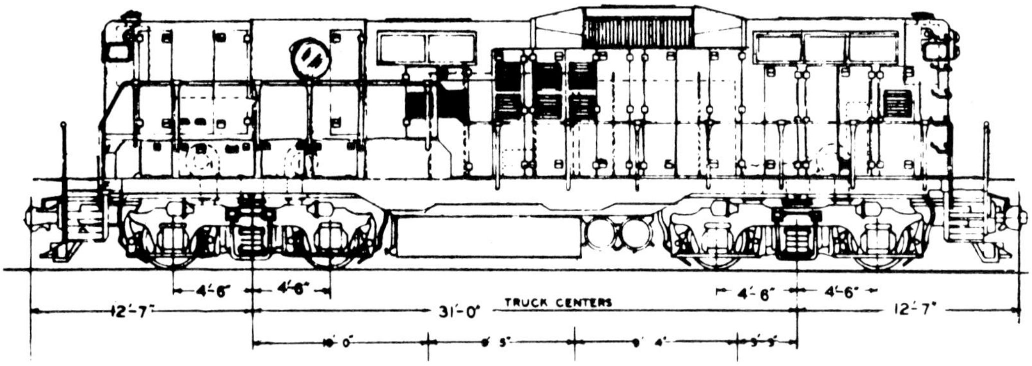

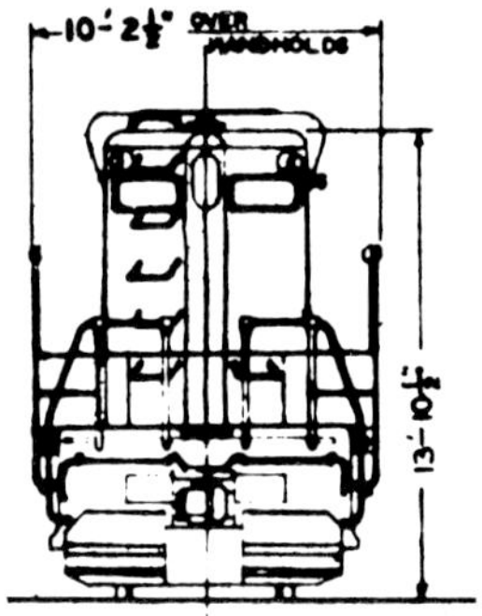

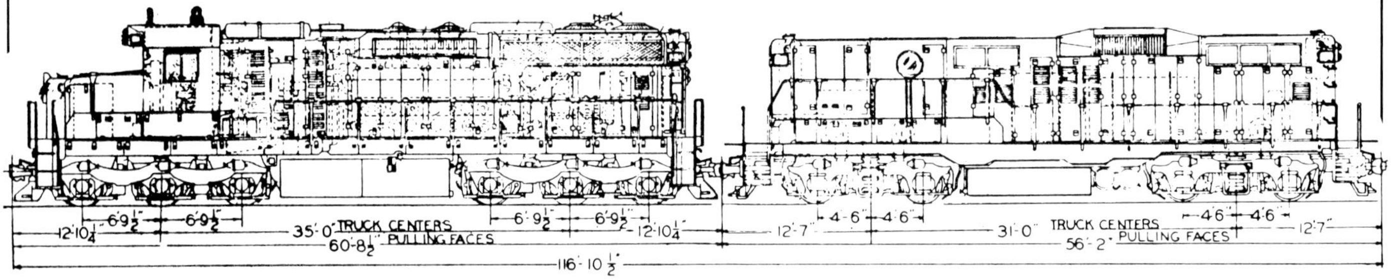

SD24 WITH 4/AXLE SLUG — 12 MOTOR UNIT

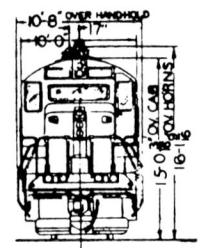

UNION PACIFIC ELECTRIC TRAILER (Slug) ROSTER

UNIT	BUILDER DATE	BUILDER NUMBER	REMARKS	UNIT	BUILDER DATE	BUILDER NUMBER	REMARKS
S1	October 1974	UP 176B	Rebuilt from GP9B (bn 19252, 3/54), Omaha Shops.	S5	March 1976	UP 314B	Rebuilt from GP9B (bn 23720, 9/57), Omaha Shops.
S2	October 1974	UP 341B	Rebuilt from GP9B (bn 23747, 10/57), Omaha Shops.	S6	September 1976	UP 306B	Rebuilt from GP9B (bn 23712, 9/57), Omaha Shops.
S3	October 1974	UP 301B	Rebuilt from GP9B (bn 23707, 9/57), Omaha Shops.	S7	January 1978	UP 406B	Rebuilt from SD24B (bn 25394, 7/59), Omaha Shops.
S4	August 1975	UP 316B	Rebuilt from GP9B (bn 23722, 9/57), Omaha Shops.	S8	December 1978	UP 444B	Rebuilt from SD24B (bn 25432, 9/59), Omaha Shops.

The first "ten-motor" slug set await its next yard duties at North Platte, NE on 22 March 1978. Electric Trailer S1 was converted from GP9B UP 176B in December 1973 and has been continuously mated with SD7 UP 459.

The second "ten-motor" slug set was also assigned to North Platte for duties in the massive classification yards. Electric Trailer S2 was converted from GP9B 341B in June 1974 and coupled to SD7 454 as its master control unit. The pair is shown at Council Bluffs, IA on 28 June 1974, ready for westbound movement to their new assignment.

Pushing a long string of cars over the "hump" is an easy task for UP S3 and 458. Electric Trailer conversion of GP9B UP 301B to S3 was completed at the Omaha Shops in October 1974. The electrical conversion to a master unit was accomplished on SD7 UP 458 at the same time. This "ten-motor" slug set has been assigned to the massive North Platte classification yard since its release from the Omaha Shops . . . where it is shown active on 22 March 1978.

The conversion of the SD24's as master control units has fared much better than the earlier SD7 arrangement. Several retired SD24's are being retained for possible slug conversion . . . either as master units or Electric Trailers.

Just back from the paint shop is newly constructed Electric Trailer S4, idling in front of the Omaha Shops on 22 September 1975. It was converted from GP9B UP 316B and mated to SD7 UP 402 with an original assignment to the California Division at Los Angeles. During the summer of 1980, it was reassigned to work on a ballast sled train in Wyoming. It was later modified with larger sanding boxes, as shown on the following page.

In its original set-up, this "ten-motor" slug set idles on a very cold night in front of the Omaha Shops . . . 8 March 1976. Ex-EMD demo (EMD 7201), UP 446 is the master control unit for S5, converted from GP9B UP 314B. This pair was assigned to the California Division for service at Los Angeles.

Formerly GP9B UP 306B, it is shown at Council Bluffs, IA on 26 September 1976 . . . just released from the Omaha Shops. This was the last electric trailer which utilized the complete body of the former unit. The master unit in this "ten motor" slug pair is SD24 UP 429. The set works at Pocatello, ID.—*Photo by Gerald J. Bosanek.*

The basic conversion of former SD24B UP 406B sees "daylight" for the first time on 18 January 1978. It has just been brought out of the Omaha Shops where it will be cranked up and put on the load tester with master unit UP 405. This is the first "chopped body" Electric Trailer and the first SD24 conversion by the Omaha Shops. Further electrical work was scheduled, with the "twelve motor" slug pair being released in April 1978. Shown in front of Omaha Shops on 18 January 1978.

Awaiting the next "push" on the hump at North Platte, NE, the crew takes a break. The Electric Trailer on this "twelve motor" slug set was formerly SD24B UP 444B. The conversion was completed at Omaha Shops in January 1979. The basic mechanical design follows the pattern of S7, which will be incorporated into several more Electric Trailer conversions planned for UP 411B, UP 430B and UP 445 currently held in storage. North Platte, NE, 8 September 1979.

Formerly assigned to Los Angeles, this "ten motor" slug pair was relocated to a ballast sled train working in Wyoming. While its performance there was satisfactory, the Electric Trailer was continually running out of sand. It was sent to Omaha Shops where salvaged DD35 sanding boxes were applied. The results were so good that all future Electric Trailer conversions will incorporate the installation of higher capacity sand boxes. Shown ready for westward movement at Council Bluffs, IA on 8 October 1980.

Based on the successful modification of Slug S4, the large sanding boxes salvaged from the scrapped DD35's were added to S7. The forward right side box mounts on the "step-up" platform; however, this platform was removed on the left side during the original conversion (see opposite page), so the box sits level on the walkway. The master unit in this "twelve motor" slug pair is SD24 UP 405. Shown active on the diesel leads at Council Bluffs, IA on 22 October 1980.

Looking back from the master unit, UP 405, the six-axle Electric Trailer is simply ballasted out to gain the most effective tractive effort for its six traction motors. The power source and control comes via the electrical harness connections from the master unit. The high mounted right side sanding box atop the "step-up" platform is taller than the cut-down body of the slug. This pair is assigned to North Platte, NE and awaits a return movement at Council Bluffs, IA on 22 October 1980.

ENERGY CONSERVATION SLOGAN SIGNBOARDS

UP 3632 on the diesel service lead, Council Bluffs, IA, 4 September 1980.

In May 1980, the Mechanical Department issued mechanical standards covering the application of signboards on SD40-2's. The most recent EMD order, UP 3609-3768, was selected to receive these distinctive boards. A total of fifteen different slogans were selected from employee submissions across the system . . . all having an energy conservation conotation.

The first application was made in mid-July to UP 8013, which was undergoing major maintenance at the Omaha Shops. When released for fleet service, it left as UP 3408 . . . regeared to standard 65-mph operation.

The initial installation provided the finite measurements necessary to produce the detailed instructions for mass installation outlined on Drawing 353-ST-10051, issued in July 1980.

Basically, the signboard is constructed from 11-gauge mild steel which measures 98.5-inches long and 30-inches high. The signboard is attached between the first three posts just below the handrail behind the cab on both sides. All sharp surfaces and edges are smoothed . . . and finished in Armour yellow paint.

The application of the slogan is made over a solid white scotchlite surface. A 1½-inch black scotchlite strip provides an edging on all four sides. The slogan is applied per the various designs. The name and location of the author is applied in 1½-inch letters under the slogan. The same slogan is applied to both sides of the locomotive.

UP 3611 points its nose west at Council Bluffs, IA on 6 October 1980. The new simplified locomotive lettering leaves off the road numbers under the cab windows. In this particular scene, where the large road numbers applied to the car body are not visible, it becomes difficult to identify the unit. The full Union Pacific scotchlite lettering, including the numbers under the cab windows, cost about $860 in early 1980.

The walkway on the engineer's side is not as deep as on the left side, making the signboard appear smaller.

An elevated front end view of UP 3723 shows off the signboard application on the fireman's side. The walkway is deeper, housing the electrical harness and piping, making the signboard appear bigger than the right side application.

The same slogan is applied to both sides.

This unit has just come in from the west and will soon be brought around the "balloon track" for servicing and assignment. Council Bluffs, IA, 8 October 1980.

THE SLOGANS

LEFT SIDE APPLICATION

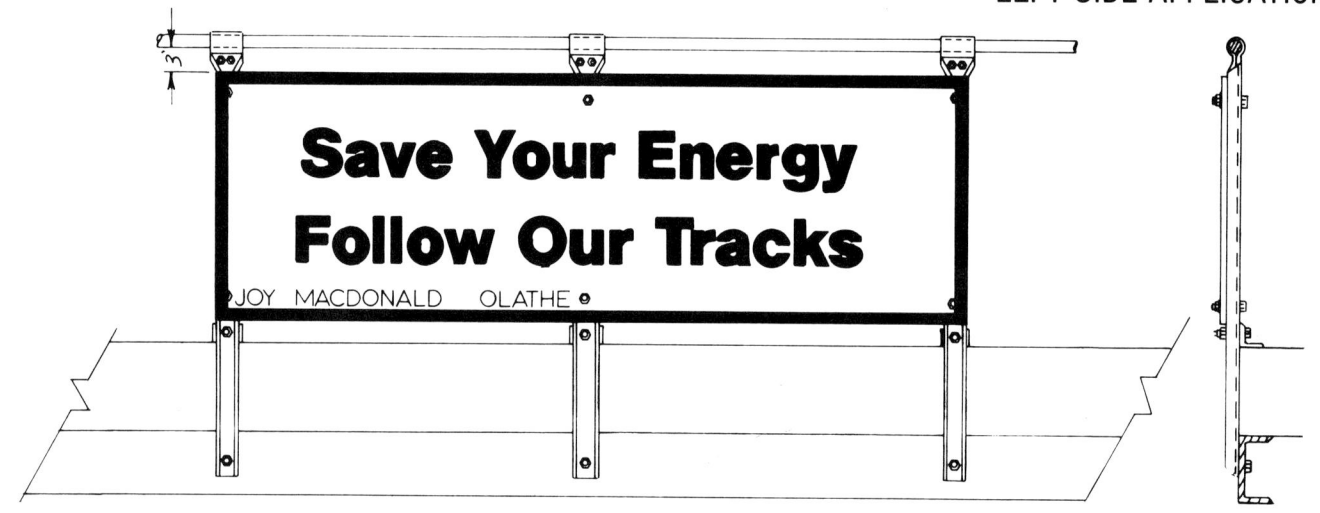

350-ST-10059

Don't Be Fuel-Hearty
HARRY E. SEEVER   ST. JOSEPH

350-ST-10060

Energy For Use But Not Abuse
LARRY W. FOREMAN   OMAHA

**Save Fuel
All Ways — Always**

350-ST-10061

KEN MOODY OMAHA

350-ST-10062

**Let's TRAIN the Nation
For Energy Conservation**

HARRY A. LEONARD AURORA

**Our Railroad Ties
Energy With Efficiency**

350-ST-10063

FRED GALATA OMAHA

350-ST-10064

**Conserve
Without Reserve**

VERLYN M. PENRY HERMISTON

**America's Salvation?
Energy Conservation!**

350-ST-10065

G. J. RIHA OMAHA

350-ST-10066

**You Don't Deserve
What You Don't Conserve!**

SANDRA KRUBACK HERSHEY

350-ST-10067

**Energy Conservation
Is More Than Conversation**

NORMA N. DUNN   COUNCIL BLUFFS

**Serving and Conserving
Serving by Conserving**

350-ST-10068

KEVIN G. GUTIERREZ   HERMISTON

350-ST-10069

**UP and Me
The Energy Key?**

BRENT R. MOWER   PORTLAND

**Save Your Energy
Follow Our Tracks**

350-ST-10070

JOY MACDONALD   OLATHE

350-ST-10071

**Fuel Conservation?
Rail Transportation!**

ROBERT S. EMPEY   OGDEN

**Make Profits Rise
Be Energy Efficient and Railroad Wise**

350-ST-10072

JOSEPH M. DUDEK   OMAHA

Let's RAILROAD This Energy Crisis Right Out of America

350-ST-10073

HELEN STRONG   OMAHA

Idling in C&NW's Council Bluffs, IA servicing area on 22 October 1980 is recently sloganed SD40-2 UP 3687. Pool power agreements on unit coal train movements find heavy usage of Union Pacific power off-line . . . always welcomed due to their well maintained mechanical condition. The energy slogans have created favorable public comment.

Serviced and ready for a westbound assignment, UP 3672 idles on the diesel service leads at Council Bluffs, IA on 2 November 1980. Sporting one of the 15 energy slogans recently applied to late model SD40-2's, Union Pacific continues its established program of using such devices to achieve higher safety, greater shipper recognition of service, employee pride and now . . . conservation of energy.

Public reactions to these slogans are quite positive, while jogging the company employees to greater consciousness . . . a well-planned double-pronged publicity program!

UNITS STORED

The DDA40X "Centennial" fleet was placed into storage in May 1980. After inspection, the units were protected by covering all openings with plastic sheeting and placed on out-of-service tracks at Council Bluffs, IA.

In late September, the units were brought back to Omaha Shops where the brushes were removed from the traction motors and prepared for movement to Las Vegas, NV for long term storage.

These are the first units to be stored at Council Bluffs, IA, 13 May 1980.

Newly delivered SD40-2's were placed into long storage lines at Council Bluffs, IA after being set-up. Here is a string of the very latest units in the 3700-sequence, all protected with plastic sheeting . . . set-out on the grain storage tracks at Council Bluffs, IA on 25 May 1980. These units were placed back into service during July and August 1980, as traffic demands started to increase. The SD40-2 fleet reigns supreme on the Union Pacific, with high requirements placed on their availability.

SERVICEABLE

The only remaining DD35's operational were brought from Council Bluffs, IA over to the Omaha Shops for class maintenance and preparation for long term storage. . . eight A-units: 71-73, 74, 76, 77, 79 and 81; and one surviving B-unit: 93B. Lined-up awaiting their turn inside the shops are five of these units. After they were released to storage, they were returned to Council Bluffs. Omaha, NE on 21 August 1980.

Another long line of DD35's and DDA40X's at Council Bluffs, IA on 17 September 1980. Most DD35's in this grouping have been stripped of all useful parts and are awaiting sale. The DDA40X's stored here will be the last ones prepared for movement in late 1980 to Las Vegas, NV for long term storage. Mixed in at the far end are some GP9 and GP20 units already ear-marked for sale and awaiting shipping instructions.

HORNS, HORNS, HORNS, HORNS

Union Pacific has been testing a wide range of horns over the last several years to determine their optimum alerting effect. Up until recently, the horns have always been mounted over one of the radiator fans, so as to prevent freeze-up during cold weather operations. Now, a forward location has been selected, so as to pitch the sound forward without being masked by the front part of the locomotive.

A variety of horns were tested on UP 3634, for both tone, audible distance and fan sound pattern. A "jury-rig" piping brought air up from the brake line to a quick-connect. Each horn was measured at various distances for their effect.

SD40X . . . UP 3049

SD40-2M . . . UP 8045

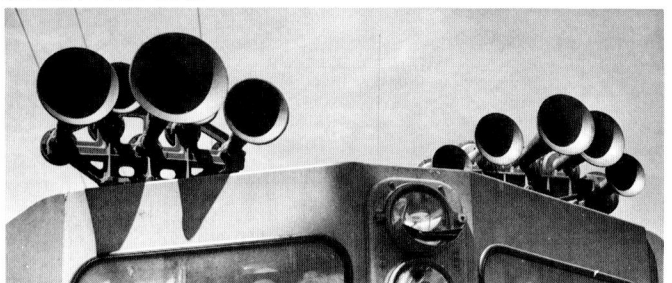

SDP35 . . . UP 1409

E9A . . . UP 951

SD40-2 . . . UP 3752

GP40X . . . UP 9000

In addition to the variety of air-operated horns used on Union Pacific locomotives, sirens have also been installed. The first such set-up was applied to UP 3049, on the opposite page. These could either give a continuous shrill or emit a varying "whelp." Not powerful enough, air-raid sirens were then installed on two SDP35's which were later reinstalled on two DDA40X's.

In order to safely operate in the west which has many road grade crossings, Union Pacific continues to improve the locomotive's audible and visual warning devices. Equal attention is being paid to trackside alerting facilities.

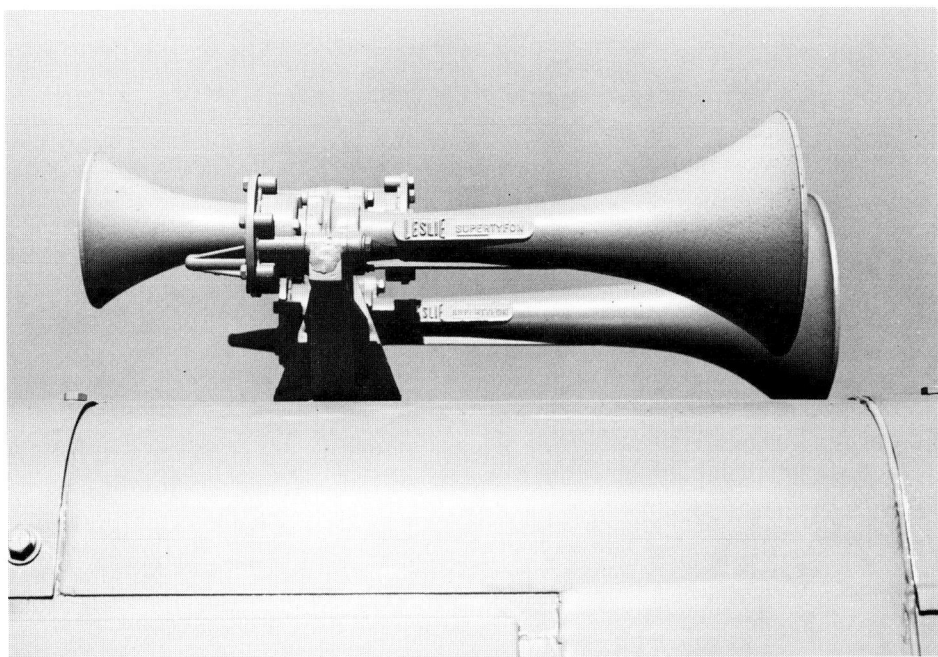

C30-7 . . . UP 2511

GP40 . . . UP 603

SD40 . . . UP 3089

SW10 . . . UP 1206   GP9 . . . UP 256

TENDER		
WATER CAP	FUEL CAP	
GALLONS	OIL	
23,500	6000 GALS.	
WT. OF TENDER		TOTAL WT. ENG. & TEND. LOADED
LIGHT	LOADED	
176,600	421,550	907,890
TENDER FRAME	TRUCK	BUILT
WATER BOTTOM	GENERAL STEEL	A.L.CO. 1944
TIMKEN ROLLER BEARINGS		

ENGINE

BOILER		FIREBOX		TUBES			EVAPORATING SURFACE-SQ FT.				
INSIDE DIA	PRESSURE	LENGTH	WIDTH	NUMBER		DIA.	LENGTH	TUBES	FLUES	FIREBOX	ARCH TUBES	TOTAL
86 3/16"	300 LBS	150 1/32"	96 3/16"	198	58	2 1/4" 5 1/2"	19-0"	2204	1578.5	442	69.5 *	4224.5

SUPERHEATER SURFACE SQUARE FT.	GRATE AREA SQUARE FT.	CYLINDERS		WHEEL BASE		WEIGHT IN WORKING ORDER - LBS.				TOTAL LT. WT.
		DIA	STROKE	DRIVING	ENGINE	ENG. TRUCK	DRIVERS	TR. TRUCK	TOTAL	ENGINE
1400	100.2	25"	32"	22'	50'-11"	102,130	266,490	117,720	486,340	443,340

DRIVING WHEEL DIA	MAXIMUM TRACTIVE EFFORT	FACTOR OF ADHESION	AIR PUMP	VALVE GEAR	F W HTR	STOKER	SUPERHTR.	ROLLER BEARINGS				BUILT
					SELLERS	STANDARD	TYPE	ENG. TR.	DRIVERS	TR. TRUCK	RODS	
80"	63,800	4.18	2-8 1/2 C.C.	WALSCH-AERTS	EXHAUST STEAM	B K	A	SKF	TIMKEN	SKF	-	A.L.CO. 1944

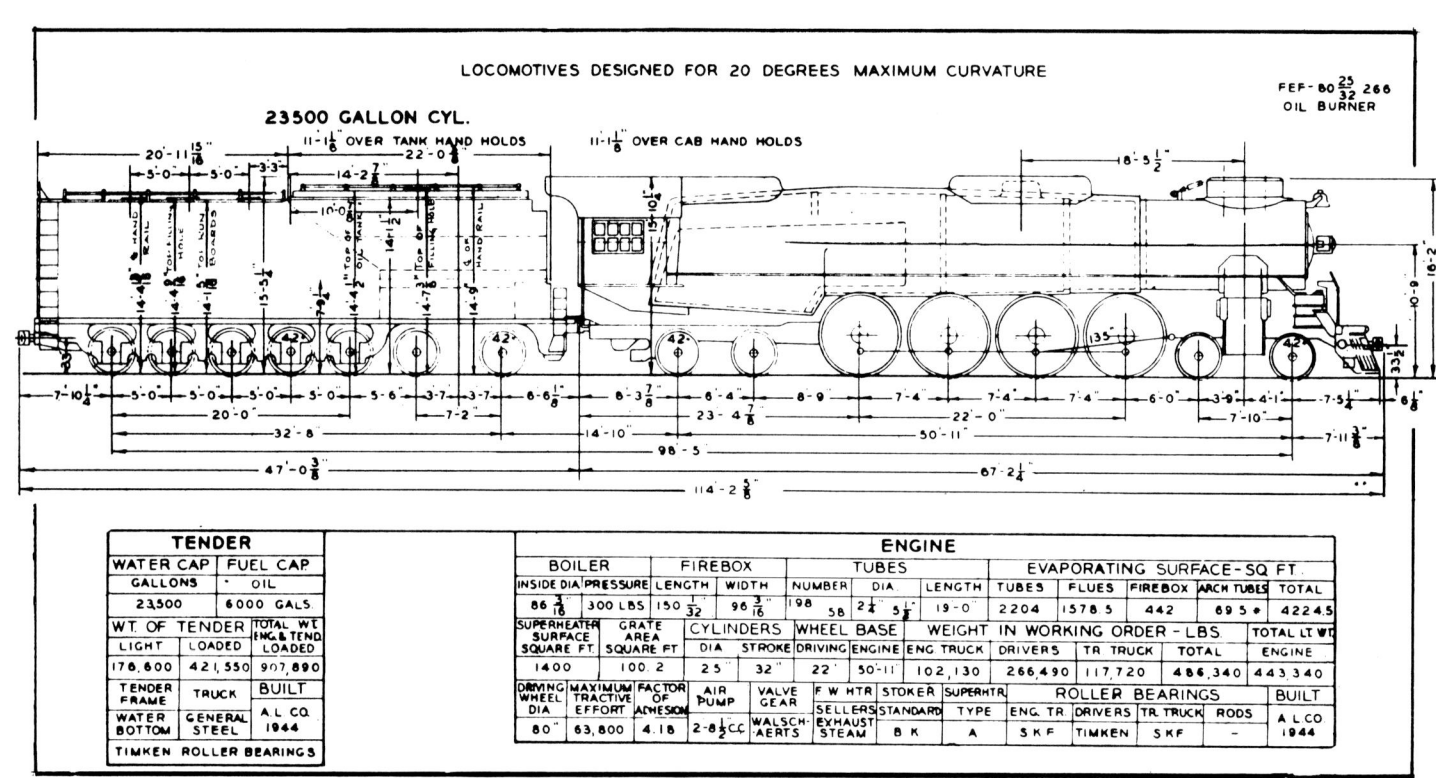

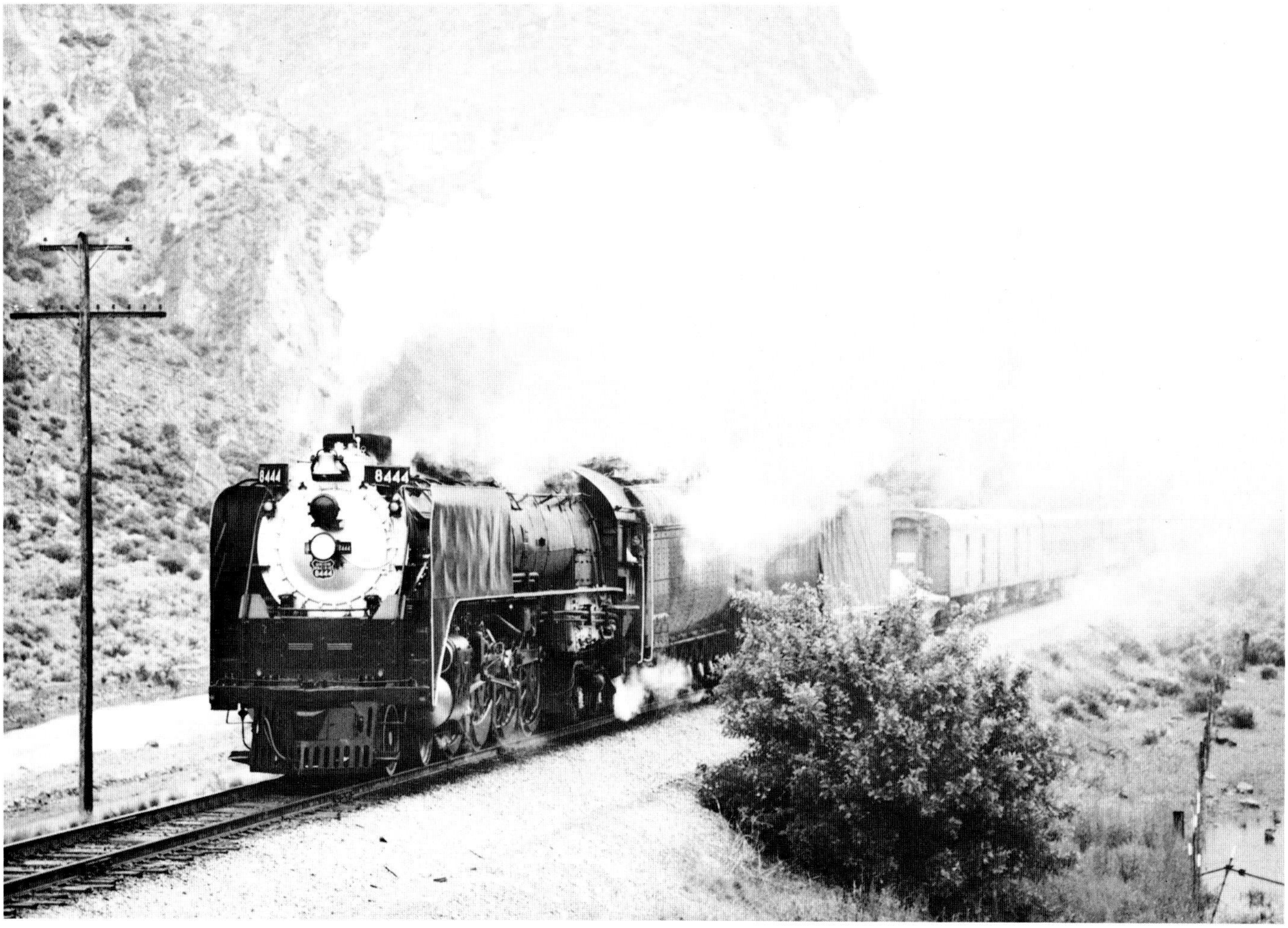

Steaming westward in light rain, UP 8444 rushes through Meadow Valley wash some 100 miles from its destination . . . Las Vegas, NV. While a popular locomotive on the Nebraska and Wyoming Divisions, this is a first time out on the Utah's Second and Third Subdivisions into Nevada. After participating in Las Vegas city celebrations and a quick side trip to Boulder, it returned back home to "Big Sky Country" . . . Cheyenne, WY.—*Photo by Martin Bosnyak.*

The *mighty* 8444 sits in the illumination of the Omaha Shops at midnight on 8 October 1975. It had come in from Cheyenne for class repairs . . . and was rushed to completion so as to double-head west with the *American Freedom Train's* ex-Southern Pacific GS4 4449 which stopped in Omaha for wheel turning before catching up and continuing with the across-the-48-states bicentennial tour.

In October of 1978 *The 3985 Committee* was organized with the purpose of possibly restoring Union Pacific's *Challenger* 3985 to special service. The committee's composition of active and retired Union Pacific employees is unique . . . the only railroad employee group in the country restoring a steam locomotive.

Concept studies were presented and permission was granted by the Union Pacific to proceed. Plans were made to move the big Mallet 4-6-6-4 from its display site next to the Cheyenne Depot over to the roundhouse. This was accomplished on 24 September 1979. It was housed in early October and work commenced.

As of October 1980, over 2,200 manhours have been spent in carefully going over each piece of operating machinery in accordance with practices outlined by the Federal Railroad Administration's *Rules for Inspection of Steam Locomotives*. It must be borne-in-mind that all manpower is contributory. The key people are full-time Union Pacific employees and are available only during their off-duty time.

Almost all the specialty equipment used to maintain these locomotives were sold for scrap when the "last fires were dropped." This places a special burden on the restoration team's ability in using today's technology to solve each problem. Many times it boils down to making a special tool or rig to ensure proper operation or installation.

The success of *The 3985 Committee* is evidenced in the successful hydrostatic test conducted on 8 August 1980. A boiler pressure of 350-psi was maintained for over 30 minutes! A thorough inspection proved the integrity of the boiler and its ability to maintain a working pressure of 280-psi.

No target date has been established to "steam-up" . . . the major variable being manpower availabililty to properly complete all mechanical tasks and operating checks. The locomotive is a coal-burner, and no plans have been made to convert it to oil operations.

The 3985 received class repairs in Cheyenne's backshop in 1956 and was operated during seasonal rushes until set aside in April 1959. It was saved from the scrapper and placed in storage at the Cheyenne roundhouse. In the spring of 1975, it was placed on display next to the Cheyenne Depot where it has remained . . . well protected and highly respected.

Congratualations are due *The 3985 Committee* and high hopes expressed to watch the mighty *Challenger* under-steam on the high-iron again.

The Ohio crane places the last section of "snap track" into position so that the big 4-6-6-4 "Challenger" can be pulled from its display location beside the Cheyenne, WY depot over to the roundhouse. Considerable preliminary planning to restore this locomotive had taken place prior to its being moved.—Photo by A. J. Wolff.

MOVING THE CHALLENGER 3985
Cheyenne, WY • 24 September 1979

Once the "snap track" was properly aligned with the display track section, the Ohio crane hooked up to the big articulated locomotive and began to ease it off the display site. As it stands, the light weight of this locomotive is 581,400 pounds . . . and represents no small effort in putting it back on working rail.—Photo by James W. Watson.

The Ohio crane continues to pull 3985 away from the display track... now on the "snap track" laid across the Cheyenne depot's parking lot... to the mainline. The 1943 ALCo "Mallet" is in surprising good condition; however, it will certainly be a *challenge* to restore the full operating status.

Photographs on this page by JAMES W. WATSON

The Ohio crane continues the slow pull towards the mainline. Walkers carefully watch the 69-inch driving wheels move along the temporary "snap track." The movement was well planned and executed with minimum problems... a high compliment to the crews!

Nostalgia ran high among the many railroad veterans who came down to the depot to see this behemoth regain the "high iron." As the Ohio crane pulled it out of the display area and onto the mainline, the chore was then handed over to a GP9 to continue the movement to the temporary storage tracks by the Cheyenne roundhouse. The tender's light weight is 172,300 pounds and measures just over 47 feet long... balanced on the 14 42-inch wheels.

The typical builder pose is assumed by the "Challenger." The Ohio crane has just disconnected and moved off so that a GP9 can continue the 4-6-6-4's movement from its display site by the Cheyenne depot to the roundhouse. The full 121 feet, 10⅞ inches are shown off to their best advantage.—*Photo by James W. Watson.*

24,000 GALLON TENDER

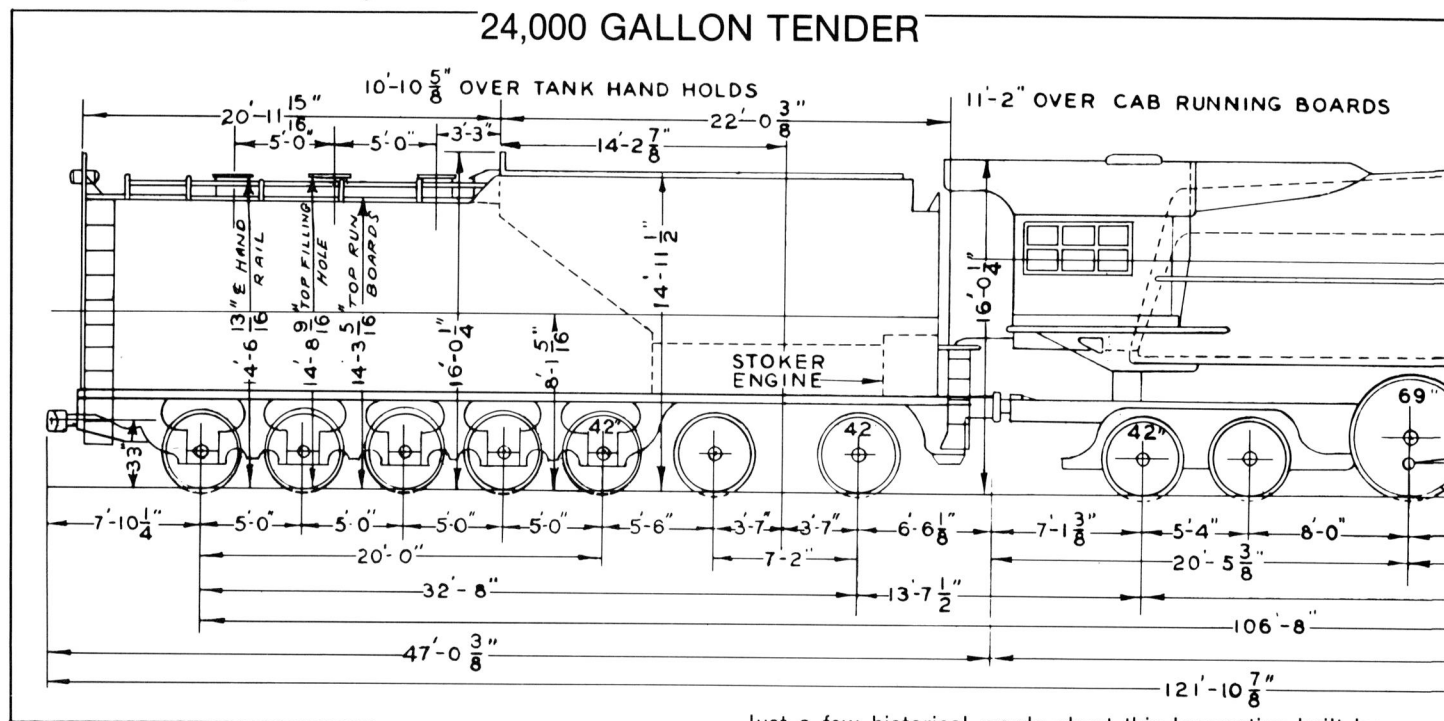

TENDER		
WATER CAP.	FUEL CAP.	
GALLONS	COAL	
25,000	LEVEL FULL 56,000 LBS.	
WT. OF TENDER		TOTAL WT. ENG. & TEND.
LIGHT	LOADED	LOADED
172,300	436,500	1,070,000
TENDER FRAME	TRUCK	BUILT
WATER BOTTOM	GENERAL STEEL	A.L. CO. 1943
TIMKEN ROLLER BEARINGS		

Just a few historical words about this locomotive built by American Locomotive Company of Schenectady, NY in July, 1943 for the Union Pacific. It is in the 3900-Class locomotive's fourth series, grouped 3975-3999. Initially team-designed by Union Pacific and ALCo designers in 1937-1938, the type proved so successful that other railroads opted on the design and ordered similar locomotives.

Classified as a single-expansion articulated engine, it was used in fast freight assignments in the Nebraska and Wyoming Divisions. On occasion, it hauled passenger "varnish" over the same territory. The 3900-Class helped establish Union Pacific's fame in handling fast freight over the continental divide.

**UNION PACIFIC RAILROAD
RESEARCH & MECHANICAL STANDARDS**

The GP9 pulls the mighty coal-burning giant west on the mainline so that it can back down the lead to the Cheyenne roundhouse where the 4-6-6-4 will be parked. It will be spotted on a storage track as room is made available to commence detailed inspections and start up a restoration program. —*Photo by James W. Watson.*

LOCOMOTIVE 3985

4-6-6-4 69 $\frac{21-21}{32}$ 407 - MB
COAL BURNER

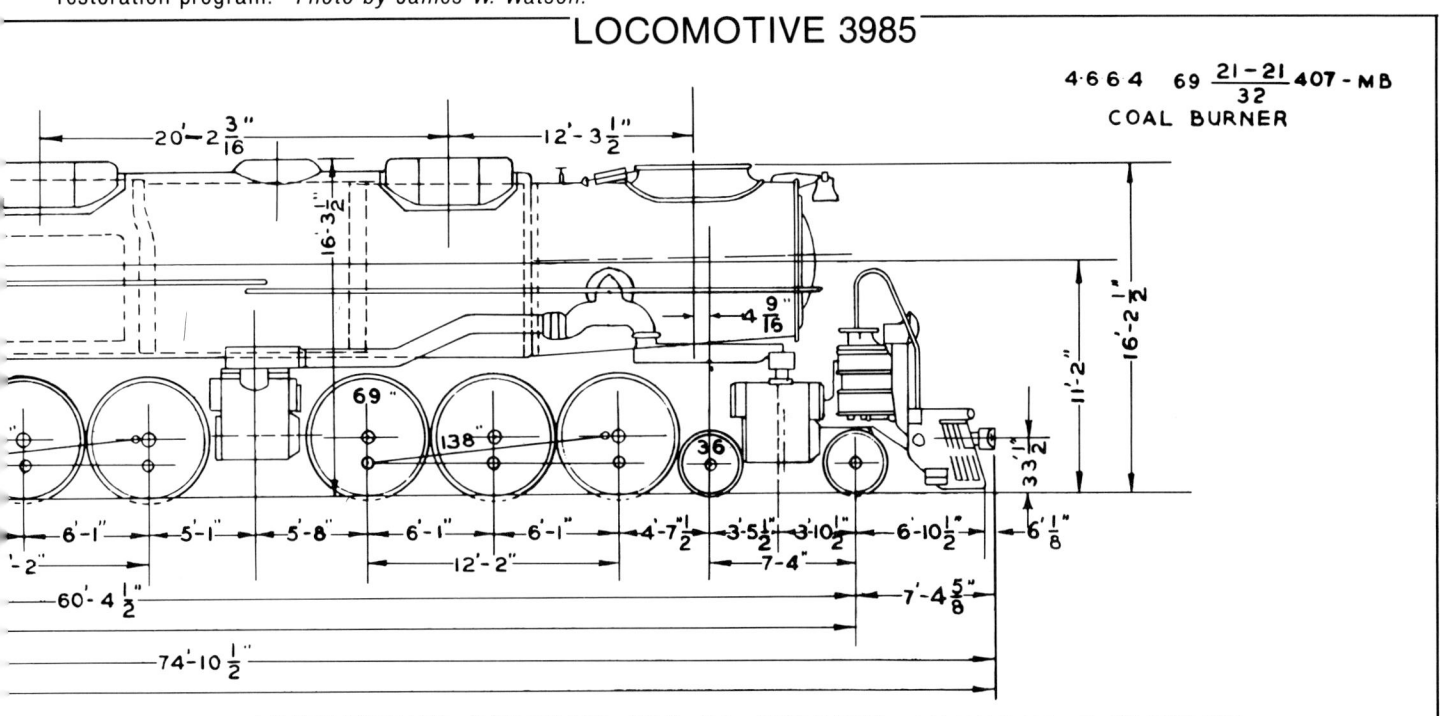

LOCOMOTIVES DESIGNED FOR 20 DEGREES MAXIMUM CURVATURE

ENGINE										
BOILER		FIREBOX		TUBES			EVAPORATING SURFACE - SQ. FT.			
INSIDE DIA	PRESSURE	LENGTH	WIDTH	NUMBER	DIA.	LENGTH	TUBES	FLUES	FIREBOX	CIRCULATORS	TOTAL
94 $\frac{11}{16}$	280 LBS.	187 $\frac{1}{32}$	108 $\frac{3}{16}$	45 / 177	2 $\frac{1}{4}$" / 4"	20'-0"	527	3688	519	83	4817
SUPERHEATER SURFACE SQUARE FT.	GRATE AREA SQUARE FT.	CYLINDERS		WHEEL BASE		WEIGHT IN WORKING ORDER - LBS.				TOTAL LT. WT ENGINE	
		DIA.	STROKE	DRIVING	ENGINE	ENG. TRUCK	DRIVERS	TR. TRUCK	TOTAL		
2,085	132	21"	32"	35'-1"	60'-4 $\frac{1}{2}$"	102,000	407,500	124,000	633,500	581,400	
DRIVING WHEEL DIA.	MAXIMUM TRACTIVE EFFORT	FACTOR OF ADHESION	AIR PUMP	VALVE GEAR	F. W. HTR. ELESCO EXHAUST STEAM	STOKER STANDARD	SUPERHTR TYPE	ROLLER BEARINGS			BUILT
								ENG. TR.	DRIVERS	TR. TRUCK	RODS	A.L.CO
69"	97,350	4.18	2-8 $\frac{1}{2}$"CC	WALSCH-AERTS		M.B.	E	S.K.F.	TIMKEN	S.K.F.	—	1943

WE'RE A GREAT BIG ROLLIN' RAILROAD

We're a great big rollin' railroad,
  one that everybody knows.
We were born of gold and silver spikes
  a hundred years ago.
We're a million miles of history
  a shinin' in the sun.
We're the Union Pacific
  and our story's just begun.

    From the great plains of Nebraska
      to the California seas,
    From the summits of the Rockies
      to the mighty redwood trees,
    We're a thousand wheels of freight train
      hear the diesel engine's power.
    We're the Union Pacific
      doin' ninety miles an hour.

Bound from Omaha to Portland
  thru Cheyenne and Laramie.
We're a headin' west for Boise
  on the mainline to the sea.
'Cross the flats at Salt Lake City
  on to Vegas and L.A.
We're the Union Pacific
  and we've got the right-of-way.

    From the green fields of the prairies
      to the blue Pacific shores,
    We deliver your great cargo
      and come rollin' home for more.
    On the backbone of our nation
      you can see us make the climb.
    We're the Union Pacific
      and we're gonna be on time.

—Courtesy of Union Pacific.  —words by Bill Fries

The old and new... UP 8444 and 8072 share the yard in Cheyenne, WY on 4 October 1978.—*Photo by A. J. Wolff.*